MISTAKE FREE LIFE

3 books in 1

Empowering Habits

Not Distractable

The Power Of Good Sleep

Marc Walker

Alexander Larkess

MARC WALKER and ALEXANDER LARKESS

EMPOWERING HABITS

How To Acquire Habits That Will Lead You To Quickly Reach Your Goals

MARC WALKER and ALEXANDER LARKESS

Table Of Contents

Introduction

Habits seem like a topic of common sense in our modern society, yet the actual reality of what habits are, how they work, and why they seemed to be something that very few people actually know about or understand. Instead, people realize that habits are things they engage in repeatedly and that produce certain wanted, or unwanted, results on a continuous basis. Often, people will make excuses for their habits, use habits to justify their behaviors, and otherwise act as though they are a victim of their habits. Of course, if you do not understand how habits work, this can feel incredibly true. That is because habits work on a deep, subconscious level within your mind, and they are designed to make engaging in repetitive behaviors easier. Once a habit is formed, your conscious mind and the majority of your brain, in general, is completely removed from the practice as it becomes an automatic behavior. This will happen regardless of whether or not the habit is positive or negative because, quite frankly, your brain does not care about that. All it cares about is creating the desired reward and making it effortless for you to experience that reward over and over again.

At this point in your life, you may have thousands of different habits. Some of these habits are good and healthy, and often contribute to you having a higher quality of life. Likewise, some of these habits are destructive and negative, and often take away from your quality of life. Knowing how to get your habits under control through your conscious effort and awareness will help you start to take responsibility for these habits, break the toxic ones, and develop a life that is more fulfilling and successful.

As you read through this book, you will quickly realize that despite how our brains work, we are not nearly as "out of control" with our habits as we tend to think we are. As well, you are not at the mercy of bad habits, and it is actually quite a bit easier to change habits or create new habits than you might think.

Rather than waiting for extraordinary events to occur in your life, such as winning the lottery or meeting your soulmate or magically landing the job of your dreams, get ready to take control of your life *right now*. Nothing and no one can have as big of an impact on your ability to take control over yourself and your actions as you can, which is exactly why you need to be ready to take responsibility for yourself and your success in life.

If you are ready to scrap the limiting belief that "habits are hard to break" or "bad habits die hard" and start learning how to ditch bad habits and formulate good ones quickly and effectively, you are in the right place.

It's time for you to officially ditch the idea of chance and struggle and start knowing with absolute CERTAINTY that you have the ultimate power over your life. Let's begin!

Chapter 1

Your Habits Drive Your Lifestyle

"Whoever becomes a slave to habit, dies slowly" Martha Medeiros

People have an overwhelming tendency to blame their habits for why they are unable to create the results that they desire in life. Constantly, you hear of people saying things like "I would work out in the morning, but I can never wake up early enough" or "I would eat healthier, but it takes too much time to shop for and cook healthier recipes, plus I don't know how." What people are really saying is that they are in the habit of waking up late, or shopping for and eating convenience meal items and they do not know how to break this habit. Rather than accepting responsibility for it, they allow that habit to overrule their lives and prevent them from achieving their goals. What's more is that these individuals genuinely believe that they are incapable of making change because of how deeply rooted these habits are and how difficult it is for them to uproot these habits. This is because, for the most part, people are uneducated on what habits actually are, why they exist, and the real neuroscience behind how you can change a habit easily and for good.

Everyone Has Unconscious Habits

Everyone, regardless of who they are, has unconscious habits. Whether you are brand new to addressing your habits, or you have been addressing them for years, you have unconscious habits that exist in your life that affect you in one way or another. Unconscious habits are habits that you develop without realizing it or habits that you unintentionally created through repetitive behavior. These habits are developed right from a very young age in your life and continue to be created for as long as you are alive. Even when you are consciously creating your habits, you will still be creating unconscious habits along the way.

Most of your current unconscious habits come from engaging in repetitive behavior without fully realizing the effect that this has on your brain. Some of them may have been taught to you by your parents, such as to make your bed and brush your teeth when you wake up, while you may have learned others on your own, such as what direction to drive to work in the morning or when to check your emails or social media updates. Either way, every single one of these habits was developed through repetitive behavior that you either knowingly or unknowingly engaged in for a period of time.

While unconscious habits can continue to be developed even after you have more conscious control over your habits, they are most prominent and affect your life the most prior to you taking conscious control over your habits. This is especially true of habits that began in childhood or that are rooted in beliefs that began in childhood, as these habits and beliefs are based on what other people told you and were developed at a time when you could not consciously dispute them. The longer a habit is carried for, or the more deeply attached it is to a deeply-rooted belief of yours, the stronger that habit will be, and the more it will affect you. In fact, it may even become so strong and impactful that you do not realize it is a habit, or that you have any level of control over it. This is often why people behave like they are victims at the mercy of their habits because they do not know any better.

It is true that unconscious habits will always exist, but it does not mean that they have to run amok in your life. When you learn how to address and navigate your habits, you will discover that it is actually easier to source and eliminate a habit than you may currently believe. Through this fail-proof process, you will be able to identify, uproot, and eliminate as many problematic habits as possible. While it will take time, and it will require you to be patient, it is possible and in due time, you will find yourself consciously in control of at least the majority of your habits. For those which you may not consciously be in control over, you will still have the strength to mindfully navigate them so as to lessen their negative impact on your life.

Your Habits Drive Your Lifestyle

The habits you keep are largely responsible for the lifestyle you currently have. People who choose to keep habits that keep them stuck or engaging in behaviors that are counterintuitive to what it is that they truly want for themselves will continue to experience a reality that fails to give them the results they desire in their lives. This is incredibly common amongst people who are unaware of and, therefore, no consciously in control over their habits.

Even when you do become aware of your habits, however, you can start to find yourself experiencing trouble with actually changing them unless you know the real secrets behind *how* to change them. Thus, you can feel as though you are trapped in an unwanted lifestyle and truly unable to escape because try as you might, you cannot bring yourself to make the necessary changes. If you are coming up against this frustration yourself, I encourage you to take a moment of pause and to celebrate yourself for being here, reading this book, and doing everything you can to learn how to change your habits and create new ones. Your devotion *will* pay off!

Anytime you desire to make a change to your lifestyle, it is critical that you drive that change first in your beliefs, and then in your habits. By creating change on these deeper levels, you are able to adjust your lifestyle in a way that is actually sustainable. Most guides surrounding lifestyle will encourage you to make changes using willpower when in reality, willpower is only intended to be used in short bursts. Attempting to make entire life changes on willpower alone will result in constant relapses, as soon as your willpower runs out. You *must* go deeper than willpower and into your beliefs and habits if you are going to make any lasting change.

As soon as you start integrating changes on a deeper level, you will start seeing serious changes in your lifestyle. At this point, lifestyle changes will no longer seem unstable or easy to shake because you will have confidence and certainty in these changes. Through this, you will be able to reliably believe in your changes and embrace them in every way possible.

How Bad Habits Keep You In a Low Quality Life

Your subconscious brain does not have the capacity to decipher "good" from "bad" which is why it can be so easy to develop bad habits, especially when you are not consciously aware of the habits you are creating. This is why, until they take control, so many people find themselves with a variety of bad habits that are affecting their lives and shaping their lifestyles.

Some of these bad habits may seem small and may seem like they have minimal impact on the overall quality of an individual's life. For example, if you don't make your bed in the morning or if you wear your shoes through the house and track mud across the floors, this may not seem like such a big deal. On an individual level, it's true; these are not necessarily habits that you need to be overly concerned about. However, if you find that you are later frustrated because the messy bed makes you feel like your room is chaotic, or because you have to put in extra effort to clean the mud off your floors, suddenly these "small" bad habits have a large impact on your life.

The culmination of bad habits in your life can lead to you driving an entire lifestyle that feels as though you are constantly cleaning up after yourself, or making you pay the price in the future for things that you are doing in the present. While this may not seem like a big deal at times, experiencing this on an ongoing basis can create a lifestyle that ultimately does not align with how you want to feel, or what you genuinely want for yourself in life.

Aside from smaller bad habits which can accumulate and create nuisances in your life, even to the point of completely transforming your lifestyle, larger bad habits can do the same. In fact, larger bad habits tend to be the ones that initially trigger people to realize that they need help in navigating their habits in the first place. You might find yourself struggling with bad habits like smoking, eating low-quality food, skipping your workouts too frequently, or spending so much money that you barely have enough to pay your bills at the end of every month. These types of habits tend to be obvious and have large, unavoidable consequences that can leave you feeling frustrated and overwhelmed with yourself and the habits you keep. Until you change them, you will continue to live at their mercy, too.

Bad habits can hold people back in virtually every area of their lives and can lead to them living a life that is unfulfilling, unaligned, and out of integrity with their authentic self, and that can even create negative and toxic consequences in their lives. The more you feed into these habits, the longer these consequences will be faced and the more emotional, mental, and physical turmoil you will likely face as a result.

How Good Habits Will Transform Your Life

While bad habits have the capacity to drive you toward having an unfulfilling and unaligned lifestyle, good habits can help you create the life of your dreams. A few consciously created and well-placed habits can transform your eating habits, your exercise routine, your success with your career, and many other areas of your life.

Good habits are designed to keep you in deep alignment with your desires and your goals, allowing you to create the lifestyle you truly desire. Through them, you are able to work effectively with your brain and your nature in such a way that allows you to consciously co-create your life by design. Everything flows easily, and it feels effortless to create the lifestyle you desire when you are working alongside good habits.

Chances are, even if you have not already been working with your habits on a conscious level, you have begun to experience the benefits of positive habits. Remember, your subconscious mind does not recognize the difference between good and bad, which means that just like you have already developed bad habits, you have already developed good habits, too. While most people do not recognize or give attention to their good habits because they are not causing any discomfort or problems in their lives, it is always a good idea to do your best to draw awareness to these habits. Becoming aware of and celebrating your good habits is a great way to recognize that you are already capable of enjoying good habits and that it is easy for you to create good habits in your life. This way, as you begin to consciously create good habits, you realize it is already easy and possible for you.

Some of the good habits you may already have include eating several times a day, communicating with your loved ones, brushing your teeth twice a day, or showering on a regular basis. These habits and any habits that contribute to you having a higher quality of life and a greater level of success in your life can all be considered good, positive habits. The more you can embrace these habits and use them to your advantage, the better your life will be. Ultimately, your goal when creating conscious habits is to create as many positive habits as possible so that you can drive a positive, happy, and fulfilling lifestyle that allows you to effortlessly and inevitably reach all of your goals.

The Eight Areas Of Your Life To Improve

In your life, there are eight primary areas that you are going to want to pay attention to when it comes to what types of habits you have and how these habits are affecting your wellbeing. Understand that as you address these eight areas of your life, you are not going to want to dive in and change or create new habits for every single area of your life all at once. In fact, you may not even want to start deeply analyzing the habits of each area of your life all at once, especially if you tend to be particularly overwhelmed by such work. Instead, you want to become aware of the fact that all eight areas of your life exist and that habits are currently affecting and influencing each of these eight areas of your life. You also want to work on taking responsibility for those habits and these areas of your life so that you can begin to have greater control over the life you are creating for yourself.

The first area of your life that you will want to consider is your health. Your health is affected by many things in your life, ranging from how you eat and how you exercise to how you set boundaries for yourself and what types of thoughts you routinely think about.

The second area of your life to consider is your wealth. Your wealth includes your finances, your budget, and any habits you have surrounding money. Wealth also covers non-money related material wealth, such as your belongings, your home, and habits surrounding other resources you have access to in your life.

The third area of your life that you need to consider is your career. Your career includes any professional endeavors you are engaged in, ranging from your full time career to your side ventures. If you are not presently employed, anything you do to seek work or in place of work qualifies as your career.

The fourth area of your life to be considered is your relationships. Any habits you have revolving relationships with family members, friends, co-workers, acquaintances, and even strangers you meet on a daily basis are all housed under the topic of relationships. These habits will include things such as how you create, maintain, manage, and end relationships in your life.

The fifth area of your life to consider is your romantic relationship or your love life. Habits revolving around how you meet romantic interests, how you engage with them, and what types of patterns you uphold in your relationships fall under this category. Your habits here may directly affect your partner or potential partners, or they may be entirely intrapersonal, such as how you think about romantic interests or the role you take on in relationships.

The sixth area of your life that you need to consider is your relationship with yourself. This includes how you talk to yourself, how you think about yourself, what you think about yourself, and the way you treat yourself. Habits revolving around how you care for your body, mind, and emotions, as well as habits that revolve around how you spend your alone time and how you feel being by yourself.

The seventh area of your life to consider is your hobbies and interests. You will need to become aware of how your habits result in you approaching your hobbies, committing to your hobbies, creating time for your hobbies, and otherwise engaging in hobbies. Pay attention to your interests as well, even those that do not manifest as hobbies or long term interests, as they can tell you a great deal about your habits, too.

Lastly, the eighth area of your life to consider is your faith or spirituality. If you are religious, this will include any habits you have around your religion. If you are of non-denominational faith or lack faith in anything at all, your habits will matter here, too. You can identify your habits based on how you approach your faith and how you tend to invest time in or share your faith with others.

Chapter 2

Quit Relying On Chance and Take Responsibility

One of the many problems with existing inside of the victim mentality that often accompanies a person that is entrenched with unconscious habits is the idea that everything in life comes down to "luck." Rather than taking radical responsibility for their lives and making changes so that they can enjoy the lives they want, they choose to believe that they are "not lucky" or that chance has yet to fall on their side to give them their dream life. Often, these individuals can be found waiting on a lottery ticket, a soulmate, or a dream job to magically fall into their laps so that their lives can change. The reality is, you and you alone are responsible for the quality of life, and waiting on the chance to create your desired results for you is a sign of laziness and a sign that you have succumbed to the victim mentality of unconscious habits.

If you have found yourself saying these things at one point in the past, even if it was in the recent past, I encourage you not to develop shame or feelings of embarrassment around having believed that chance was your one shiny hope for a better life. Our society is presently structured in a way that largely promotes the idea of banking on chance and getting comfortable in a not so comfortable life. Arguably, the circumstances that lead to you feeling that way are not entirely your fault. What you do now that you realize this is completely absurd and untrue, however, is your responsibility.

Chance Is Not Worth Betting Your Life On

Your life will only ever happen once. There is no guarantee that you will get a do over, or that you will be able to make up for the things you did not take advantage of or act on in the past. New opportunities are arriving every day, but if you never take advantage of them, then what does it matter? If you are so busy waiting on the chance to drop you with an extraordinary experience that you ignore or deny those opportunities, then the only person responsible for your misfortune is *you.*

Your life is precious, your time is precious, your energy is precious, and everything about your existence on earth is precious. If you do not yet believe that to be absolutely true, then trust that as you begin to take responsibility for yourself and your life, this will change, and you will find yourself having an entirely new outlook on life. Regardless of whether you are there or not, though, you need to start acting like your life is the most important thing that you have in this world – because *it is*. Banking the entire quality of your life on chance is one of the worst gambles we can take. If you take this type of chance with your life, you are setting yourself up with the odds stacked wildly against you, and with no chance of redeeming yourself from the constant misfortune that comes with this untasteful bet. The only way to free yourself of this misfortune and to start experiencing the luck you wish to experience is to take responsibility for yourself, your life, and your actions and to start changing your lifestyle on your own terms.

As Oprah Winfrey says: "Luck is preparation meeting opportunity." Luck is not things magically falling into your lap without you going out and doing something to make said things happen. Even if you wanted to win the lottery, find your soul mate, or get that great job, you would have to go out and make it happen. You would have to buy the ticket, start taking dating seriously and put the work in to ensure that you were qualified for your dream job. *Nothing* in your life happens without you first doing something in order to make it happen.

When you start to realize that even the extraordinary events that you are waiting on require action on your behalf, it no longer seems so unreasonable for you to put in the work on situations that are far more likely to work in your favor. For example, putting the work in on changing your diet, exercising more, keeping your home cleaner, learning new skills that support your career, or communicating in a way that is more harmonious with the loved ones in your life. All of these, plus many other wonderful changes can be made by realizing where you ought to be investing your faith, hope, and energy in order to actually create the results you desire. This way, you can stop being a victim of bad habits and luck and start being the creator of your own destiny.

Extraordinary Events Don't Make Extraordinary People

Before we dive into how you can begin to take responsibility for yourself and your habits, I want to dig a little deeper into the reason behind why most people wait on extraordinary events to change their lives, and why this is a bad idea. The concept of waiting for something extraordinary to happen before you are willing to make a life change is both lazy and absurd. In regards to laziness, this choice to wait on something special to happen gives you a great opportunity to justify why you are not taking action in your life and, therefore, why you do not see any results. It is a great copout for anyone who is afraid of the work or energy that it might take for them to see the results they desire, or for anyone who is afraid of failure or obsessed with perfectionism. As long as you always hold onto this concept of waiting on something special, you can continue to argue that it is "not your fault" that nothing has changed in your life. Of course, this is not true, but it can be easy to justify your lack of change in this way, and therefore many people cling to it.

In regards to absurdity, it is important that you realize that extraordinary events do not make for extraordinary people. For example, winning the lottery will not suddenly improve your life or give you everything you ever wanted. Likewise, finding your soulmate will not magically heal your romantic woes, and landing your dream job will not suddenly inspire you to start taking your work more seriously. Contrary to popular belief, these types of events do not inspire true change in anyone and, the change that is experienced will rapidly be lost when the novelty of this new change wears off, and the person realizes that they themselves never actually changed. As a result, you will quickly realize that these perceived fortunes were never the reason why you had not yet managed to change your life. The real reason is that you decided not to engage in change is because you did not want to, or you were unwilling to learn how.

The only way that you can experience true change in your life is if you put the work in to make change happen. You have to be willing to become aware of what it takes to make change happen, and you have to be willing to put the work in to actually create this change so that the change can be long lasting. If you are unwilling to become aware of the process or put the work in, you are going to find yourself constantly experiencing more of the same old same old, because you yourself have chosen that. As far as the effort required to make changes, that is up to you. You get to decide how easy or how hard it will be for you to engage in change based on how much effort you are willing to put into finding a solution that works for you, and how committed you are to believing in that solution and seeing it through.

Taking Responsibility For the Quality Of Your Life

Now that you understand why waiting on extraordinary events for your life to change is absurd, you can start to take true responsibility for yourself. First, you need to start by taking responsibility for the quality of your life. Right now, all of the experiences that you are having in your health, wealth, career, relationships, love life, relationship with yourself, hobbies, and faith are all because of choices you have made. You, and you alone, are responsible for the quality of life that you are experiencing.

When I say this, understand that I am not trying to blame you for things beyond your control. Chronic illness, economic crashes, and certain hardships, for example, are not all your fault. Often, our lives are affected by external things that we truly cannot stop or change, and there is no way that we could even begin to. What I am saying, however, is that it is your choice whether or not you do the most within your capacity to ensure that you live the best life possible. For example, if you have a chronic illness, you are the one deciding whether or not to take your medicine or engage in habits that are going to support you in improving the quality of your life, no one else. Or, if you are experiencing poverty due to the economy, you are the one deciding whether or not to do something about it so that you can find new opportunities or at least offset the amount of hardship you are facing. No one can force you to talk to someone, take your medicine, look for new jobs, develop new skills, or try out new opportunities if you are unwilling to take action yourself. Furthermore, no one *will*. Even if you happen to be someone who has people in your corner pushing you to do better if you continually choose not to then eventually those people will give up and let you go about creating more of your own misfortune. Everyone has their limits.

Rather than blaming your family for how they raised you, or your friends for how they treated you, or your education for how it failed you, or your job for laying you off, or whatever else you can think to blame, start taking responsibility. Realize that within your realm of opportunities in every situation lie two things: your judgment, and your voluntary actions. This means that you get to decide whether you are going to view something as a misfortune or a lesson, and you get to decide how you are going to navigate the cards you have been dealt. Many people navigate challenging situations in such a way that enables them to create seemingly miraculous circumstances, all because they believed it was possible, and they created the necessary habits to make it happen. Many others, however, navigate challenging situations in such a way that creates more challenges because they believe they are unlucky and that they are a victim of misfortune. As a result, they often also develop negative beliefs and habits that continue to draw them further away from the life they desire.

Taking Responsibility For the Habits You Have Created

In addition to taking responsibility for the quality of life you are presently experiencing, you also need to take responsibility for the habits that you have created. Now, this may seem challenging as some of those habits may be rooted from your youth or connected to beliefs you created as a young child. You may also want to argue that since you had no idea how habits were created, you could not possibly have stopped any unwanted habits from taking root. While all of this can be true, again, it is up to you to choose to take responsibility starting right now. You may not always be the one "at fault" for why things happened, but you can certainly take responsibility for the outcome and start taking action to improve your outcome.

As far as your habits go, realize that in taking personal responsibility for every single habit you have created, you also take back your personal power, which supports you in undoing every single unwanted habit and creating new, healthier habits. When you are the one in control, you get to decide what happens. Until you are truly taking responsibility for where you are at in life, you will only be using your control to place that control outside of yourself where it is not useful.

You need to decide as of right now that every habit you have created is your responsibility. Finding out where that habit came from, why it exists, and what drives it is your responsibility. It is your responsibility to understand how to shift that habit or replace that habit, or how to ensure that you are engaging in said habit consciously and with intention. You are responsible for any circumstances that habit produces, and for the results of your own actions. Even if it feels like you cannot help yourself or it seems impossible to stop engaging in said habit, it is your responsibility.

The more you can take radical responsibility for your habits, the easier it will be for you to start making serious changes to your habits so that you can begin shifting them. The best way to start taking radical responsibility is to say, "I am responsible for this" every single time you witness yourself engaging in a habit, and during every step of the way. For example, when you realize a habit has been triggered, say, "I am responsible for this." When you carry out that habit, say, "I am responsible for this." When you experience the aftermath of engaging in your habit, say, "I am responsible for this." This way, you can start getting into the mindset of taking back your power and you can set yourself up to start truly making changes in your life.

Identifying Damaging Habits You Have Been Holding Onto

As you begin to take responsibility for your quality of life and habits, it may feel particularly challenging to identify and take responsibility for damaging habits. After all, damaging habits have been creating chaos in your life, and taking responsibility means that you realize that in the past, you contributed to that chaos and that in the future, you are responsible for any chaos that is created, too. Most of us do not want to admit that we are responsible for our own suffering, which can make it easy to reject the idea of damaging habits being our responsibility. In the end, though, this only hurts you and worsens your suffering.

For now, let's lean into the process of working with your habits in a way that promotes you taking radical responsibility for the habits you are carrying. You are going to do this by identifying at least one damaging habit that you have been holding onto, uncovering the entire habit itself to the best of your ability, and taking responsibility for that habit. Once you have done this for one habit, you will want to start doing it for every single habit you have, destructive or not.

You can start to identify your damaging habits by looking for symptoms of destruction in your life. Look at areas of your life where you experience hardship, toxic patterns, or drama on a regular basis. This may be in your relationships, in your health practices, or anywhere else in your life, where you find yourself continually struggling to enjoy a positive and healthy experience. Once you have located an area of your life with said symptoms, write it down and write down all of the symptoms you have noticed. Then, start looking at all of the actions you take around these symptoms that either contribute to them, cause them, or come after the symptoms have been experienced. You will likely begin to notice a pattern of how you tend to behave and contribute to said situations that will allow you to begin to witness your own role in them. Now, you need to take responsibility for this pattern. You need to accept that, in one way or another, you have agreed to continue acting on this pattern, and that you have been responsible for this pattern continuing. In taking responsibility for it, you also need to take responsibility for the outcome this habit has had on your life, and for the way it has affected your overall quality of life. It may take you a little while to accept full responsibility for your role in a certain habit, but as long as you continue working toward owning it, you will find yourself taking full responsibility for it. Then, you will have accepted full power over your ability to shift it so that you are no longer being affected by this pattern anymore. We will talk more about how to do this in *Chapter 10: How To Break Bad Habits.*

Chapter 3

The Facts About Habits

Now that we have done some work around your mindset surrounding your habits let's dig into some cold hard facts surrounding what habits are, where they are formed in the brain, how they form, and why habits exist in the first place. This fact-based approach to dealing with habits helps you understand the neuroscience behind a habit which, in many ways, will give you a deeper sense of awareness around why habits are so important to your wellbeing. This will also support you in understanding what is going on when habits are being developed, or removed, which can remove a great deal of the mystery around habits themselves. This way, rather than wondering why breaking bad habits can be so hard, and why willpower alone is not enough when it comes to breaking bad habits or starting good ones, you can have the exact answers you need to navigate your habits effectively.

Note that the neuroscience and facts in this book are as up-to-date as possible at the time of writing this, but science is constantly evolving, and there is always more to be learned. For that reason, it is always a good idea to keep an eye out for the latest research studies done on habits so that you can further improve your understanding of how habits work and how you can leverage habits to your benefit. Even if you think you have the process down pat, refining it even just a little more at a time can make it easier and easier for you to reach your goals and truly embrace the life you want to live.

What Is a Habit?

One great quote that can help you understand the power of habits and the importance of habits was by Mahatma Gandhi. In it, he said, "Your beliefs become your thoughts, your thoughts become your words, your words become your actions, your actions become your habits, your habits become your values, and your values become your destiny." This quote truly outlines the power that habits have in our lives, as well as the general outline for how they are designed and how they affect us, and our long term wellbeing.

It is no secret that habits are powerful and that they are influenced by you, but what *are* habits exactly? The most direct description of a habit is "a behavior pattern acquired by frequent repetition or physiologic exposure that shows itself in regularity or increased facility of performance," which can be found in the

Meriam-Webster Dictionary. Ultimately, habits are a series of behaviors that you engage in on a regular basis, in the exact same way every time, for the same reason, and with the same immediate benefit.

There is often some misconception around what constitutes as a habit, and what does not. Some researchers like to view habits on a spectrum that shows a different range of "dedication" to a habit that you may have. On one end of the spectrum, you have a behavioral pattern that has not yet become routine, meaning that it is a chosen behavioral pattern that you have to consciously choose to engage in and that may change from time to time. On the other end of the spectrum, you have a full blown addiction that is so deeply ingrained in your brain and life that you repeat it at the same time, the same way, without fail, and if you do not, you experience serious repercussions for skipping the habit. For example, people who have a habit of smoking will often experience migraines, anger, and tell-tale symptoms of withdrawal if they skip a cigarette break.

Certain habits are reinforced by behavior and natural chemical reactions within the brain alone. These habits are ones where no substance is introduced to the body, and therefore there is no alteration of consciousness or state of being when the habit is engaged in, beyond what the body naturally produces itself. Other habits are reinforced by behavioral and natural chemical reactions within the brain, as well as by addictive substances that can magnify the natural habit-creation process. These types of habits are far more likely to become addicting because of the added substances that cause the habit to "hook" much deeper into the brain and to have much more significant consequences if it is not engaged.

For the purpose of this book, we are talking about habits that are non-substance related, although those that are substance-related can still be benefited by the material within this book. However, anyone can benefit from this information and can use it toward breaking habits. I only ask that you ensure that you have the proper support and medical care if you are working through habits that involve addictive substances to avoid dealing with any negative medical repercussions by following this process.

Where Are Habits Formed In the Brain?

Deep in the cerebral hemispheres of your brain, there is a group of structures known as the basal ganglia. These structures include the putamen, the caudate, and the globus pallidus in the cerebrum. They also include the subthalamic nucleus in the diencephalon and the substantia nigra in the midbrain. The basal ganglia has a strong connection with the cerebral cortex, the brainstem, the thalamus, and other parts of your brain and are therefore involved in many different functions of the brain. Some of these functions include voluntary motor movements, habit learning, procedural learning, cognition, eye movement, and emotion.

As far as habit learning goes, the basal ganglia works by identifying a system of routines that can be repeated based on a specific trigger, and that produces a specific emotional reward. Upon identifying this system of routines, it begins to recognize it, learn it, and integrate it as a habit into your brain. Some of the more practical habits that your basal ganglia has helped you learn include exercising, parallel parking, brushing your teeth, and driving your typical route to work. That's not all, though. Every single habit you have *ever* made was formed within the basal ganglia.

Once a habit is identified, the basal ganglia works to memorize it perfectly, almost like a machine-learning computer learning a piece of code. As soon as the "code" is memorized enough, your brain integrates it as a habit. This process effectively removes the conscious thinking and decision making patterns from that particular behavior so that you no longer have to consciously think about how to do something, or make decisions around it. Instead, your brain already knows what to do and what decisions to make, and it does so automatically. As a result, the habit is formed and executed.

The process of your conscious thinking and decision making patterns being removed from the habit is largely what makes navigating the process of changing or breaking habits so challenging. At this point, a habit is truly wired into your brain, and it will take a lot more than some willpower and elbow grease to get it out of there. Now, you need to understand how the "coding" of your brain works so that you can essentially change the code within your brain. This may sound easy, but when you realize that all of these pieces of code coincide with each other and that one single habit affects so many areas of your life, as well as so many other habits, you begin to see how changing or breaking a habit can become so difficult. At this point, you are not just changing one thing; you are changing multiple things. For this reason, the most effective approach is the one that has the least disruption to the existing code, yet has enough of a disruption to be able to eliminate the unwanted habit itself.

How Long Does It Take To Form a Habit?

There is a lot of mixed information on how long it actually takes to form a habit. At one point, it was popularized that it only takes 21 days for a habit to form, but the truth is that after 21 days, the habit is still in its infancy. At this point, you have begun to develop a strong habit but it would still be incredibly easy for you to break or disrupt this new habit. As soon as it was broken, it would be easy to abandon the habit and would take a great deal of effort to reintegrate it. While it would not be quite so hard because you had put effort into learning it in the first place, and therefore neural pathways had been formed, it would still be very challenging.

Recent science has shown that it takes an average of 66 days for a habit of becoming automatic, although there are a lot of variables that can affect the validity of this. For example, an individual's behavior, beliefs, personality, and circumstances can all impact how quickly they are able to integrate a new habit and maintain that habit as a true automatic behavior. Because of these variables, it is generally agreed upon that it can take anywhere from 18 to 254 days for a new habit to be properly formed. Once a person has reached the 254 day mark of repeating the behavioral pattern of the new habit, regardless of where they fall in the range of variables, there is a very strong chance that they have embraced a true habit, making the behavior automatic.

What Is the Benefit Of Habits?

Despite the fact that bad habits can lead to unwanted results and hardships in your life, habits themselves actually have a very important and beneficial role in your life. Habits themselves are used to help you engage in life in a way that results in your brain using less energy, leaving you with a greater ability to divert your conscious awareness toward something else. For example, when you go to the bathroom, you do not have to think about how to sit down, how to go to the bathroom, how to wipe, how to flush, and how to wash your hands. Instead, all of this is a habit and you likely do it in the same way (or close to) every single time. As you are doing this, you may be thinking about what you need to do after you have finished going to the bathroom, or daydreaming about something new that you want to try.

Practical habits exist in all areas of your life as a way to make important and necessary behaviors easier while also reducing the amount of energy they require. From a neuroscientific point of view, if a behavior is automatic, then it requires less of your brain function in order for that behavior to be executed. This way, you save energy. Believe it or not, your body uses up the majority of your daily calories when you are resting, *not* when you are actually exercising, which means reducing your energy usage during rest is still vitally important for your body.

In addition to habits helping you through practical things in life, they can also help you through mastery, or through progressive development. For example, let's say you are an artist, and your chosen medium is drawing. If you had not developed habits on how to hold your pencil, how to draw basic lines and shapes, and how to engage in other seemingly basic drawing skills, it would be virtually impossible to master the art of drawing. You would have to relearn the basic behaviors over and over again, thus preventing you from being able to build on them by developing habits that are more aligned with mastery levels of drawing.

Habits also help you when it comes to consciously choosing your lifestyle and achieving your goals through various points in your life. If you develop good habits, you can help yourself achieve certain goals and outcomes effortlessly because you do not have to consciously think about taking the actions that will get you the results. Instead, your brain *automatically* engages in these actions, thus making it virtually effortless for you to create the success you desire. In many ways, your success is inevitable because you have wired your brain to make it happen.

Can We Live Without Habits?

Given the nature of habits, it is impossible to completely rid your life of habits. Furthermore, you would not want to. While some people may claim to live habit-free, what they are generally talking about is being free from bad habits, or from habits that are non-essential to standard everyday life. For example, they may live free of habits surrounding TV usage, reading, engaging in hobbies, and performing other non-essential behaviors. However, they will still have habits that support them in driving, cooking, using the washroom, cleaning themselves, and otherwise taking care of their livelihood. While they may be bringing conscious awareness to these habits through mindfulness, they are not breaking the habits or defying the habits per se. Instead, they are simply becoming aware of the habits, their benefits, and the steps involved in completing those habits.

Instead of trying to rid yourself of all habits, you can focus on eliminating and shifting habits that are giving you negative results, or that are not giving you the results you truly desire. This way, you are no longer carrying ineffective habits that are going to create unwanted outcomes in your life. You can also eliminate any non-essential habits that are not bringing you positive results, even if they are not bringing you negative results, either. In doing so, you create the capacity for you to develop habits that will be far more effective, and that will bring you far greater benefits in your life.

As you work to shift your habits, you can also work toward increasing your mindfulness so that while you are engaging in habits, you are able to bring your conscious awareness to them. This way, you are able to be mindful of each step in the habit and you can take inventory on how helpful the habit is, or whether or not it is truly worth it for you to engage in the said habit. You can also use this mindful awareness to decide whether you want to keep engaging in the habit, shift it, or change it altogether. Working alongside your habits in this more mindful manner is far more productive than attempting to truly live habit-free, as doing so would require a significant amount of conscious awareness and energy and, ultimately, would not be ideal.

Chapter 4

Three Step Habit Loops

As your basal ganglia works toward identifying behavioral patterns that can be developed into habits, it works through what is called a three step habit loop. This three step process can be broken down into a few sub steps. However, each of these three primary steps must be completed in order for a habit loop to be developed. Once a habit loop is developed your brain recognizes it and keeps it in its awareness so that it can spot any repetitions of this habit loop that you may be engaging in. The more times you repeat your habit loop, the more times you will reinforce said habit and the stronger it will become. Eventually, you have reinforced it so many times that the necessary neural pathways have been developed, strengthened, and put on autopilot.

Having a clear understanding of what this three step habit loop is, what it entails, and what sub steps are included in the habit loop helps you begin to identify how you can develop your own habits by working with your brain instead of against it. This is the first major step toward creating habits that will be effortless to maintain, sustainable, and effective toward helping you develop the lifestyle you desire.

The Three Steps Of a Habit Loop

The three steps of a habit loop are as follows: a cue, a routine, and a reward. Your basal ganglia will work together to identify these three steps through your everyday behaviors, whether you are consciously aware of it or not. Essentially, anytime you engage in a pattern, your brain, through your basal ganglia, will spot the three steps of that pattern including the cue, the routine, and the reward. Patterns with a larger reward will be more prominently memorized, whereas those with a smaller reward may not be memorized until they have been repeated a few times over.

After the initial memorization of a pattern, your brain will be looking for that pattern and will recognize anytime it has been repeated. It will then measure the number of repetitions to the size of the reward to determine the benefit of that habit and, the better the reward, the more likely it will be for you to continue engaging in that habit. This is how all habits are designed, whether they are designed consciously or unconsciously.

To consciously design a habit, your goal is not to change the habit loop, but instead to identify what it is and to consciously create a cue, routine, and reward that is worthy enough of your brain memorizing it and integrating it as a habit. As long as you continue to consciously engage in this habit, your brain will continue to reinforce it until, eventually, it becomes automatic. From there, you will no longer have to exert as much conscious thought or decision making into the process because it will happen all on its own.

Step One: The Cue

The cue of a habit is often the most elusive part of unconsciously designed habits because it is a random trigger that your brain has identified and associated with your habit in question. In some cases, the cue may become obvious, whereas, in others, it could remain a mystery for some time until you do some sleuthing to identify what the cue actually is.

A cue is any trigger that will encourage your brain to start engaging in a habitual process. For example, when you wake up, you may find yourself immediately going to the bathroom, and then going to the kitchen to make a coffee. The cue here is waking up, while the routine is going to the bathroom and then making your coffee.

Unconscious cues can be associated with anything that can affect your five senses, which is why they can be so challenging to uncover. A smell, sight, sound, touch, or taste could all trigger the response of a habit loop. Cues can also be associated with specific behaviors or with other habits, thus adding to the complexity of cues. For example, you may be in the habit of eating dinner and then immediately having a dessert after your dinner. In this case, the habit of eating dessert is directly associated with the habit of eating dinner. If you eat dinner at a certain time, then that time would trigger the habit. If you have dinner immediately after getting home from work, yet you get home from work at different times of the day, then getting home from work would be the trigger for dinner.

As you can see, cues can be rather complex and can be associated with just about anything. The best way to identify the trigger of an existing habit is to begin to pay attention to exactly what you are doing the moment you begin to engage in said habit, as well as exactly what you were doing in the moments before you engaged in that habit. Be sure to explore all five of your senses, as well as your circumstances, to ensure that you have a full understanding around what it is that is the cue for your habit.

When you begin to consciously create habits, you are going to want to intentionally develop your cue.

Through this, you can decide what specifically will result in you engaging in your habit. Then, you will go ahead and consciously interact with your cue immediately before following through on the routine so that your brain makes the association. At this point, the unconscious work going on in your basal ganglia will be exactly the same; the only difference is that you will be directing it with your conscious mind.

Step Two: The Routine

The routine of your habit is the part where you engage in the habit itself. This isolated part of the habit routine is often seen as the habit in its entirety by people who are unclear on what a three step habit loop actually is, or who are unclear on how the brain works when it is developing habits.

The routine of your habit is the behavioral pattern that your basal ganglia is looking out for so that it can keep track of the actions you are taking that are associated with the developing or developed habit. Here, your basal ganglia wants repetition that happens in the exact same way every single time. This means that you are going to complete each step of the routine in the same way, in the same order, every single time you engage in your habit loop.

For unconscious habits, your basal ganglia may start by getting a general idea of what it is that you are doing, and in what order you are doing it. Over time, it will start to help you "refine" these steps until they have been designed in such a way that it is easy to repeat in the same way, in the same order, every single time. At this point, each step is as much a habit as each overall routine is. The basal ganglia knows the routine is over when your brain experiences a reward. This reward is typically a chemical reaction in the brain that produces a positive feeling, thus making habits addicting and easy for you to repeat.

When you are looking to consciously develop new habits in your life, you want to identify a set routine that you can do in the same way, in the same order, every single time you consciously engage in your routine. For added benefit, you should be consciously thinking about each step that you are engaging in and the order you are engaging in it through so that you can draw your direct attention and awareness to this information. This way, your subconscious mind is more likely to absorb that information in its intended order and, through that, create your desired habit.

It is very important that you do exactly the same thing in exactly the same way to the best of your ability every single time. You must also consciously engage in your cue *before* the routine so that your brain begins to associate the routine with the said cue. This is how you can start to form a real habit loop in your brain that will become automatic and effortless. If it is easier for you to remember, consider your cue as "step one" of your habit every single time, and in every single habit you create.

Step Three: The Reward

The reward is perhaps the most important part of the entire habit loop. Within the reward, your brain determines whether a habit is worthy enough of its attention, and whether or not it deserves to be turned into a habit. The better the reward, the more likely a habit will be developed, and the stronger that habit will become.

In your brain, there is a portion known as the "reward system," which is responsible for what is known as "incentive salience." Incentive salience refers to motivation and wanting desire and craving for a specific reward. Whenever you engage in a habit, your brain produces a rewarding effect and, then, begins to crave that rewarding effect which encourages you to engage in the behavior again and again. Rewards are generally experienced in emotions such as joy, euphoria, or ecstasy. During the process of a reward, your brain produces dopamine which is responsible for developing those positive and oftentimes addictive emotional experiences.

There are three types of rewards you will experience when you engage in a habit, primary rewards, intrinsic rewards, and extrinsic rewards. Primary rewards are ones that facilitate the survival of one's self and offspring, which can include eating, engaging in sexual contact with your partner, and raising your child. Intrinsic rewards are considered to be unconditioned and create a deep sense of inner and personal pleasure whenever they are fulfilled. Extrinsic rewards are those which are conditioned and are attractive but are not inherently pleasurable and include things like making money or watching your favorite sports team win a game.

Through the reward center in your brain, you learn to engage more positive behaviors and refrain from engaging in harmful behaviors. From a primal point of view, this helps entire species continue to thrive by allowing them to engage in behaviors that positively affect their survival and wellbeing and avoiding behaviors that could cause damage or kill them off. Of course, it is not perfect, and many species, humans and non-humans alike, will engage in behaviors that can have harmful side effects because they are capable of producing a reward-like experience in the brain. For example, eating junk foods or consuming harmful substances that are able to support your reward system in producing addictive rewards.

The Anatomy Of a Strong Reward

As you begin to take responsibility for your own habits, you will find that you need to learn how to effectively navigate the reward center of your brain in order to cement habits in. Rewards are the entire motivator behind habits, and, arguably, they are as uniquely complex as the entire habit loop itself. Knowing how to pick positive rewards as a way to reward yourself for engaging in your chosen habit is important, as it will allow you to trigger an actual chemical reaction in your brain that rewards you for your experience, and motivates you to do it again.

Primal rewards are unlikely to be relevant or even remotely helpful in most of the habits that you are going to want to create for yourself. Extrinsic rewards, while enjoyable, are often not nearly as motivating as intrinsic rewards, meaning that while they are important, they are unlikely to provide you with the motivation that you need. As well, you may not have the resources to provide yourself with extrinsic rewards every time you engage in a new habit, which means this form of reward may be unrealistic for you. Intrinsic rewards, then, are the last route and are the best way for you to go.

Intrinsic rewards are any rewards that provide you personally with a deepened sense of joy and fulfillment. They can be elicited by external events, but they rarely give you a lasting, tangible reward. Instead, they give you a deep inner feeling of joy, euphoria, or ecstasy that allow you to feel incredibly positive for the activities that you have engaged in. Thus, your goal when creating a positive reward for your habit loop is to identify rewards that are going to give you unlimited intrinsic reward.

The key to picking an intrinsic reward that is going to rapidly and effectively cement your new habits into place is to choose one that is going to make you feel incredibly good, and one that can be completed immediately after engaging in the new habit. This way, your basal ganglia immediately recognizes the cue, routine, and reward, and your reward center is able to be abundantly boosted in order to create the results you desire.

Some ideal rewards you could use to reinforce your new habits include: calling a loved one and having a positive and enjoyable phone call, having a few minutes of you-time where you give yourself unconditional attention and care, a pep talk to yourself in the mirror, a happy dance as soon as you complete the new habit, or a moment for deeply felt and expressed gratitude. These are all rewards that can be engaged in quickly that are not contingent upon resources, and that will provide an abundance of joy, euphoria, or ecstasy in your brain so that your habit loop is complete and strong enough to motivate you to complete it again.

Chapter 5

Diverting Your Desire

While habits are often seen as a repeated routine of behaviors by your conscious mind, the real driving force behind habits is the reward cycle for your subconscious mind. For that reason, knowing how to work with your desire in a proper and healthy manner is far more conductive than attempting to work against your desire in order to change your habits. This is a key factor that many people miss because they do not realize how truly powerful and necessary the reward and desire is for their ability to effectively create, shift, and break habits.

To put it in layman's terms, your brain creates micro-addictions to things that are enjoyable for you so that you will do more of them. It also creates aversions to things that are not enjoyable so that you will do less of them, exactly as you learned when we discussed rewards. In order to effectively develop new habits, then you need to be able to identify how to create the same form of desire through a new system of actions. If you fail to complete this process, any habit you are attempting to form will be driven solely on willpower which will inevitably run out and result in you no longer following through on this new habit. For many people, this pattern will also create a feeling of shame within you as you continually fail to achieve your desired result and have to face the embarrassment of admitting defeat on yet another goal. As this shame cycle grows, it becomes harder and harder to embrace new habits because your willpower dwindles *and* you grow to stop believing in yourself and your ability to engage in new habits.

Fortunately, shifting your approach to include a redirection of your desire rather than attempting to deny your desire is all you need to correct this experience. This way, you can begin to experience new habits, achieve your desired goals, and break the cycle of shame as you realize that the problem was not with you but with your approach to the habit-forming cycle.

Resisting Desire Creates Relapses

Let's explore what the average approach to changing a habit looks like before an individual is educated on how to effectively work with the nature of their brain to facilitate change. Say you decide you want to change your diet so that you can reach your ideal weight and stamina, so you go to the bookstore and find a book that discusses a diet that can help you reach your needs. You educate yourself on this book, you get excited about the recipes and the extrinsic reward, and you are thrilled to get started. Amidst all your excitement, you toss out all of the food in your kitchen that does not fit the diet and you immediately begin eating this new way. For the first few days, or maybe even the first couple of weeks, everything is going great. You are pushing through cravings, you are eating every meal, and you are reaching all of your targets that you have set out for yourself. Things are *awesome*.

And then suddenly the momentum drops. You stop feeling so excited about the diet, and your cravings start feeling a little stronger. The novelty of this new diet has worn off; maybe you have seen some of the rewards for your change but not all of the rewards you had hoped for or it feels as though they are taking far too long to arrive. You think "just this once I'll eat something that does not adhere to my diet" and you cave. And suddenly, you can't stop. You held out on fulfilling that desire for so long that now, not only are you eating what you shouldn't be, but you are eating way more and you can't seem to reel yourself in. Your relapse, as we will call it, may even be worse than your original habit because the abstinence of desire made the fulfillment of desire *so* much better. And thus, your diet is broken and you are back where you started, if not worse.

Anytime you resist desire, you are setting yourself up for failure. Your brain is not wired to resist desire, and there is no good reason for you to attempt to resist desire, either. You can work within the realm of observing, being mindful of, and even delaying desire to a degree, but attempting to resist it indefinitely will create incredibly negative feelings around your new habit, which will eventually lead to you ditching the habit altogether. It may seem like you did so because you were lazy or not strong enough to keep going, but the opposite is actually true. You were incredibly strong to go as long as you did, because you were literally denying your brain of the thing it was craving, meaning that you denied your very nature. This requires magnificent strength and required you to use your willpower alone to push through for as long as you did. Eventually, though, that strength ran out and as soon as it did the new behavior fell apart.

Whenever this happens, you can feel confident that what you were creating was *not* a new habit. In order for it to have been a new habit, you would have needed to fulfill the craving for desire by engaging in a positive reward. Instead, you were engaging in a chosen repeated behavior that was running entirely through your conscious mind, thus defying the very point of a habit, which is to sink a chosen behavior into your subconscious mind so that it becomes automatic.

The only way to stop engaging in this battle of willpower and to prevent yourself from experiencing yo-yo like behavior as you bounce back and forth with new "habits" is to introduce desire back into the mixture. The key is to introduce desire intentionally, mindfully, and in such a way that promotes your desired outcome so that you are far more likely to actually reach it. When you can do this, then you will create true habits that are easy to build, easy to maintain, and that are far more likely to actually sink into your subconscious mind with the support of your basal ganglia and your reward system.

While creating a new habit in this manner will reduce the instance of relapses, it is important to note that it will not prevent them altogether. Once a habit loop has been established in the brain, it is extremely easy for that habit to be reengaged at any point in the future. While it does become less and less likely for it to be engaged, it can be, and thus, you must always be mindful of your behavior to ensure that you are never slipping into an old habit loop again. Remember, habit loops are triggered by a complex system of cues and, for that reason, it can sometimes be hard to ensure that you effectively rewire your behavior around every single cue associated with any given habit. The most effective way to navigate these potential relapses is to be mindful of your behavior, to witness anytime you see yourself slipping into old habits, and to use willpower to help you shift back into your preferred habit. Then, rely on the cycle of cue, routine, and reward (desire) to allow you to carry on with that new habit. Through this, you will be effectively balancing mindfulness, willpower, and desire to create strong, lasting habits that support you in reaching your goals in life.

Identifying Your True Desire

Much like how cues can be rather elusive at times, identifying your true desire can be elusive at times, too. With rewards existing in three forms, primal, intrinsic, and extrinsic, we can summarize that there are also three forms of desire: the desire to fulfill primary rewards, the desire to fulfill intrinsic rewards, and the desire to fulfill extrinsic rewards. Generally speaking, when it comes to developing new habits, the best approach is to focus largely on intrinsic desire while also recognizing extrinsic desire. This way, you are focusing on the most deeply fulfilling desire and reward system that is within your control, as well as an additional desire and reward system that has a positive impact on your life and your capacity to reach your worldly goals.

If you have been living your life with unconscious habits, you may not clearly understand what your desires are or what actually motivates you to engage in new habits. It may also feel challenging for you to identify each specific desire attached to each specific habit so that you can effectively navigate the redirection of that particular desire. As with discovering cues, some sleuthing can be helpful as it will support you in discovering what your actual desires are and how you can use those desires to create strong and positive habits.

One way you can begin to identify desire and the specific reward being gained from a habit you are engaging in is to identify what you are thinking about during the fulfillment of that habit and what you are most fulfilled by immediately after it. See if you can keep a log of each time you engage in that habit for the next few days or weeks, depending on how frequently you engage in said habit and keep track of this information. You should begin to see a pattern in desire or motivation and rewards being gained from your habit relatively quickly, allowing you to realize what it is that you are looking for and gaining every single time you engage in this behavior.

Another way to dig into what your desires are is to start paying attention to your emotions. Through your emotions, you can start to identify your general desires, which will allow you to gain a stronger understanding of what drives you in general. This way, you can begin to use this to understand what is likely to be driving you in each individual habit, thus narrowing down that which may be affecting you and supporting you with shifting your habits more quickly.

Jealousy is a very important emotion to watch for when it comes to desire, as you will often experience jealousy around people who have something that you want. You may be jealous of a specific person, or of something in particular that many people may have in common. For example, you may be jealous of your friend, or you may be jealous anytime you see someone in a positive, healthy romantic relationship. When you witness yourself experiencing jealousy, start asking yourself questions to identify why you are jealous, or what it is that you wish you had that someone else has. Anytime you feel jealous, it is because you desire something that someone else has, which can help you uncover a desire that you are experiencing that seems as though it is going unfulfilled.

You should also pay attention anytime you feel uncomfortable or anytime you experience a "no way" response; for example, "there's no way I could do that!" Discomfort shows you anytime there is something in your life that you do not want, which allows you to then examine what it is that you do want. For example, maybe anytime you talk to a certain person you experience discomfort so you try to push through it or avoid that person in order to avoid the discomfort. Upon further examination, you may realize that the reason why that discomfort exists is that this person tends to cross your boundaries when you are talking to them, which means that you desire for more boundaries. The "no way" response is a specific form of discomfort that means that you feel a level of intimidation and admiration from something that you are being faced with. If you were truly disinterested in something, your response would be less emotionally charged because you would not care about the experience or event. When you experience this emotional response to something that makes you uncomfortable through intimidation and admiration, this means that there is likely an unexpressed or unexplored desire hidden in there that you need to explore.

It is also important to realize that after you have had a particular habit for any given period of time, it may begin to develop new rewards unto itself that continue to reinforce that particular habit. One big reward in particular that tends to be experienced by people who engage in long time habits is the reward of familiarity. Familiarity keeps us comfortable by keeping our surroundings and our lives familiar and predictable, which means that we can switch off of surveillance mode and relax from time to time. In these settings, your primal brain knows that you are unlikely to be at risk of experiencing any incoming threats, so you can simply relax and be at ease in your life. Be aware of these secondary rewards when you are looking through existing habits to ensure that you are truly seeing the entirety of what you are gaining from each habit you explore. This way, you know exactly what needs to happen in order for you to fully shift away from that habit.

As you begin to identify these general desires that you have, you can use them to help you develop new habits, or to change existing habits that you already have. This is an excellent way to step out of the practice of denying your desire and into the practice of leveraging your desire to create positive habits.

Redirecting Your True Desire

Once you uncover your true desire, you need to start identifying ways that you can redirect your desire. This is going to be a two-step process: first, you are going to identify what the desire is and how it could be fulfilled in different, healthier ways. Then, you are going to define a specific routine that is going to help you achieve the fulfillment of that desire, and it's reward in a way that is far more positive and healthy for you.

Understand that true desires are often rooted in emotions and, therefore, are easy to be redirected. For example, let's say you have a habit of eating junk food because when you do you feel a sense of comfort from eating it. In this case, your desire is for comfort, and your reward is experiencing that comfort. To redirect this reward, all you would need to do, then, is to identify healthier methods for achieving comfort. Perhaps you could identify comfort through listening to a guided meditation or relaxing music, through confiding in a trusted friend, or through massaging your body with a pleasant smelling lotion.

Anytime you are redirecting your reward, it is important that you understand exactly where that reward is being experienced in your life. Elaborating on comfort, for example, is the reward of comfort eating bringing you physical, mental, or emotional comfort? Or a combination of all three? When you begin to understand what specifically is being comforted, or rewarded, when you engage in habitual behavior, you gain the capacity to understand what specifically needs to be done to fulfill that reward in a new way.

Right now, I want you to take just one of the habits that you wish to change in your life. Then, I want you to write that habit down on the top of a piece of paper, or on a note in your phone. Under it, write down the cue and the step by step actions you are taking to fulfill that habit. Then, write down what you believe the reward is for fulfilling that habit. Now, I want you to write down all of the positive and negative side effects that you are experiencing in your life surrounding that particular habit. With all of this written down, you can now plainly see how this particular habit is serving you, how it is affecting you, and what benefit you are gaining from this habit that keeps you engaging in it time and again.

Now, I want you to brainstorm at least 3-5 different ways that you could fulfill this reward in a manner that is much healthier for you, and that will support you in achieving the results you desire. Be mindful of also identifying routines that will minimize unwanted or negative side effects so that you are not causing harm to yourself in any way whilst changing your existing habits. You will use this list of brainstormed routines to help you fully redirect your desire and habit in the next step.

Finding a Healthier New Routine

Finding a healthier new routine for any habit you have been engaging in for any period of time is important, and it takes some effort on your behalf. You need to adequately way the pros and cons of potential new routines so that you can see which ones are likely to give you the best benefits and which ones may keep you in a negative habit loop. At this point, your entire goal is to find a new routine that is going to give you a new experience with your old desire and reward. This way, you are able to continue to fulfill your needs without creating all of the unwanted side effects and patterns that your old routine was creating.

Once you have identified the best possible routine for you to engage in as a part of your new habit, you can write that routine down. Then, you want to break that routine down into a step-by-step process that you can follow in the same way and in the same order, every single time. Write that process down in order now so that you can see it out in front of you.

For the last part of redirecting your routine, you are going to want to honestly look through the routine to ensure that it will help you reach your desired goal. Then, you need to look through it and honestly assess whether or not this is a routine you will engage in. Consider your likes, dislikes, preferences, and personality, as well as what types of resources you have access to and whether or not this routine will actually fit in with your everyday life. You must make your new routine reasonable, realistic, and achievable in order for you to engage in it. Otherwise, you are giving yourself every reason to stop engaging in it, rather than every reason to keep going.

The ideal routine for your redirected desires will be one that promotes your ability to fulfill your desire, achieve your reward, and do so in a way that has as few negative impacts on your life as possible. It should also be one that you are going to enjoy engaging in, that is going to be easy for you to engage in, and that will be sustainable for you to engage in. If your redirected routine fulfills all of these criteria, then you can feel confident that you have found a redirection that is going to maximize your potential to shift your bad habit for good.

Remaining Conscious Over Your Desires

You may have noticed I mentioned that no matter how effectively you create a new habit, or how long you engage in the new habit, it is possible that your old habit could emerge at any given point in an effort to achieve your desires and rewards the old way. This can happen anytime, an unrecognized cue is triggered, if the new habit has not been repeated enough to be strong enough to override the old habit, or if you are under stress and are suddenly in need of something familiar and comfortable. It can also happen if you begin to remove your conscious awareness from your habits, as you may find yourself slipping into old patterns unintentionally, and with no seeming rhyme or reason.

If you are going to effectively maintain your new habits and achieve your desired goals, you are going to have to remain conscious of your desires and your habits at all times. While this may seem counterintuitive, realize that this does not mean that you have to remove any level of automation from the new habits you have developed. You do not have to push yourself to consciously remember and engage in that habit over and over every single time. After all, it would not be a habit if you were engaging in this form of behavior.

Instead, your goal is to ensure that you are regularly consciously checking in with your habits and being mindful of your desires to ensure that your habits are continuing to fulfill your desires at all times. Over time, your desires may shift. As well, a change in your circumstances could give rise to new desires, or possibly even old desires that resurface. Being mindful and aware of this can support you in navigating your desires so that you can continue to empower and improve your positive habits and discourage and shift your negative habits. Through this, you will drastically minimize your risk of experiencing a relapse and falling out of your new habit.

Chapter 6

Planning Your New Habits

Shifting habits and creating new habits are quite similar, although the process does vary slightly. When it comes to shifting unwanted habits, your focus is on identifying your existing desire and reward and shifting the way that you fulfill that desire and reward. While it may seem like a new habit, you are still engaging in an old pattern; you are simply approaching it in a new way. Creating new habits altogether occurs when you uncover a new desire and the potential for a new reward and choose to develop a habit that will allow you to routinely fulfill that desire and reward. During this process, you truly do gain the opportunity to play master creator in your own life as you decide what your habits will look like and what lifestyle they will help you create.

Identifying the Need For New Habits

The first thing you must do when it comes to creating new habits is identifying the need for habits in the first place. When your brain automatically designs habits for you, it's number one focus is to identify what habits would optimize your daily or weekly experiences to ensure that you are able to get through them quickly and easily, every single time. Since you are taking the habit-making process off autopilot and putting it in your own hands, you are going to need to do this detective work for yourself to identify what habits are going to help you optimize your life.

In this unique scenario, you have the capacity to foresee how habits are going to affect you and, therefore, you can identify which habits are going to help you create the lifestyle you want rather than merely help you maintain the lifestyle you have. This gives you a sense of leverage in that you can identify and decide upon your chosen lifestyle in advance and then begin cultivating habits that will help you get there over time.

From this unique vantage point, you need to start identifying habits that are going to support you with cultivating the life that you actually want to be living, or developing the skills that will help you reach your desired goals. At this point, you can brainstorm some ideal habits that will help get you there, and you can break down that list and choose the one that you will start with based on what you think will get you the furthest. When it does come time to decide which one you will start with, make sure you only choose one as this is going to be your primary focus until you integrate it. Attempting to integrate too many new habits at once can be overwhelming for your brain, especially when these habits are designed with respect to what you anticipate or what you are creating, rather than what you are experiencing right now. Taking your time will ensure that you are able to be more thorough and that your new habits will be sustainable and effective.

The Anatomy Of a Positive Habit

With your list of potential habits brainstormed, it is time to start comparing those brainstormed habits to the anatomy of a positive habit. This way, you can identify which habit is going to be best suited to be your main focus for the coming weeks and possibly months as you place all your focus on the development and creation of this habit.

Positive habits should have these main elements: clarity, significance, low risk, simplicity, relevance, and desire. If these six elements are present in your ideal habit, you are looking at a habit that is likely going to support you in many ways as you begin to put it into action.

Clarity in a habit means that you can clearly identify what the habit is, what it will look like, and how it is going to benefit you. It should be simple for you to define the habit and each step of the habit itself to ensure that it is easy for you to follow and replicate. A habit that has not been clearly defined is one that may not provide you with the best results because you will not clearly understand what needs to be done. If you have only discovered the need for a habit, or for improvement in an area, but not an actual habit itself, you need to do more brainstorming.

Significance means that your new habit is going to offer you maximum impact, and as many benefits as possible. When we want to simplify something and integrate it as a part of our regular routine, it is important that we choose things that are going to go a long way. This does not mean that the biggest part of your day or the most important part of your goal needs to be turned into an automatic practice. It does, however, mean that the habit you are choosing to embrace is going to go a long way in helping you create results. For example, getting into the habit of making coffee before you start work every day is unlikely to affect your ability to achieve your goals, but getting into the habit of turning off distractions and getting focused will have a huge impact on your results. Make sure that the habits you choose will help create as many results for you as possible.

In addition to bringing you many benefits, you should also be focused on developing habits that are low risk.

Habits are often considered a "bad" thing because many times we roll toxic behaviors into our habits, which in turn makes them bad. This is not inherent to habits, though, and the toxicity factor does not have to be relevant to every habit in existence. Make sure that any habit you create has as few risks as possible, and that it is not going to have detrimental or unwanted side effects that will ultimately negate from the point of the habit itself. If you do notice potential for something toxic to come of your new habit, adjust your habit to eliminate the risk.

Simplicity is a key factor in making any habit stick. The easier your habit is, the more likely you will be to see it all the way through and, therefore, the more success you will experience in developing that habit and truly turning it into an automatic behavioral pattern. Ideally, you should be able to clearly identify the process of the habit, and it should be effortless for you to access the resources and complete each step of that process.

The habits you are seeking to create should also be relevant to who you are and what you are and are not willing to do. Attempting to create habits that are not relevant to you because they clash with your personality or your preferences is going to result in you struggling to see them all the way through. There are many ways to adapt habits so that they fit with your personality and preferences, and so that they are relevant to who you are and what you prefer. This way, you are creating habits that are realistic to you and that will actually get you the life that you desire and help you fulfill the goals that matter to you.

Lastly, you need to think about your desire factor around the habits you want to create. Remember, desire and reward are the number one things that drive us to create and maintain habits, and without them our habits will likely never stick. Identify which desire it is that is driving your potential habit and see if you can tie it in with a significant desire and a meaningful reward that will help you see your habit all the way through.

Giving Your Reward Significance

As desire is what drives the creation of habit, it is important that we address which desire it is that you are going to be tapping into, and what reward you are going to be using, to develop consistency within your habits. If you are going to be switching one habit for a new habit, all you need to do is change the routine while keeping the trigger and reward the same. If you are going to be creating an entirely new habit around an unexpressed desire, though, you are going to need to explore how to amplify that desire and create a strong enough reward to warrant the creation of a new habit.

By following the process of uncovering your desires in chapter 5, you have likely gained insight into what it is that you truly desire in your life. Through this, you can start to identify at least one strong desire you have that you can associate with your new habit and a potential reward that you can use alongside that desire to make that habit stick. In order to truly amplify the power of this desire, though, you need to teach your subconscious mind that it is a desire worth working toward. If you do not, your subconscious mind will ignore that desire because it does not know what it is missing.

A great way to get started with strengthening your desire and identifying a positive and strong reward for your new habit is to indulge in your unexpressed desires for a while. Try out new methods for pursuing and fulfilling those desires, and relish in the positive emotional and mental experience you have upon fulfilling them. Let yourself increase your desire through curiosity and exploration, and continue to do so until you find yourself incredibly excited about fulfilling that desire again and again. Then, turn that into a desire that drives your new habit.

By building up to the desire this way, you are training your brain to see that this particular desire is worth your attention, and that it is worth fulfilling. The subconscious then begins to realize that there is a positive intrinsic reward associated with this particular behavior and recognizes that a habit in this area of your life would be valuable. From there, when you begin to consciously implement intentional habits into this area of your life, you will have the support of your subconscious mind as it attempts to latch onto a habit in this area, too, so that it can continue to experience the desired reward.

Planning Out Your New Habit, Step-By-Step

Now that your subconscious mind is activated and ready to help your conscious mind implement your new habit, it is time for you to fit your new desired habit over the three step habit loop. You are going to start this process by identifying a simple, easy to identify the cue that will indicate when it is time to engage in your new habit. For example, a time of day, the ending of a different habit, or any other cue that you know without a doubt will reliably appear when you need it to in order to remind you to engage in your new habit.

After you have identified your cue, you need to go ahead and identify a simple to follow step-by-step method for the routine. Here, you need to clearly identify each part of the process you are going to follow, how, and in what order. It can be helpful to organize the steps of the process in chronological order on a checklist so that you can refer to it and complete the habit in the same way, and in the same order, every single time. Make sure this part is simple to follow and that it will be reasonable for you to complete each step the same way every time by ensuring that the necessary resources will be available for you to use.

Lastly, associate your routine with your reward by identifying how you will consciously tie your reward into the habit. This could be through intentionally recognizing and indulging in the fulfillment of your desire as you engage in the habit and then exaggerating the reward when you receive it, or it could be through taking necessary action to draw forth the reward. Either way, make sure you clearly tie the routine into the reward so that you can guarantee its fulfillment every single time you engage in your habit. And, if possible, enhance the reward in a simple and repeatable manner so that you can increase your subconscious mind's desire to anchor in this new habit.

After you have identified the cue, routine, and reward for your habit loop, you are going to need to look your entire habit through from start to finish to ensure that it flows smoothly and effectively. If you notice any area of the habit that needs to be strengthened or reinforced, or that could be made simpler or more effective, work through that right away. You should also maintain some flexibility so that you can adapt your new habits as needed until you find the proper routine that works best for you.

Planning the Execution Of Your New Habit

The last step in planning your new habit before you can move into actual execution of that habit is to plan the execution itself. The execution of any new habit comes in two steps: the trial period and the official subscription. A trial period with a habit reflects the first few executions of the habit where you are trying out your plan for the habit and ensuring that it works, that it flows well, and that it gets you the results you desire. At this point, you are going to work through the habit a few times to ensure that you are getting exactly what you need out of it and that you are going to be able to engage in it over and over again for the foreseeable future.

The trial period of any new habit usually lasts for around the first 3-5 executions of the habit, as this is when you are really going to be going through the motions. At this point, you may realize that some of the steps you planned out need to be improved or that a step needs to be added or even removed in order for you to create the results that you desire. Be flexible during this time and be open to adapting your habit as needed, so long as the adaptation continues to help you achieve the results you desire.

Once you have effectively made it through the trial period, you will move into the subscription of the habit. This is where you officially subscribe to the method you have planned out for yourself, and you commit to seeing that habit through in the same way, and through the same order, time and again. At this point, you do not want to adjust the habit at all unless it is absolutely necessary, as doing so will result in you disrupting the natural habit making process in your subconscious mind. Remember, your subconscious mind does not care about good or bad; it cares about repetition. You want to repeat something as much as possible, and through that consistency, you will find yourself naturally integrating that habit into your life.

Through your continued subscription to your habit, you will find the habit slowly slipping into your subconscious mind until you no longer have to think about fulfilling that habit. Instead, it will automatically be fulfilled through the natural habit process of your subconscious mind. At this point, you will have completed your work with the habit, and all you will need to do is work toward maintaining that habit so that nothing in your life disrupts it or derails it. This is the part of the process where your habit fulfillment becomes virtually effortless and you can easily move on to creating and implementing another new habit to complement the one you have already implemented.

Chapter 7

Executing Your New Habits

While a great deal of the habit creation process revolves around rewards, anyone who has attempted to implement new habits into their lives will know that the reward is great, but it is virtually meaningless if you cannot get yourself started in the first place. Motivating yourself to begin a new habit or to engage in a new habit can be challenging, no matter how positive or rewarding you know it will be. That is because, arguably, you are in the habit of *not* engaging in that habit, and so you have to work toward breaking that cycle and getting into the action *as well as* get through the new habit. This may seem small in your conscious mind, but to your subconscious mind, that is a lot of work to sort through which is why it is so hard for you to get into action in the first place.

Fortunately, there are many things you can try to help you get motivated and get started so that you can leap into action and integrate your new habits. Each of these processes are designed to work *with* your nature, instead of against it, effectively supporting you with creating the motivation you need to engage in your new habits. As you approach these methods, it may be beneficial to turn the process of motivating yourself into a habit itself so that it becomes easier for you to continually engage in new habits. This can also help you draw away from the need for you to continually call on willpower so that you can stop exerting so much mental effort into the practice of getting motivated and start relying on a less mentally demanding experience.

Willpower and the Motivation To Engage

Willpower is a form of mental control that is exerted to help you do something or refrain from engaging in impulses. A great way to think of willpower is to consider it your mental turbo boost. When you are in need of that extra kick or mental strength, you can call on willpower to help get you through whatever it is that you are working through. With that being said, just like a turbo boost, it can only offer so much boost before it needs to recharge so that it can offer you more again in the future. In other words, relying on willpower for long periods of time is an ineffective and unsustainable way to approach your habits.

Rather than attempting to rely on willpower for long term support, it is more productive to rely on willpower to get you in the habit of getting started with your new habit. Use it to support you with creating the motivation to get started during the trial period and for the first few times that you work on your subscribed habit. Then, as you begin to move into a more full-time experience with your new habit, you can go ahead and start relying on other things to keep you going.

When you use willpower in this more sustainable method, you are leveraging it for what it is intended for rather than relying on it for more than it has the capacity to accomplish. In the meantime, as you use willpower to get you going, make sure that you are also supporting yourself in creating thoughts and beliefs that are going to keep you going so that you are fostering a positive can-do mindset toward your new habit.

Turning Motivation Into a Habit

When we address the creation of new habits, it can be easy to focus on the actual habit itself. For example, if you want to get into the habit of eating healthier, reading more, or exercising on a regular basis, you may focus exclusively on this new area of focus. However, if you really want to create sustainable results, it can be beneficial for you to focus on turning motivation into a habit, too. In fact, many people will focus on the habit of self-motivating before anything else, as this is a habit that can be relied on to create even more self-motivation in the future.

You can turn motivation into a habit by applying the same methods of habit creation to the habit of self-motivation, and by using that habit every single time, you need to motivate yourself to do something. Even if you are not motivating yourself to engage in a new habit per se, you can call on this habit to motivate you to mow the lawn, cook supper, or get a chore done that you have been putting off for a while now.

Each time you successfully motivate yourself to get something done, be sure to recognize your motivation and to emphasize your success that you experienced in motivating yourself to get into action. The more you can celebrate, amplify, and integrate this habit, the easier it will be to motivate yourself to begin new habits in the future as the process of even getting started with that new habit will bring a great sense of reward to your mind. In this way, you are creating smart habits that will go a long way in helping you achieve your goals.

Forming Your New Habits Around Existing Ones

During the trial period of your new habit, while you are still relying on willpower to get you started, it can be helpful to create other correlations that motivate you to get into action. These correlations begin to anchor into your subconscious mind that a habit needs to be engaged, which means that rather than relying on your willpower to get you started, you will feel a deeper need to engage in your habit due to the correlation itself. If you continue to create these correlations and act on them when you feel compelled to, you will effectively support your new habit with integrating into your subconscious mind. In other words, you will be supporting those early stages of creating and maintaining a new habit.

The best way to develop correlations to help you maintain your new habits is to create correlations that are easy to remember and follow. For example, attaching your new habit to an existing habit that you already have. This way, you are already up and in action, so moving into new action is easy because you do not need to summon the energy to get there. As well, at this point, your existing habit is already cemented in, and therefore, it is likely that you are going to engage in it no matter what. This way, you can feel confident that you are going to see it through and, therefore, you can feel confident that the cue to start your next habit will exist every single time.

To begin forming your new habit around existing ones, consider which habits will make the most sense to attach your new habits too. This way, you are organizing your habits in a way that makes sense and is reasonable, thus meaning you will be far more likely to see those habits all the way through. Make sure that the existing habit you choose is one that you have been doing for a long time, as attempting to attach a new habit to an immature habit can lead to you losing two habits rather than just one if you do find yourself falling off the wagon at any point. So, for example, attaching your new habit to a part of your morning, afternoon, or evening routine that you have had for a long period of time so that you are far more likely to actively engage in these new routines. When you build your schedule out wisely in this way, you are far more likely to see all of your habits through and create the results you desire.

Rewarding Yourself For Motivation

As you are turning motivation into a habit itself and calling on that habit to help you get into action on other habits you want to create, it is important that you consider the reward of this habit itself. In this case, you are going to be rewarding yourself for getting motivated to engage in your new habit *and* for completing the new habit, which means technically you will be experiencing two rewards to get you through the new habit you are engaging in.

The best way to reward yourself for motivation is to award your motivation efforts with your attention and awareness. In other words, every single time you motivate yourself into action focus largely on how proud you are of yourself and what you have been able to achieve in your life as a result of your motivation. Many times, people find themselves taking away from their own motivation rather than adding to it because as soon as they notice the need for motivation, or act on it, they flood their minds with negative thoughts. They think things like "I don't want to be doing this" or "this sucks" or "I can't wait until this gets easier," which tells their subconscious mind that engaging in this new habit is dreadful and that the reward is not worth it in the end. If, however, the thoughts you were flooding your mind with was positive, your brain would start to associate your new habit with positive things and, as a result, it would feel rewarded for getting motivated. This would start to formulate the positive foundation for your belief system that would then support your ability to move away from willpower and into habitual motivated action.

As you begin to cultivate new habits, start being particularly mindful around the mental dialogue you are experiencing anytime you go to engage in these habits, or as you are engaging in them. Be particularly cautious about any negative dialogue you are experiencing and mindfully move away from that negative dialogue anytime you find yourself engaging in it so that you can move toward positive dialogue instead.

You can also reward yourself for motivation through actual tangible rewards if you feel the need to ramp up your reward system. A quick little happy dance you do for yourself, or a few minutes spent singing or humming to your favorite song are great ways to show your mind that getting motivated is a great way to go. You can also try recognizing any tangible benefits from your motivation, such as having a completed task checked off of your to-do list, or some form of new extrinsic reward in your possession that you gained as a result of your motivation. By taking the extra moment to acknowledge and build excitement around these things, you work toward effectively rewarding yourself for getting motivated, which makes it even easier for you to get rewarded in the future.

Steps For Staying Consistent

Motivating yourself to get motivated is an important part of getting started with your new habits, but there is plenty more that you can be doing to help you stay consistent with your new habits, too. The more actions you can take to help yourself stay motivated, the more likely you will be to get into action and complete your new habit every single time. This way, you will have a much easier time integrating this new habit into your subconscious mind, effectively making it a real habit.

One of the best ways that you can stay consistent with your new habit is to have some sort of alarm or reminder set that will tell you when it is time to engage in your new habit. If you find that you are the type of person who tends to put reminders off until a later time, you might consider putting a few on just to make sure that you really do get up and get into action. Oftentimes, when we engage in new habits, it can be easy to completely forget about said habit until it begins to develop some level of automation. This is because you are simply not used to engaging in the habit and so it is incredibly easy for the habit itself to slip your mind. If you were to have a reminder, however, you would not have to worry about forgetting to engage in the habit because you would already have the reminder you need to get started.

Another great way to help yourself stay consistent is to motivate yourself to get into the habit of keeping everything as simple as possible. For example, make sure that all of the supplies you need to complete your habit are readily available, easy to access, and easy to use. This way, when it comes time for you to engage in your new habit, you are less likely to make any excuses or complain because you already have everything you need in place to help you get started.

Another way that you can help yourself stay consistent with new habits is through a personal accountability system that acts as a form of reward all on its own. To understand what I mean, think back to when you were a child, and recall how people used to motivate you to see things through. It is likely that your parents or teachers used things like stickers as a little reward to help you stay motivated to get something done. This way, the reward of actually seeing the new habit through was amplified by the reward of the sticker or the other accountability method. Creating these accountability methods for yourself is a great way to amplify your motivation, add an extra layer of rewards, and keep yourself on track.

If you do choose to use a personal accountability system, you should be cautious about how you approach periods where you fail to see your new habits. With these systems, it can be easy to start to feel bad and get down on yourself if you miss a few days, but that is actually the worst way to approach your new habit when you have made the mistake of breaking your consistency. Rather than getting down on yourself and making yourself feel bad for not seeing that habit through, you would be better to acknowledge anytime you have not been seeing your habit through and use willpower to get yourself moving forward again. If you find that this alone is not enough, you can sit and brainstorm why you do not see your habit through and what needs to change in order for you to get back into action with it. The more you can continue to address and adjust your habit when this happens, the more likely you will be to create a habit that is easy for you to see all the way through. As you do this, be sure to keep a positive or, at the very least, neutral mindset toward your ability to fulfill your habit as bullying yourself or being negative toward yourself will only further deter you from getting back into the habit of your new habit!

Chapter 8

How To Pamper a Habit (and Why)

New habits are high maintenance, no matter what you do to try to make them easier. While there are many ways that you can make your new habits more approachable or simpler for you to embrace, there is nothing you can do to entirely erase the fact that new habits require effort and work on your behalf. The sooner you can accept this, the sooner you can begin to discover how you can nurture your new habits so that they are more likely to stick.

Pampering a new habit essentially means that you are going to acknowledge the fragility of this new habit, recognize that it is easier for you to drop this habit if you are not careful, and then do everything in your power to nurture the habit. The more you can continue to nurture this habit, the more likely you will be to find yourself maintaining consistency so that you can see this habit all the way through to becoming a true habit.

Rest assured that while pampering a new habit does mean that you are going to put added effort into maintaining your new habit, it does not mean that you are going to be babying your habit forever. It simply means that until your habit is rock-solid and less likely to fall apart, you will continue to nurture this new habit and remain mindful of it so that you can feel absolutely confident that you will be able to see this habit all the way through.

Why New Habits Will Always Be More Fragile

New habits are incredibly fragile when you first take them on, and they remain fragile for quite some time after that. While their level of fragility will slowly decline over time, it is important to note that even after years of engaging in a habit, it is still at risk of being abandoned for a habit that has been around for much longer than that habit has been. The more mindful you can be of this fact, the more you can prevent yourself from sabotaging the new habit or losing it in favor of an older and more deeply embedded habit.

The fragility of new habits largely comes from the fact that your brains neuropathways are much stronger for habits that have been around longer, or that have been anchored in deeper. These stronger neuropathways are far more likely to be executed than the more fragile and fresh neuropathways of your younger habits, as your brain can guarantee their results. Plus, they are so worn in that your brain can execute them easily without having to exert too much effort. As a result, they are preferred over newer habits.

If you do not develop the mindfulness of this fact and instead rely on your subconscious mind to help you navigate your habits, it is likely that your new habits will be canceled entirely in favor of older habits that your brain deems as being more effective. As a result, you will constantly find yourself breaking new habits in favor of old ones and struggling to recreate any new habits. While the ones you have worked to create will be easier to recreate than even newer ones, they will still be more fragile than the ones that have been around longer.

Over time, your newer habits will have existed long enough that they will count as older habits and, as a result, they will not be quite so fragile compared to other habits you have been working on creating. However, any habits you have consciously created will always be at risk of being canceled in favor of older habits if you are not careful. If you recall, there are typically countless cues that indicate when a habit should be acted on and, when you consciously create habits, it can be hard to identify and adjust the habits surrounding every single cue your subconscious mind has picked up on. In fact, it may be downright impossible as you cannot examine your subconscious mind to identify what is inside of it. Furthermore, the cues it picks up on are often ones that fall beyond your conscious awareness and could include anything from a certain smell or voice to a certain time of day or emotion you experience. This makes navigating and deleting or rewiring your cues nearly impossible, meaning that you must always be mindful of your habits to avoid accidentally slipping into old patterns and canceling new ones.

What Happens When You Don't Pamper a Habit

When you don't pamper a new habit, it shows. The simplest way to identify a lack of pampering with a new habit is to look for the habits that disappeared as quickly as they appeared. This is because, eventually, the willpower-based momentum that supported these habits in coming to the surface stopped, and the habit was abruptly canceled when your brain then decided to rely on an old habit. Since you were unlikely to be aware of why this was happening, or what you should do about it, you may have found yourself navigating this situation feeling as though you failed yourself or your new habit when, in reality, you simply did not know how to work with the nature of your subconscious mind.

New habits that are canceled due to a lack of pampering can be witnessed as having been cancelled at any phase during their creation. They could be cancelled within days, weeks, months, or even years of being created. For example, let's say you got into the habit of waking up and exercising when you were living abroad, but as soon as you returned home three years later, you abruptly stopped exercising in the morning and now it is challenging for you to start again. Or, let's say you were eating healthier for three months and then you abruptly stopped and went right back to your old eating patterns. These abrupt stops happened because something triggered your old patterns and, you not being aware of what was going on, had no way of knowing how to navigate these situations mindfully.

When you learn how to pamper a habit, you learn how to spot weaknesses in your habit, as well as identify possible situations that could prevent you from effectively navigating and maintaining your habit. Through this, you find yourself being able to mindfully navigate all weaknesses and situations that may cause you to cancel your habit so that, instead, you can strengthen it and keep it alive and thriving.

The goal here, then, is not to turn your habit into anything high maintenance or that will require a long period of ongoing effort and attention so that you can keep it running. After all, this would be no different

MARC WALKER and ALEXANDER LARKESS

than trying to run a habit on willpower rather than subconscious power, which we already know is ineffective. Instead, your goal is to simply be mindful of all of your habits and continue to navigate them as intentionally as possible during periods where they may be jeopardized so that your brain never cancels them in favor of an old pattern.

What It Looks Like To Pamper a Habit

To pamper a habit means to shower it with attention and intention and to keep your focus on maintaining that habit for as long as it takes for that habit to become automatic. This means that you are going to remain dedicated to the habit and that you will do anything you need to in order to see it through and fulfill it every single day. You may even go so far as to doing research to identify new ways to improve your habit, maintain your habit, or even develop smaller "side habits" to help you maintain this habit even more effectively.

In addition to remaining as dedicated to seeing the habit through as you possibly can be, you will also use some of your conscious awareness to ensure that you are doing everything in your power to support that habit. This means you are going to do the extra little bit to ensure that everything is organized so that it is easier for you to do the habit when the time comes. It also means that you are going to continually analyze to ensure that you are doing it properly and to the best of your ability, and that should you notice any weaknesses or setbacks in the development of your habit, you will do what you can to improve the situation.

Should you find yourself experiencing any sort of setback with your habit, you will immediately begin to pamper that habit once more and will jump right back into action as though you never missed a beat. When you are truly pampering a habit, there is no time to sit around and wish you had not quit or to get down on yourself for not keeping up with your habit. This would mean that you had accepted defeat and that you had decided to permanently give up your habit. Instead, you acknowledge the habit has taken a stumble, and you immediately work toward finding a way to repair that stumble by identifying what went wrong and fixing the circumstances. This way, you are not accepting defeat over your habit, but rather, you are staying committed to seeing the habit all the way through, effectively pampering your habit.

While you will not need to pamper a habit quite so long, the longer you maintain it, you will need to continue to pamper it for as long as you wish to have that habit. Over time, however, the habit will require less and less of your attention as you become more capable of engaging in it in a subconscious way. Even so, you should be prepared to check in on your habit from time to time to ensure that it is continuing to work for you and that you are continuing to follow it in the best way possible. If you find yourself slipping, recognize a need for it to be improved, or realize that you have stopped engaging with it altogether, this would be the best time to reinforce that habit and place a greater focus in it so that you can continue maintaining it long term.

How To Pamper Your Own Habit

As far as pampering your own habit goes, there are a few things that you need to consider. If you are going to effectively pamper your habit enough to ensure that it sticks and you do not end up with a canceled habit, you are going to need to put effort into making sure that you have a plan in place for *how* you are going to pamper that habit.

Each habit is designed differently with different cues, routines, and rewards, and different purposes. For that reason, it is best to ensure that you address each unique habit and create plans for how you are going to measure your level of success with that particular habit. Once you have identified how you are going to be able to address and measure each habit, you are going to want to create a plan for how you are going to keep up with these measurements. This way, you know exactly what to expect as far as how you are going to need to manage your new habit to keep it active and effective.

Since you want to focus all of your energy into actually building the habit, it is useful to put your pampering methods on autopilot so that you are not in need of adding any additional habits into your life. Ideally, you should put reminders in your phone to check in on how your habit is doing so that you can receive these reminders automatically. This way, all you need to do is sit down and mindfully think about how the habit is going each time a reminder goes off. You could also use that moment to get everything ready so that it is easier for you to engage in the habit itself when the time comes. At first, you may want to have these reminders scheduled daily. Once you start to notice the habit getting easier and easier, though, you can start to set the reminders a few days apart, and then weekly, and then every few weeks. Eventually, you may only need to check in with your habits on a month to month basis to ensure that everything is running smoothly. During these periodic check ins, you may even check in on multiple habits at once to ensure you are continuing to create the results you desire. Then, if you find that you are not, you can take the necessary measures to begin pampering your habit all over again.

Being Mindful Of High Stress Periods

One of the most important elements of effectively pampering a habit is being able to anticipate periods where you are likely to stop engaging with your habits. Knowing how to anticipate when you are going to experience stress or overwhelm that could throw your habits off means that you can create measures in advance that will prevent you from having your entire system thrown for a loop. This way, you can mindfully navigate these high stress periods or periods of change in such a way that allows you to continue to maintain your habits to the best of your ability. Then, as everything begins to settle again, you can start to go back to only checking in on your habits casually.

It is important to understand that periods of high stress can interrupt habits of any magnitude, no matter how long you have had them or how meticulous you are at engaging in those habits. Some things to look for include: large moves, changes in your lifestyle, job changes or transitions, or changes to your relationship status or family, such as with the introduction of a new family member in the household. High stress periods such as those when you are experiencing heightened pressure from work or your personal life, those where you may be facing issues with your health, or those where you may be facing any other types of stress even if it does not seem all that significant can also impact your ability to maintain your habits.

Anytime you recognize yourself going through one of these phases, be sure to immediately address your habits and consider what you are going to do to ensure that you continue to maintain them to the best of your ability. You may even find that you need to adapt them for a period to ensure that they serve your needs during periods of stress or change. The more mindfully you do this, the more likely you will be to maintain the changes and refrain from developing bad and difficult-to-change habits during periods of stress.

Chapter 9

Making Habits As Simple As Possible

One of the best things you can do for yourself when it comes to making new habits is making habits that are as simple as they can possibly be. When habits are simple, it is easier to motivate yourself to get started with that habit, and it can also be easier for you to see that habit all the way through. This way, rather than having to train yourself to complete a series of complex steps in a specific order, you can focus on practicing simple steps, or you can simplify complex things to make them easier for you to remember.

When it comes to habit creation, there will be some situations where you can easily simplify the process, and there will be others while simplification will not be so simple. For example, you may be able to simplify your morning routine, but you may not be able to simplify certain processes at work, which may need to be done in a specific way. In this case, the best thing you can do is simplify the process to the best of your ability to ensure that you are getting everything done properly.

In situations where you do have more control, learning how to make things as easy as possible will help shed away the need to exert unnecessary energy, as well as the need to attempt to remember complex processes. It can be natural to want to make things more challenging if you believe the added few steps will get you greater results, but the reality is that those added few steps may make the habit unreasonable when it comes to executing it day in and day out. If those steps are absolutely necessary, or they really will have a huge impact, you can always add them into the habit at a later date, once you are in the habit of the basic practice itself, first.

In situations where you have no control over how things are done, you can develop habits by simplifying what you can and by starting with just a few habits here and there while continuing to do everything else intentionally. Over time, you can add more habits into your "base habits" to make it even easier for you to create the results you desire over time. Doing it this way will ensure that it is easier for you to create true habits and the results you desire with those habits.

Effective Methods For Simplifying Your Habits

Choosing how to simplify your habits is going to depend on whether you are simplifying a brand new habit that you are creating for yourself or one that you have already been engaging in for some time. In both cases, you are going to need to put your detective skills to work and analyze the routine aspect of your habit to ensure that it is as simple and easy-to-follow as possible.

For habits that you already have, simplifying them can be a great way to adjust the routine to ensure that you are still getting your desired reward fulfilled, but that you are also not expending any unnecessary energy in doing so. Sometimes, when we have habits for a long period of time, it can be easy to overlook ways that we are wasting energy by doing things that are not necessary with those habits. For example, you might still be following an outdated system for filing your invoices at work because that is the habit you are in when, by now, there is a much quicker and easier way of doing it. Simplifying your habits whenever possible, even long-time habits is a great way of ensuring that you are never wasting energy when it is not needed.

As you begin to create new habits for yourself, it is also a good idea to look through those new habits to see how you might be able to simplify them. In particular, pay attention to the routine itself and see if there is anything you can do to make the routine easier, to make it pack a bigger punch, or to help it do both. Do your best to look at your routine from a practical standpoint, too, and see if it flows effectively. Sometimes when we are in the planning process of things, it can be easy to get carried away with how things *could* be and we find ourselves forgetting how they *are*. Ensure that your simplified plan is realistic. Otherwise, you are going to have a hard time seeing it through. While you will certainly be able to work out the kinks during your trial period, you do not want to have so much to sort out that it is challenging to even get through the trial period of your new habit in the first place.

If you are unsure about how a routine might be simplified, try researching similar habits that people have. These days, there are countless self-help blogs full of different habits people have that contain plenty of great details about what those habits are and how they look. Getting an idea of how other people are navigating their habits can be a great way to identify new opportunities to create and simplify your own.

How To Ensure That You Still Get Your Desired Results

As you simplify your habits, it is important that you do not simplify it to the point where you no longer get your desired results out of the habit. After all, this would be a waste of your time and would render the habit completely useless. Your goal whenever you are navigating the creation of a habit should always be to create the biggest impact through the fewest steps possible. The more you can master this balance, the better your habits will be, and the greater your impact will be toward reaching your goals through your habit.

The perfect way to ensure that your habits are still functional after you have simplified them is to compare them to your goals and see if you can realistically see how your habits are going to take you toward your goals. If it seems like they will do so in a positive and powerful manner, you have likely done an effective job of making your habit simplified while still being able to reach your goals. If, however, it seems as though your goal will be unreachable, you will want to adjust your habit to ensure that you can make a meaningful impact. After all, the entire purpose of this book is to create habits that are going to help you reach your goals!

Chapter 10

How To Break Bad Habits

Bad habits are something that every single one of us is familiar with, and something we have all wanted to break at one point or another. Dealing with bad habits can be frustrating, troublesome, and even overwhelming or embarrassing. If we are not careful, they can also overrule our lives and leave us living a lifestyle that we truly do not want to be living, all because we have felt committed to or trapped within bad habits.

It may seem impossible to break your bad habits, especially if you have been living with them for a long period of time, but rest assured that like any habit, a bad habit can be broken. The number one reason why most people *don't* break their bad habits is that their mindset surrounding their bad habits is one that makes it seem as though change is impossible and improbable. As a result, they lack the mental strength they need to see the trial period through and get into the process of truly changing their bad habits. If you can shift this belief system within yourself and empower yourself to change your bad habits, then you will see yourself effectively breaking free from every single bad habit you may experience in your life.

Getting Real With Yourself About Bad Habits

The first thing you need to do when it comes to dealing with your bad habit is getting real with yourself about them. Start by acknowledging that they are bad habits, that you are responsible for them, and that you need to be responsible for changing them. Now, you need to start to acknowledge what your mindset is like around your bad habits. More often than not, you will notice that your mindset is disempowered and full of beliefs that leave you feeling as though you have no control or say over the matter. This very mindset is what makes navigating the process of breaking your bad habits so hard because you have given them so much power and control that it feels as though there is nothing you can do to change the situation.

If you are going to find the strength to break apart bad habits and eliminate them for good, you are going to have to first address your mindset around these bad habits so that you can take back your power. This way, you will genuinely believe in yourself and in your ability, and through that your subconscious mind will begin to pay attention and support you with creating the results you need when it comes to eliminating these habits.

As soon as you have identified your mindset around your bad habits, you need to start empowering yourself to believe that it is possible for you to break these habits and find new ones that will serve you in a bigger way. The best way to get started with these is to get real about your bad habits and put some perspective around them. Notice that your bad habit is likely not nearly as bad as you make it out to be and that it doesn't really need to be that big of a deal in your life. Rather than giving your bad habit any emotional charge, see it as just being an experience you are having that you are ready to change so that you can have an experience that is more useful to you. It may take some time for you to make this adjustment in your beliefs and emotions, so do not be afraid to give yourself time to navigate this shift in your mindset.

Once you start to see your bad habit through a neutral perspective, you need to start building up your belief in your ability to create new habits. At this point, you want to avoid focusing on the bad habit as much as possible and instead focus on what positive you can create in your life. Focus on how easy it can be for you to create new habits, how fun it can be to try new things, and how much better your results and rewards will be when you try these new habits. You can also start looking around for evidence about how effectively other people have broken habits similar to yours to realize that it is entirely possible, and it is well within your ability to do so.

Your entire goal at this point is to take away any attention and focus you give to your bad habit and start focusing entirely on new habits and your potential and power. Stop listening to people who say you can't, or people who make it seem like bad habits are inevitable, unavoidable, and unfixable, and start listening to people who tell you that it is possible and who gives you guidance to support you along the way. As you continue to make this shift in your mindset that focuses less on getting away from your bad habit and more on moving toward your healthier habits, you will find that it becomes easier and easier for you to make shifts in your life. That is because, to put it simply, whatever you focus on grows.

Fitting a New Routine Over Your Habit

Once you have navigated the practical mindset aspect of breaking your bad habits by eliminating any negative beliefs you are carrying around them, you can begin to focus on the actual breaking down of the habit itself. At this point, you can start following the same steps from previous chapters in this book to create change in your habits. To do this, you will want to identify the cue and reward associated with your formerly bad habit and start focusing on effective routines you can use to navigate your new habit. This way, you are able to break up the habit and create new results for yourself.

Remember, your goal should be to maintain your cues and rewards but focus solely on changing your routine, as this is where your power lies. The less you try to fight against desire and nature, and the more you can focus on working with your existing nature, the more effectively you will be able to break your bad habits.

As you create your new routine to replace your habit, it is imperative that you are thoughtful and considerate about the routine you plan. Realize that with all habits, the routine is important and carries a great weight around whether or not you will be able to integrate it as a habit. By replacing bad habits, however, the routine is extremely important as you have built up a significant belief system suggesting that it is not possible for you to change your habit. Even if you have been doing work to shift your belief system, pairing that with a meticulously planned routine that will promote your success will ensure that you have far higher chances of creating success with this changed habit in the first place.

Be sure to follow all of the standard practices of clearly defining the routine, breaking it down into simple-to-follow chronological steps, and making it as simple and thorough as possible so that you are more likely to follow it. If you can, you should also put measures into place to prepare yourself for any emotional or mental setbacks you may have that could prevent you from engaging with the changed habit. This way, you are far more prepared to handle the emotional and mental challenges that may be presented from attempting to get through this particular habit change.

Mindfully Navigating the Breakdown Of Your Bad Habit

As you begin to break down a bad habit and transform it into something positive, it is important that you are mindful of navigating this process. Bad habits in and of themselves tend to be harder to break, particularly because of the intense connection they can have to your belief system, values, and emotions. Knowing what to expect and navigating these situations mindfully is an important way to help yourself get through the harder mental and emotional parts of breaking down bad habits. When you can mindfully navigate these parts of the process, you can release yourself from the idea that the suffering you experience will be unbearable or will last forever, allowing you to experience a greater sense of peace during this process. Most often, this peace and the realization that the discomfort and any suffering associated with breaking bad habits will end minimizes the suffering and ensures that it passes much quicker.

Realize that the first week of changing a bad habit is usually the hardest week. This is the week where you are going to be navigating strong cravings or urges to engage in your old habit, and you may struggle to feel any level of fulfillment or satisfaction from your new habit. Even if it is designed to fulfill the same reward and need, you will find yourself feeling as though the need itself is not fulfilled because it has not been fulfilled in the way that you are used to having it fulfilled. It will take some time for your subconscious mind to acknowledge that the same need is being fulfilled, just in a different way. You are also going to navigate many firsts during this week, including several cues that will go unfulfilled because of your conscious choice to switch your habit to something different. This first week can bring about great emotional and mental frustrations and even distress as you find yourself getting used to this new normal.

The second and third week into this process, you will find yourself slowly beginning to relax, although it will still be challenging. At this point, you may begin to feel more at peace with your new habit, but you will continue to experience a heightened risk of backsliding into your old ways. The more relaxed you feel about your new habit, the more at risk you become, so it is important that you navigate this time mindfully to refrain from experiencing a setback. At this point, cues are going to continually arise and trigger the old habit, and if you are too relaxed, you may engage in it accidentally, or find yourself in a position where the emotional and mental urge to engage in it are too strong and it feels impossible to deny it.

As time goes on, you will continue to feel random periods of emotional and mental frustration surrounding your changed habit, but it will grow easier and easier. Still, you must always be cautious as you never know when an old cue will be unexpectedly presented, potentially causing room for a setback. The more mindful you can be of this possibility, the more you can navigate these situations in such a way that it will not cause you to slip back into old patterns.

It is also important to realize that this timeline is merely a guideline for what to expect. How you experience this will ultimately depend on you, your personality, the unique habit you are breaking, and many other variables that may be outside of your control. Still, the more mindfully you can navigate this, the more success you will have in completely breaking down your old habit and replacing it with a new one.

Chapter 11

Habits You Should Have

Working together to develop stronger habits for you to reach your goals has me wanting to impart wisdom on what goals have supported me in reaching my own goals over the years. These habits have proven to support me in my ability to stay motivated, get everything done, and see things through so that I am able to achieve the results I desire. Including these habits in your own day to day experience can help you experience greater success with your habits, too, while also supporting you in achieving your own goals.

Some of these habits may seem generic, so I want to underline something important. Each of us, no matter how unique we may be in personality and expression, has a basic set of needs that our bodies and minds require to be fulfilled in order for us to do anything. If these basic needs are not fulfilled, we may find ourselves falling into default and unconscious patterns as a way to fulfill them, which can result in us taking up habits that take away from our ability to either consciously or habitually reach our goals.

The more you can learn how to incorporate these habits into your everyday life, the more effectively you will be able to support yourself in creating a solid foundation for you to generate success. In many cases, these habits alone will amplify your success in a way that no other habit can. As well, developing new habits that are specific to you, your needs, and your desires will become a lot easier once you have these habits in place. So, it is well worth it to research these habits and discover how you can implement them in your own life in a way that fulfills your own needs.

Getting Up Early Each Morning

While there is a lot of speculation around how early you should wake up in order to have a successful day, I don't believe there is one golden hour that will fit everyone. Instead, I believe that each of us has our own hour that serves as the best time for when we should rise every single day. Finding your "golden hour" can be done by identifying how much sleep you need in order to feel rested, discovering how much time you need in order to get your day started every single day, and figuring out what generally feels right for you. You may want to play around with your waking hour for a little while until you find what feels best.

Once you have found your "golden hour," aim to awaken at that time every single day, regardless of what you have going on for that day. This way, you can start every single day off right, ready for whatever may come your way. Plus, if any great opportunities to make advancements toward your goals present themselves, you can take advantage of them as you are in the perfect frame of mind to turn them into a success.

Giving Gratitude For Each Day

Gratitude is a powerful emotion that can literally rewire your brain and set you up for success. People who approach their lives from a point of gratitude tend to be more positive, open minded, and curious about life itself. When they are presented with new opportunities, rather than immediately worrying about whether or not they are capable of fulfilling those opportunities or becoming skeptical about the quality of the opportunities, they accept them with gratitude. Then, through gratitude, they generate a level of belief in themselves that enables them to embrace and utilize those opportunities to their advantage.

Creating a habit surrounding gratitude in your everyday life is a great way to help provide you with these same benefits so that you, too, can create a sense of positivity and optimism in your own life. A great gratitude habit you could include in your life is one that can be included in your day immediately upon waking up. As soon as you awaken, express gratitude for 3-5 things that you are grateful for in your life. Try to choose something new every day so that you have to consciously think about what it is that you want to express gratitude for, as this will allow you to create a stronger sense of gratitude. Watch how this simple habit drastically shifts your mindset and, as a result, your life.

Making a List Of Your Goals

Although many of us can recite what our goals are, very few of us write those goals down and turn them into plans that we are working toward. There is something profoundly impactful about writing your goals down on paper and reviewing those goals every single day. In fact, some people, such as Grant Cardone, will write their goals down every single time they are feeling doubtful, uncertain, or unmotivated, as this enables them to get back into the mindset of remembering what it is that they are working toward. This way, they can stay motivated and keep going.

Rather than holding onto your goals in your mind, turn them into something tangible. Write your goals down on paper and review that piece of paper every single morning, and anytime you find yourself feeling uncertain, doubtful, insecure, or unmotivated. The more you can refresh yourself on these goals, the more motivated you will remain to reach them in your everyday life.

Exercising Daily

Your body is an important part of you, and if you fail to take care of it, you will find yourself struggling to fulfill your goals largely due to the fact that you are in too ill of health to be able to pursue them. Rather than letting your health fall to the wayside and finding yourself too ill to pursue your goals, take your health seriously. Exercise for at least 30 minutes every single day, even if you are not capable of engaging in intense exercise. Walking, jogging, biking, swimming, yoga or even doing at-home cardio workouts are all great ways to get your body moving on a daily basis.

There are countless studies that show how your body thrives when you take proper care of it, so doing this is important. If you are someone who has never had a consistent workout routine or who struggles to work out on a regular basis, you might consider working together with an accountability partner or a personal trainer until you get into the swing of things. Once working out comes more naturally to you, you can adjust your plan as needed.

Eating a Healthy Diet

In addition to taking care of your body through movement, it is also important to take care of your body through nutrition. Eating is about far more than just satiating a hunger craving that you get a few times a day. Eating is about learning which foods are going to nourish you best so that your brain, organs, and body are all able to function at maximum capacity. Highly successful people know that the better they can nourish themselves, the better they will be able to get through their day to day lives.

If cooking or preparing food is not something you enjoy, find a dietary guide that looks tasty for you and teach yourself how to master a few recipes from that dietary guide. Then, rely on the habit of being able to make this food as a way to help yourself eat healthy on a routine basis. You might also try meal prepping as a way to prepare healthy food for yourself, as this is another great way to nurture your body and take care of your wellbeing.

Managing Your Money Properly

Many people believe that they are bad with money, or that they are experiencing a level of lack or poverty because of reasons that are beyond themselves. While this may be true, there are also countless other people who are relying on these two reasons as excuses when, in reality, they could be experiencing far greater success with their funds. All they need to do is get out of the habit of spending all their money so that they can get into the habit of saving and investing their money.

The more effective you are at managing funds, the more successful you will be at saving money so that you can allocate those funds toward things that are more meaningful to you, such as retirement or large purchases like cars and homes. Get into the habit of budgeting your money every month and sticking to that budget meticulously throughout the month. Stop engaging in habits that result in you spending pointless money throughout the month, too, such as purchasing your coffee from a drive-thru rather than making it at home, or eating out because you are too lazy to cook. These simple shifts can go a long way in helping you make your funds go further, which can create security, comfort, and an added ability to reach your goals.

Keeping a Precise Agenda

Your time is the most precious resource you have, precious even more so than the funds in your bank account. Rather than wasting all of your time engaging in habits that do not add to the quality of your life, start taking your time seriously and keeping a precise agenda. The more effectively you can schedule your time and stick to that schedule, the more effectively you will be able to get through the day and reach all of your goals.

Start keeping an agenda with you, and every time you agree to do something make sure you schedule it into your agenda. Then, make sure you spend time each month, week, and day scheduling out how your time is going to be spent so that you know exactly what you need to be doing and when. The more you can get into the habit of keeping track of your time and directing your time meticulously, the more you will get done on a day to day basis. This way, rather than sitting around doing nothing, you are intentionally using up every minute of your time to support yourself in achieving your goals.

Enjoying an Hour To Yourself

It is important to educate yourself on the difference between wasting time and investing time into yourself. Many people feel like sitting around enjoying time by themselves is time wasted because they are not productive. On the contrary, spending time on your own, even if that time is spent staring at the ceiling being bored, can actually be incredibly supportive of your mental and emotional health. This time is a great opportunity for you to enjoy your company, unwind, process any residual thoughts or emotions you may be carrying with you, and otherwise take a good moment to relax.

Get into the habit of spending an entire hour to yourself every day, or as close to an hour as you possibly can. During this hour, do whatever feels good for you, and notice how much it transforms your mental and emotional health. There is a great deal of benefit that can come from giving yourself absolute permission to enjoy time by yourself, knowing that you are not putting anything off and that your day is not suffering based on your decision.

Checking In With Yourself Each Evening

Making the mistake of carrying your day with you to bed can create heightened stress, reduced quality of sleep, and long term mental health struggles as you find this day to day stress compounds and feels worse over time. Rather than carrying everything with you to the pillow, set aside some time for yourself to check in with how you are doing. This time in the evening spent releasing your thoughts and emotions, and bringing closure to your day will help you go to sleep feeling peaceful, which will allow you to feel well rested and ready for a wonderful day ahead.

If sitting and simply thinking is not enough for you, you can incorporate other routines into this nightly check in, too. Consider meditating, engaging in a calming yoga session, journaling, or drinking a calming tea as you enjoy this time to relax your mind and release the weight of the day so that you can rest deeply and thoroughly later that night. If, during this time, you realize that you wished something had gone differently during the day or that something was left incomplete, make a note of it and take care of it the next day.

Reading For 30 Minutes Before Bed

Studies have shown that anything you learn in the 30 minutes before bed is learned faster because of how your brain processes information as you sleep. With this information, we can assume that what we think about before we go to bed is tremendously important, and choosing our thoughts intentionally can go a long way toward helping us not only learn but also feel better. Use the 30 minutes you have before going to sleep as an opportunity to educate yourself on skills that could support you with achieving any goals you are working toward in your life. This way, you are learning information that is conducive to your growth and your success. While some people prefer to read in bed, I suggest reading next to a lamp on a chair or the sofa in your living room. This way, your mind associates your bed only with sleeping and when your head hits the pillow you are able to fall asleep quicker and easier.

Chapter 12

Habits You Should Quit

Just like you are going to want to pick up new habits that will help you navigate a healthier life, there are also some bad habits that you should consider eliminating from your life so that you can pursue your goals even more effectively. For me, there have been many habits that I have had to eliminate from my life so that I can experience greater success. Although it seemed hard to break these habits at the time, I have come to realize how powerfully my life has changed since I left them behind. Plus, over time, it does get much easier to go without these habits, meaning that the suffering and discomfort does end.

If you have any of these habits in your life or any others that you can clearly observe as having a negative impact on your life and your ability to reach your goals, you are going to want to recognize these goals and begin eliminating them from your life. With that being said, I recommend only working toward breaking one bad habit as a time, as trying to break too many can be overwhelming. While focusing on one at a time means the others may linger for a while longer, it also means that your ability to eliminate them will be far more sustainable and likely to remain permanent, which will have a far more positive impact for you in the long run.

Smoking

Smoking is a habit that comes with many obvious negative side effects. From damaging your health to draining your wallet, smoking can seriously set you back. For most people, smoking is either a way of getting some quiet time to themselves, a way of navigating stress, or both. If you can learn how to fulfill these needs in other, healthier ways, letting go of smoking will become much easier for you.

With that being said, smoking is an addiction that includes a dependency on a substance that you are introducing to your body. For this reason, smoking will be a harder habit for you to break. As you are working on breaking the habit in your subconscious mind, you will also need to navigate the physical detox you will go through at the same time. This combined experience of denying pleasure while willingly choosing pain can be incredibly difficult to navigate, so you are going to want to take your time and do so intentionally. It may be useful to buy a smoking cessation book, join a program, or work with your doctor to increase your ability to successfully navigate breaking this bad habit.

Biting Your Nails

Biting your nails, or any other habits that are borne out of nervousness, such as sucking your hair, picking at your skin, or chewing your lips, are all habits that need to be rectified. These habits are often developed as a way to experience a positive release from negative emotions through the form of self-soothing. They can also indicate to your brain that there is a reason to be nervous in the first place, even if there is not, which can worsen your nervousness and, in turn, worsen your habit as well.

Rather than letting these self-mutilating habits continue, it can be helpful to learn how to self-soothe in other ways so that you are more likely to experience a positive release from negative emotions, rather than a release that actually worsens these emotions. Consider trying things like talking, humming to yourself, journaling, distracting yourself for a few minutes, meditating, mindfully breathing, or grounding, which are all healthier ways to combat nervousness in a positive and healthy manner.

Sleeping In

Sleeping in is a bad habit that you can get into that can result in you missing out on many things in life. When you sleep in, rather than helping yourself rest better, you usually end up oversleeping which can actually leave you feeling even more tired. As well, if you are sleeping in on days where you have to be somewhere by a specific time, you are also sleeping during time that could be used preparing your mind, body, and emotions for the day.

Rather than sleeping in as long as you possibly can, get into the habit of waking up and engaging in a positive morning routine that allows you to completely prepare for your day in every way possible. This way, you are well rested, energized, and ready to face the day ahead of you.

Leaving Late

While waking up at a reasonable hour can help offset tardiness, there are many other reasons why you may be leaving late and, thus, arriving at appointments late, too. A lack of punctuality is something that can increase your own stress, while also pushing off any possible opportunities you may have access to because you are showing people that you do not care enough to take advantage of them. Learning how to leave on time and show up on time is a great way to take a load of stress off of your own mind while also proving to people that you are reliable and that you can handle any opportunity handed to you.

Since there are so many reasons why you might be tardy, it is a good idea to look into your own tendency of being late and discover what habits may be contributing to your lateness. This way, you can target your own habits and create solutions that will help you show up on time more often.

Relying On Temptations

Temptations are something we often put in our lives in an effort to make life easier for ourselves when, in reality, all we end up doing is making life harder. While relying on temptations to "save time" or for those "just in case" moments may seem ideal, the more likely reality is that they become crutches and we find ourselves actually sticking to convenient yet bad habits, rather than putting in the effort to achieve our desired habits. A great example of this would be buying convenience meal items for those nights where you may not feel like cooking. This may seem ideal, but what often ends up happening is that you rely on them more and more until you are no longer preparing healthy, homemade meals for yourself.

Rather than relying on unhealthy or less than ideal crutches as a way to help you get through times where you may not want to put the effort in, find healthier and simpler alternatives that will continue to help you get to your desired goal. For example, while purchasing convenience meals may not be a good habit to get into, meal prepping so that you have healthy meals made in advanced might be. The less you can rely on temptations, or keep them around as a backup option, the more likely you will be to stay on track with what you truly desire in your life.

Saying "I'll Do It Later"

Putting things off is about as bad as being perpetually late for everything in life. When you continue to put things off by saying, "I'll do it later," what ends up happening is you never actually get around to doing what you said you were going to do. As they say, "later never comes." Instead of waiting for later to never come, consider getting out of this habit by either shifting your language or shifting your follow up.

In situations where you do not actually want to do something, and you have no need to do it, rather than saying, "I'll do it later," try saying, "it is not a priority to me right now." This way, you can stop letting it nag at you and you can be honest about how you feel and what you need.

In situations where you do actually want to do something, or you need to do something, rather than saying, "I'll do it later" make actual plans for when you are going to do it and then put those plans down in your agenda. This way, rather than putting it off you are scheduling a specific time for when things are going to happen, and they are far more likely to get done.

Not Taking Your Wellbeing Seriously

Many of us are in the habit of neglecting our health to the point where it is somewhat of a punchline in a societal joke. With that being said, not taking your wellbeing seriously can lead to you experiencing incredibly ill health, which can lead to you not being able to achieve *any* goals, even your basic ones. You must get beyond the habits that keep you contributing to your ill health and begin taking your health seriously by adopting new, healthier habits that are going to support your wellbeing.

When it comes to how you take care of yourself, it can take quite a while to break down any bad habits you may be carrying, especially if you have many bad habits surrounding caring for yourself. It can be helpful to start tackling them one at a time and aiming for continuous improvement rather than immediate perfection. This way, you can take some of the pressure off of yourself, making it easier for you to do better and better over time.

Spreading Negativity

Another bad habit that you need to break, if you have it, is spreading negativity. Negativity can be spread by choosing to think negative or unhelpful thoughts, through gossiping, through saying rude, hurtful, or unhelpful things, and through otherwise choosing to spread negativity around between yourself and others. Spreading negativity only breeds more negativity, as it leads to you creating more reasons to be grumpy, pessimistic, or frustrated, rather than positive and supportive.

Instead of spreading negativity around, get into the habit of saying positive things to yourself and others, and staying quiet when you have nothing kind or positive to say. This way, you are spreading around positivity, and, as a result, you are attracting more positivity into your life. This is a great way to improve your mindset and open yourself up to the potential of new opportunities.

Conclusion

Thank you so much for reading *EMPOWERING HABITS!* This book was designed to help you understand habits and navigate them more effectively so that you can easily achieve your goals. In order to effectively achieve your goals, you need to understand the anatomy of a habit, the method for creating and changing habits, and the process for breaking bad habits.

I hope that after reading this book, you are feeling confident in all of this and more, as I truly believe that following the science of habits is key when it comes to achieving all of the lofty goals you set for yourself. The more you can embrace the power of your habits and leverage them to your advantage, the more likely you will be to reach all of your lofty goals and enjoy the life that you dream of having. In fact, it is my firm belief that this is the main difference between people who achieve their goals and people who don't.

Whenever it comes to achieving what you desire in life, especially when you desire big things, it can be helpful to work *with* your nature, rather than against it. In fact, in anything you do in life, it can be helpful to understand and work with your nature rather than against it, as this is often the most effective way for you to achieve a greater level of success in your life. After all, why put all of the work into trying to swim upstream against your natural current when, instead, you could subtly shift the flow of your current and achieve what you desire with greater success and ease?

After reading this book, I hope that you continue to learn about habits and how they work, and that you begin doing a deep exploration into your own habits and how they have been affecting you in your life. The more effectively you can begin to understand and navigate your habits, the more you will find yourself breaking down any habits that are no longer serving you and creating ones that help you make your way toward your goals.

It is important that you remember that no matter how long it has been since you have broken down an old goal or replaced it with a new one, there is always going to be the potential for you to slip back into old patterns. For that reason, you should always take the time to be mindful of your habits and what you are doing so that you can prevent yourself from slipping into old patterns and losing all of your progress. In fact, it may even be helpful for you to develop a habit of reviewing your habits at a set time every week, month, or year. The better you can navigate your new habits and remain mindful, the more likely you will be to achieve your desired results in your life.

The process of self-improvement, especially as far as our nature is concerned, truly is a lifelong process that we will need to continue to address and nurture over time. The more effective you are at taking this on as a lifelong journey and embracing each step of it without rushing to the "finish line," the more likely you will be to see great improvements. The goal is always to continue improving and never to be perfect. If you can embrace this goal, you will fulfill every single other goal you ever set for yourself. That, my friend, is the secret to success.

NOT DISTRACTABLE

How To Avoid Distractions Preventing You From Achieving Your Goals

Table Of Contents

Introduction

Achieving anything in life is made exponentially more challenging when you have a constant stream of distractions preventing you from achieving any level of success.

When you are constantly giving into temptation, or focusing all of your energy on avoiding temptation, it can be challenging for you to ever have enough energy and focus to actually create the results you desire. In the end, you may find yourself so wrapped up in a world of distraction that your goals don't stand a chance.

Rather than succumbing to this reality and allowing distractions to overrule your life, it would be wise of you to discover how you can improve your resiliency toward distractions altogether so that they are no longer interrupting your success. Enter: *NOT DISTRACTABLE*. In this book, we are going to dive deep into the seedy underbelly of the many distractions we face as a collective, and as individuals, every single day. Together, we are going to dissect what distractions are, why they are so distracting, and what keeps you giving into them over and over again. Then, we are going to uncover how you can stop living your entire life around your distractions and start creating practical, reasonable, and effective tools to help you eliminate and move away from all of the distractions that have kept you trapped in your current life.

Throughout the chapters of this very book, you will discover everything you need to know to kiss distractions goodbye and finally take control of your energy, attention, and results. This way, you will no longer find achieving success to be a challenge, but instead something that comes easily and naturally when you work in tune with your natural needs, desires, cycles and interests.

Truly tapping into what it means to be not distractable is something that will change your life in more ways than one. Through this practice, you will discover that everything in your life comes so much easier when you learn how to focus your energy, attention, and efforts and quickly create the results you desire. From being able to see your goals all the way through to the end, to being able to finish an email or watch an entire episode of your favorite TV show without getting distracted, there are many ways that your life is about to improve.

One thing I wish to recommend to you ahead of time is that you keep this book on hand and that you resolve to read it again at some point within the next few months to two years. Rereading this information at a later date, when you have already been effectively practicing some of what you have learned, will allow you to deepen your understanding of what it means to become not distractable and will support you with truly absorbing all of the information contained within it. This way, you do not just tap into your potential, but you truly *unleash* it.

If you are ready to explore a world where distraction is no longer an issue, and your goals are met effortlessly and easily no matter how large or how small they may be, let's begin!

Chapter 1

We Live Under a Bombardment Of Stimuli

Our modern life significantly differs from the way things used to be and, as a result, we are still learning about what that means and how it affects us. While we are beginning to develop some concrete understandings around these changes, so much is left unknown and we are still actively working toward understanding it and using that as an opportunity to improve our lives even further. Even so, some people might argue that this constant thirst for knowledge is exactly what is wrong with the world, or what is causing so much chaos and destruction for so many of us.

Me, I'm somewhere in the middle. I don't believe that it is wrong or in any way bad for us to want to advance as a species, or to advance our collective and individual knowledge bases so that we can understand more and do more in our lives. I also don't believe that it is ideal for us to allow the stimuli to rule our lives, and so it is important that as individuals we learn about how the stimuli affect us and what we can do about it.

The more you understand what a stimulus is and how it affects you, the easier it will be for you to understand why it is so important for you to navigate the stimuli you receive on a daily basis in a more resilient manner so that it can be a benefit without being a hindrance. Learning how to cultivate this deeper level of self-awareness and self-mastery will ensure that you can tap into the abundance of knowledge and information in the world to support you in your endeavors, while also being able to remain in control. Through this, you will become far more likely to achieve your goals and fulfill your desires in life.

What Was Life Like Before All Of the Stimuli?

There was never a time in our history where we had zero stimuli, but there was certainly a time where we had fewer stimuli than we do now. These days, our stimuli have grown exponentially as we have begun to see the development of many people's interests, curiosity, and creativity manifest in physical ways, which ultimately adds to the abundance of stimuli that surrounds us.

At one point long ago, the only stimuli we had were our inner stimuli which are responsible for arousing things like hunger, curiosity, interest, intrigue, desire, sexual urges, and more. These inner stimuli drive us to begin looking for external stimuli, as well. The external stimuli we experienced back in these early primal days likely included things such as the rising and setting of the sun and moon, any threats we may have faced, as well as the primal interactions we shared with others from our species, or other species.

As our species began to develop, our stimuli began to expand. We invented various things and, through those inventions, more curiosities and cravings for expanding knowledge continued to be developed. Over time, we have created so many different inventions that they can be found all around us. In fact, our inventions have completely overhauled our once primal lifestyles by giving us an entirely manufactured life that was developed through the curiosity and creation of early human beings.

The realization that early human beings would have contributed to the development of our now overly stimulated world suggests that we have always had a deep desire to understand, learn, and grow. We have also had a deep desire to act on our inner urges or stimuli to create an outer world that reflected our inner need to be stimulated. In many ways, our ability to act on these inner urges and stimulate ourselves by creating things that are fulfilling and enjoyable to use has driven our society and helped our species grow. However, it has also completely changed the landscape of our lives, our societies, and our world as a whole.

How Does All Of This Stimuli Affect Us?

At one point in the past, the stimuli we experienced and the stimuli we created were fairly balanced. We had not yet fulfilled the need for stimulation to the point where our lives were being overruled by all of the things, we created for ourselves. These days, that reality is entirely different. These days, we have so much *stuff* that has been manufactured as a result of people's curiosity and need for stimulation that we have become bombarded with it. Everywhere you look, there is something stimulating and fascinating to look at which, ultimately, creates massive distractions for all of us. In fact, many of the things we have created as a need to feel stimulated now go so far as to intentionally stimulate us to do things. For example, our phones have notifications that stimulate us to check our phones so that we can see what those notifications are and act on them.

While at one point in the past people could engage in stimuli until their need to be stimulated was fulfilled and then move on to relaxing and doing nothing afterward until their own inner desire to be stimulated was enough to arouse them again, that is no longer the case. These days, rather than sitting around waiting for primal urges, we have stimuli calling us into action and pushing us to fulfill something new nearly constantly.

Overly packed agendas, noisy cellphones, computers filled with notifications, websites covered in pop up ads, and highways littered with billboards are just a few of the many stimulating things we come across on a day to day basis. We are constantly having our inner desire stimulated far more than we ever have in the past and, for many, it is resulting in people becoming addicted to stimulation. This addiction to stimulation can ultimately lead to things like anxiety, depression, and other mood disorders that affect people in a deep and sometimes disastrous way. Beyond the anxiety and depression, we are feeling on an individual level, we are also seeing people develop mental conditions that affect their ability to focus entirely. Conditions like ADD and ADHD are not entirely understood, yet they are conditions that result in people experiencing hyperarousal to stimuli and struggling to focus between the many stimuli that are around them nearly constantly. As you can tell, a constant stream of stimuli is anything but helpful, and it can have detrimental and troubling effects for many of us who are living in this overexposed society.

Where Is All Of the Stimuli Coming From?

The stimuli we are being bombarded by comes from way too many sources at this point. We are no longer effectively tuned in to our natural world, or even our natural way of existing. In fact, some people struggle to even find enough time in the day to sit outside for a few minutes or connect with nature. In some metropolitan areas, people go years without spending any significant time outdoors, except to zoom off from one place to the next. We are the only species with this problem, and it continues to affect us on an individual level, and on a collective level.

Arguably, every single invention we have ever made has become a stimulus for us. The couch you sit on, or the chair you sit in is a stimulus, and it can become a significant stimulus if you struggle to get comfortable or if it makes a squeaky sound that you do not like. The food you eat, this book you are reading, the car you drive in, the radio you listen to, the television you watch, these are all stimuli. And, while they are not all inherently bad, they can overwhelm your brain and create incredibly troubling side effects if you are not careful.

The particular problem we are facing right now as a society is that the stimuli are getting more intuitive, louder, noisier, and more distracting. Our cell phones are now able to effectively provide us with the exact apps that keep us hooked to them all day long. Social media websites are designed with algorithms that keep us plugged in and scrolling endlessly for hours, even if we have already seen the posts we are scrolling through. Our laptops are full of millions of websites that can provide us with access to any knowledge we desire, and the advertisements on these websites are specifically chosen with the sole purpose of attracting our interest.

Every single piece of technology we are using is getting better and better, which also means it is getting better at distracting us, keeping our attention, and preventing us from getting through our lives as normal. And, the more we use this technology, the more we empower the people who create it to continue creating it in such a way that is better, more distracting, and more addictive.

How Much Control Do We Really Have?

When it comes to stimuli in our world, we have quite a bit of control, and yet in many ways there is not a lot we can do. Understanding how much control you really have over the stimuli in your life is an important opportunity to show you where you can begin to make a difference, and where you simply need to develop a thicker skin. This may not seem like the *exact* answer you desire, but the truth is that knowing what you can do about the abundance of stimuli means that you can start taking clear, conductive, and effective action to eliminate the stimuli from your life. Or, at the very least, reduce the amount of control it has over you.

When it comes to your level of control, you can control how you choose to perceive and engage with the stimuli in your life. You have the power to decide whether or not you are going to acknowledge stimuli, engage with it, or do anything about the stimuli you are experiencing. If you choose to acknowledge and engage with it, you can also decide how you are going to acknowledge it and how you are going to engage with it. Many people do not realize they have this level of control and so they have failed to cultivate the right tools that will support them in taking advantage of this control. Fortunately, you are here today to figure that out so we can start to make a difference for you.

Beyond your control lies the existence of all of the stimuli. You cannot control the fact that the stimulus exists, or how it exists. While you do have influence over how it exists in your life and you can do certain things like put your phone on silent mode or shut off your laptop, the fact that they continue to exist in your life will remain. For many of us, the idea of getting rid of our laptops, phones, and other devices that are particularly more stimulating is unreasonable as we have grown to rely on them for communication, work-related purposes, and other important parts of modern life. Rather than trying to eliminate them from our lives, then, we must learn to control how they affect us through our thoughts and voluntary actions surrounding the stimuli.

What Will It Take To Alleviate Some Of The Stress?

In truth, it will take a lot for you to alleviate the stress you are experiencing related to the stimuli in your life. The reason for this is because the stimuli themselves are not healthy for you, and yet they have an addictive quality, and so chances are they have become a bit of a bad habit in your life. Many of us have fallen into the habit of mindlessly scrolling social media or engaging in cell phone games to stimulate ourselves during periods where we would, and should, naturally be bored. Others fill quiet time with stimulating music, television, or even reading which can result in their quiet time becoming delegated to a task, rather than simply being quiet and still. No matter how you do it, chances are you have become addicted to stimulation like the majority of the population has.

While being stimulated and intentionally engaging in stimulation is important, there is a point where it is no longer helpful. That is, when you need to be stimulated at all waking hours of the day from the moment you wake up until the moment you go to sleep, you are no longer engaging in stimulation for a positive reason. Even if you are spending that time reading, learning, and growing in some way, shape, or form, chances are you are still bombarding your mind and emotions with an overwhelming amount of stimulation.

The human mind was made to be bored, as boredom is when we take rests. When you lay around and stare at the ceiling or look out the window, you are not wasting time by doing nothing. You are feeding your body and mind's natural desire to be at rest and to take a break. However, we have not been taught this to be true. Instead, we have been bullied and manipulated into believing that we should be in action and behave as productively as possible at all times of the day, from morning until night. And, it shows, largely in the amount of stress and stress-related illnesses that we each carry. By learning how to effectively and intentionally engage in proper rest periods throughout the day, and learning how to embrace boredom, you will actually be significantly improving your resiliency toward stimuli. In this way, you will learn to intentionally ignore distractions, and you will preserve and rebuild your energy so that you can have an abundance of energy to bring into new stimulating situations when *you* feel ready to be stimulated again, rather than when a stimulating piece of technology prompts you into action. Through this, your stress will significantly reduce, and your productivity will significantly increase. Meaning, if at the end of the day your goal is to be more productive, it can help to stop trying to be so productive.

When Are Stimuli Good For Us?

Stimuli are not an inherently bad. What makes the stimuli in our modern world so bad for us is that they are bombarding us and that they are designed to make us addicted to stimulation so that we are constantly craving more. When you find yourself constantly reaching for your phone or your laptop, feeling frustrated or angry when you are "unplugged," always wanting to buy something new or feed into consumerism, or otherwise constantly feeling deprived unless you are engaged, then the stimulation you are experiencing is a bad thing, and the stimuli you are surrounding yourself with are likely toxic. Stimuli are not bad at all, however, when you are in control of your behavior around the stimuli. When you can be around your phone without feeling obligated to check your messages, be around your laptop without needing to respond to emails, pass by stores or advertisements without feeling the need to purchase something, or otherwise experience stimuli without feeling obligated to engage with them, then stimuli are not bad for you. When this happens, you are in control around stimuli and they no longer command your life. At this point, you can choose when you are going to engage with stimuli and when you are not. Then, stimuli become tools that you can leverage rather than bad habits that you feel you can't kick. At this point, you can intentionally choose which stimuli you are going to engage with, and you can do so in such a way that advances your knowledge and your capacity to fulfill your desires *when you feel like it*. Through this capacity to intentionally choose and use stimuli to your advantage, *then* stimuli become positive things.

Chapter 2

Learn To Recognize Inputs That Remove Focus

Unscrambling the mess that comes from being bombarded by stimuli is something that takes time and effort. Understand that reaching a point where you are experiencing frequent or constant distractions that take away from your capacity to achieve your goals in life is a complex process that requires many things to take place. As this entire process is going on you, unfortunately, are largely unaware of what is happening and so you have no capacity to intentionally intervene and prevent yourself from taking up this experience.

Before you can even begin to actually take action on eliminating your problematic distractions, you need to understand why they are problematic for you in the first place. And, no, I'm not just talking about the stress you have accumulated or the anxiety, depression, or multiple failed goals you are experiencing as a result of your distractions. I'm talking about understanding what was going on inside of your brain as these problematic distractions were becoming problematic and recognizing the mess that this has created for you now. The more intimately you can understand this mess, the easier it will be for you to understand the process we are going to use to undo it so that you can get back to a point of having control over your mind and, therefore, resiliency toward any distractions.

Becoming Addicted To Stimuli – The Stages

From an external or conscious awareness point of view, getting distracted is something that happens gradually over time. First, you find yourself interested in stimulating things, then you find yourself using them regularly, and eventually you find yourself using them nearly constantly or to the point where it is a challenge for you to put them down and enjoy yourself without them.

In those early stages, you are only just becoming aware of the existence of the stimuli that will eventually become problematic for you. Someone may have told you about something, or you came across it in a well-placed or targeted ad, and it caught your interest. At this point, you show interested in it and you begin to draw it into your life. You may borrow the object in question from a friend at first, or buy one "just to try it," and you start exploring what it is like to have this stimulus in your life.

After a while, you begin to grow fond of having this particular stimulus around so you purchase your own, or maybe you purchase a better one so that you can get even more out of it. Now, you are being affected by its existence as it is fulfilling this inner desire to be stimulated in a way that this particular piece of technology has to offer. You may find yourself using it on a regular basis at first, and over time that begins to increase as you use it even more frequently. Soon, you are using the piece of technology daily, or multiple times a day. Or, maybe it is not centered around any specific timeframe but instead you find yourself being distracted anytime you try to engage in something that is relevant to that distraction. For example, maybe you do not use your laptop every day, but when you do have to use it for work you find yourself getting distracted by everything else on the laptop that seems to be far more enjoyable than the work you need to get done.

By the late stages of stimulus addiction, you find yourself struggling to step away from something that has given you a positive experience with stimulation in your life. Now, rather than being able to easily put the phone, laptop, TV remote, book, tablet, or other distractions down, you find yourself feeling a sense of despair when you put it down and an immediate craving to pick it back up again. When you go too long without it, you begin to feel a deep need to check in on it. If you do, you feel a sense of reward as you have reinforced your perceived need. If you don't, you feel a sense of frustration and you may stimulate yourself in some other way, such as by fidgeting with something or engaging with a new stimulus that will provide a similar feeling of fulfillment.

While you will not reach this complex level of addiction for every single stimulus in your life, this need to be stimulated will exist and it will drive you to find stimuli in any way possible. At this point, you will likely find that it is hard for you to stay focused on things, especially things you deem boring, because your brain is craving that rush that you get when you engage with something stimulating. As a result, you will find yourself constantly falling into states of distraction and looking for that next hit of stimulation because your brain needs it, and you have no idea how to stop it.

A Complex Network Of Distracted Habits

While, on the surface, you could witness your descent into a state of distraction, there is still a lot that you may not realize about what was going on inside of your brain at that time. Essentially, at the time of you finding yourself falling into a state of constant distraction, your brain was developing habits that supported you in becoming distracted. To your brain, the stimuli that were promoting your distraction was fun and was giving you a sense of reward and fulfillment, and our brains our wired in such a way that is intended to satisfy that state of reward. To understand this on a deeper level, I encourage you to check out my book *EMPOWERING HABITS*.

In many ways, the people who created more complex stimuli like our phones and social media know the power of our inner reward system and use that to their advantage. They attempt to reward us for using their devices or technology so that our brains experience that inner reward system being triggered and, as a result, begin to formulate addictive-like behaviors surrounding that stimulus in the form of habits. Some of those habits can be fairly intense and challenging to break.

These habits were not only created by devices like cell phones and technology like social media, though. Long before they came around, people were experiencing chronic states of distraction and struggling to see things all the way through. That occurred because of one major desire that we all have and the massive reward it provides us with when we fulfill it. This specific desire and reward are fulfilled by technology and devices, but it can also be fulfilled in many, *many* other ways. The desire is for instant gratification, and the reward is to have that instant gratification fulfilled.

Any time you experience a circumstance where you have a desire for instant gratification and the fulfillment of instant gratification, your brain is going to acknowledge this and crave more. Hence all of the distractions. The distractions you have accumulated in your life, if you will notice, give you a sense of fulfillment nearly immediately. When you click on the back of the pen, it makes a noise, and you can control that noise to make it sound like whatever you want. When you scroll social media, your curiosity for what your friends are up to is fulfilled. When you call a family member or friend, rather than focus on your task at hand, you receive immediate fulfillment of instant gratification *and* emotional fulfillment from that phone call. Anytime you engage in a distraction, it is because that distraction has the capacity to provide nearly instantaneous fulfillment of your desire for instant gratification. And as you do, these distractions become habitual, and it becomes incredibly challenging for you to stop.

At this point, you will likely notice that the habits that lead to your distraction are just as problematic as the habit of distraction itself. This means that you may notice that you have specific distractions that you seem to fall for every single time, but that you also find yourself looking for other means of distraction of those specific methods are not currently available to you. At this point, you have developed a complex network of habits that promote your distraction, including the very habit of distraction itself. This self-feeding habit continues to grow as it encourages you to develop more and more habits that lead to your distraction. As all of this happens, it becomes increasingly more complex for you to stay focused and get anything done, let alone see your goals all the way through.

The Cues Associated With Your Habit Network

When it comes to the process of habit creation, cues are one part of the three-step cycle that creates and integrates habits into your subconscious mind. Cues are the initial interaction that triggers your brain to launch a habit loop. After the cue comes the routine, then the reward. In the case of distraction, your cue would be whatever it is that triggers you to become distracted, the routine would be the distraction itself, and the reward would be the instant gratification you experience for engaging with that distraction.

Once you have begun to develop a complex network of habits, such as the one associated with distraction, it is hard to say how many cues exist in this network.

MARC WALKER and ALEXANDER LARKESS

Chances are, there are countless cues that contribute to your state of distraction and they may exist on many different levels within your capacity to be stimulated. This means that your sense of touch, taste, smell, sight, and sound will likely all be working together to create cues that induce your state of distraction.

The trouble with having thousands of possible cues that trigger these habits is that it will be virtually impossible for you to identify all of the cues and effectively create new routines to fit those cues. When it comes to the process of changing habits, the most effective approach is to maintain the same cue and reward, but to change the routine. If you cannot identify the cue, however, it can be challenging to prepare yourself for the implementation of the new routine because you are unaware of what specifically is causing you to want to engage in the old habit in the first place. With such a complex network, it is also virtually impossible and pointless to attempt to identify and fix every single cue that you experience.

What It Takes To Unpack These Habits

If locating and fixing the many different habits you have that are contributing to your distraction is nearly impossible, then this means that you have to unpack your habits in a different way if you want to be successful. At this point, rather than attempting to understand every single specific cue that is triggering you to want to engage in your old habit, you need to dig your level of awareness even deeper and start looking specifically into how you are feeling and how you are behaving. Through this, you may not be able to prepare for your new habits as effectively, but you will begin to find ways to implement new habits that will support you with eliminating the impact of your old, distracting habits.

This may sound complex, but on the surface the process is actually quite simple to understand. The execution, however, will take more work as you need to prepare yourself through a deepened state of self-awareness. Essentially, what you are going to need to do is cultivate a level of self-awareness that allows you to immediately begin to recognize the moment any level of desire has been aroused around your need for instant gratification. At these points, you are going to find yourself already feeling a deep and strong urge to fulfill that need in a familiar way, which means that it is going to take quite a bit of effort on your behalf to overcome that urge and fulfill it in a different way.

The point of self-awareness becomes particularly challenging around this network of distraction habits because the level of awareness you need is something that your brain has naturally been designed to deny. If you have been engaging in a habit of distraction for any period of time, your brain has already sunk that habit into your subconscious level with the intention of no longer having to consciously think about it. This way, your brain can engage in it automatically and provide attention and energy to other things. For this reason, you may find yourself absent-mindedly engaging in distractions because your brain has literally turned this into an automatic behavior. In order to regain self-awareness around this particular behavior you are going to need to do quite a bit of work so that you can sink that self-awareness in deep enough to bury it under the roots of the distracting habit and hoist it right out of there.

As you begin to engage in this level of self-awareness, you can start breaking down your bad habits that lead to distraction one by one until eventually they are no longer overruling your life. At this point, you will begin to experience a deepened state of self-awareness which accompanies a greater level of focus and a stronger capacity to ignore distractions that are attempting to interrupt your attention span. With that being said, it can be a fairly slow process at first, but once the momentum builds you will begin to notice rapid change and improvement in your life.

Creating an Environment Of Give and Take

As burdensome as this entire process may seem, the entire practice of breaking down your distractions so that you can cultivate more focus is not centered around breaking down bad habits. The opposite side of this coin is that you are going to be spending time creating new ones, which means that in order to be highly effective in navigating these inputs you are going to need to engage in a give-and-take system.

On the taking end, you are taking away energy from your old habits that are leaving you distracted and preventing you from getting anything done. You are also taking into account your awareness so that you can deepen your capacity to eliminate these habits, effectively creating a sense of peace within your life. This side of the entire process can seem negative and burdensome at times, especially when you acknowledge the difficulty and frustration that can come along with it.

On the giving end, you are giving the energy you gain by eliminating distractions to something more positive. This is the side where you will likely experience a heightened sense of optimism, as you will be pouring your attention and energy into things that are going to support you with creating stronger habits that are more resilient toward distractions.

So, while you are focused on breaking something down, you are also focused on building something up. This combined effort of eliminating bad habits while creating positive ones will support you with your capacity to enjoy a higher level of focus and a greater ability to achieve your goals. It will take time, and it will take effort, but as you begin to tip the scales in a more positive direction the momentum will grow and, soon enough, you will find yourself creating the results you desire.

Chapter 3

Tune Into You

Self-awareness is the biggest key in breaking down distracting habits, yet the lock to your subconscious mind can be mysterious and, in many cases, rather challenging to find. Many scientists and psychologists argue that truly accessing your subconscious mind is not possible, which is why we must acknowledge the reality that you will never gain the capacity to identify every single cue that you have that contributes to your state of distraction. While you may not be able to gain that deepened level of awareness where you can reach into your subconscious mind with ease, though, you can cultivate a level of self-awareness that enables you to understand what is going on in your subconscious mind. Through this understanding, you can tap into a level of self-awareness that provides you with the capacity to recognize anytime you are engaging in an old pattern so that you can flip the switch and engage in a newer, healthier pattern over time.

It is important to understand that breaking down habits in this way tends to be more challenging and, as such, you may find yourself experiencing a heightened level of emotional and mental protest toward your desire to change. Increasing your self-awareness around these responses, too, can support you in navigating them more effectively so that you can see them through and find your way into a level of higher success surrounding your capacity to focus.

The more you deepen your self-awareness, the more you will not only find yourself breaking down old habits, but also growing your ability to direct your awareness. Through this, the entire give-and-take process of breaking down old habits to develop new habits surrounding focus will become even easier.

Receptive Self-Awareness For Digging Into Your Subconscious Mind

Receptive self-awareness is a form of self-awareness that will allow you to become aware of the symptoms of your subconscious mind, rather than the thoughts that are actually occurring within your subconscious mind. This way, while you may not be able to know exactly what your subconscious mind is thinking, you can begin to break it down through acknowledging the symptoms and applying logic to figure it out.

In order to cultivate a state of receptive self-awareness, you first need to create an anchor that represents what you are looking for. In this case, you are looking to uncover what your distracting habits are and what is contributing to the creation of your distracting habits so that you can shift away from them. So, your anchor would be any distraction that you want to stop habitually engaging in.

As soon as you identify your anchor, you want to begin to become self-aware of any thoughts, behaviors, and patterns you notice that surround this anchor. Write these thoughts, behaviors, and patterns down in a book so that you can keep track of them and recognize how they are affecting you. You may also want to jot down what types of long-term side-effects you are noticing from these behaviors, as well as what emotions you are experiencing in relation to these behaviors. Before you begin to officially attempt to change anything, you may also play around with these behaviors by attempting to engage in them differently, or not at all. At this point, you can become aware of how this shift in your approach to these behaviors affects your mind, your mood, and your energy.

It may take several days or even weeks for you to become consistently aware of the experiences you are having in relation to your distracting habits. Remember, if they are embedded deep in your subconscious mind, you are literally wired not to think about them, or even really notice them unless something changes. For that reason, you might start to develop this self-awareness retroactively, by sitting down and recalling any time you engaged in that habit throughout the day and retroactively taking note of what you were feeling, thinking, and doing. Or, if you are constantly distracted, you may take note every hour so that you can keep track of your distractions and how they are affecting you. While this retroactive analysis may not be as thorough and complete, it will begin to train your mind to become more aware of these habits which will eventually allow you to consistently recognize them in the very moment they are happening. At that point, you can take real-time inventory as to what is going on and how you are feeling so that you can gain an accurate understanding of your habits and how they are affecting you in the very moments that they are playing out.

Breaking Down the Evidence

Now that you have managed to tap into receptive self-awareness so that you can begin to uncover information surrounding your habit and the many cues and routines associated with the reward of instant gratification, you need to do some sleuthing. This sleuthing will allow you to use logic and reasoning to determine what the root cause of your distraction is, what is triggering your distraction and how you are becoming distracted, and what you can do about it. Realize that each of us is distracted for slightly different reasons, and our thoughts, beliefs, emotions, and feeling from the reward of instant gratification are all different. For this reason, the way you approach breaking down your craving for instant gratification will be somewhat different from how someone else does it.

The best way to begin sleuthing your habit is to start with the anchor piece of your self-awareness and begin to build your understanding of your habit out chronologically, from the moment you realize it is being triggered to the moment you feel fulfilled. This chronological order of your habit should take you through the feeling of being triggered, the routine itself, and the feeling and thoughts you have associated with the reward you gain from fulfilling the habit. Try to get as much detail into your habit as you possibly can so that you can gain a greater sense of context around what the habit is, how it works, and what you are gaining out of it.

Once you have laid out your habit in chronological order, you can begin to apply logic and reasoning to the habit to see if you can uncover the entire reasoning behind the habit itself. We already know that habits are largely driven by reward and that your reward is associated with instant gratification, but you want to see if you can go even deeper into that to better understand what this means for you, for this particular habit. In other words, what specific form of instant gratification are you looking for? What type of fulfillment are you seeking, and why are you drawn to this particular habit, or these particular habits, to fulfill it?

You want to get as close to understanding the exact desire and reward you are gaining from this reward as possible so that the habit itself begins to make more sense to you. This way, you can gain a deeper understanding of why you are engaging in this habitual distraction, which is going to allow you to completely recreate your routine surrounding your habit so that you can stop being distracted and start getting everything done!

Creating Real-Time Self-Awareness For Habitual Patterns

Now that you have begun to develop self-awareness surrounding what is going on in your subconscious mind and you have uncovered what it likely means, you need to start developing self-awareness around your habitual patterns. At this point, you are no longer trying to identify what is going on in your subconscious mind, but instead you are working toward deepening your self-awareness around what you have already discovered. This is going to allow you to really begin to grasp the extent of your distracting habits and develop the most intricate level of awareness around them so that it becomes far easier for you to navigate the process of eliminating these habits.

The coolest perk of consciousness when it comes to developing self-awareness is that once you put something into your conscious mind, it becomes incredibly easy for you to notice it in real-time. A great example of this phenomenon is shown in experiences such as when you think about a yellow car and then, suddenly, you begin spotting yellow cars *everywhere*. This happens because the topic of a yellow car was recently brought to your attention and, now, your subconscious mind will draw your conscious awareness to every single yellow car you see. It essentially draws a connection between the present moment and a memory that you have surrounding "yellow cars" being of some level of importance.

You can intentionally drive this phenomenon by becoming aware of your habit and choosing to acknowledge every time your subconscious mind draws your conscious awareness to the occurrence of the habit itself. When this happens, all you have to do is lean in and allow your conscious mind to become aware of said habit, and then mindfully pay attention to anything you notice occurring as the habit takes place. At this point, you are going to be looking for much of the same things as you had previously when you were unburying this habit from your subconscious mind. This will include searching for your motivation behind engaging in the habit, understanding the step by step process of the routine associated with this habit, and acknowledging your reward that you are experiencing from fulfilling this habit.

Developing Self-Awareness Around Your Mindset and Emotions

In addition to uncovering the practical steps surrounding the habit, you are going to want to draw your self-awareness into your mindset and emotions surrounding your habits that are feeding your distractions. Emotions in particular are the number one driving force behind every habit you have, which means understanding what your own emotions are can help you understand your motivation behind fulfilling said habit. While you have already done a great job at uncovering what your reward is and how it feels, at this point we are going to go even deeper into what you are thinking and feeling around your habit as this is going to increase your clarity and make navigating changes easier.

When it comes to your emotions, studies have shown that your emotions are driven by thoughts. This is why it is so imperative for you to understand your thoughts surrounding your habits, as these thoughts are driving your emotions and those emotions are driving your habit. By uncovering all three layers, you are giving yourself the best opportunity to navigate the destruction of these habits so that you can replace them with habits that motivate your focus, rather than take it away.

You can approach this phase of self-awareness in one of two ways, and it is best to choose the one that comes naturally for you as this will make untangling your thoughts and emotions surrounding your habit easier. This way, you can really tune into yourself and find the answers for how you are going to stop being so distracted and start creating deeper levels of focus and clarity for yourself.

On the one hand, thoughts precede emotions, so if you find it more natural to become aware of your thoughts than emotions, you can begin paying attention to your thoughts so that you can become aware of the way they are surrounding your habit. Notice what you are thinking when you first initiate the habit, what you are thinking throughout the entire execution of the habit, and what you are thinking after the habit has been fulfilled. Then, see if you can identify what emotions are being driven by this thought pattern. This way, you can start drawing self-awareness to your emotions as well.

If you find that it comes more naturally for you to identify your emotions rather than your thoughts, see if you can start to develop a self-awareness around the emotions you experience in association with the three steps of your distracting habits. Then, see if you can identify what thoughts you were experiencing immediately before those emotions were experienced. This way, you can start to recognize how your thoughts are driving your emotions.

Once you have developed clarity around how your thoughts are driving your emotions, and how your emotions are driving your habits, you can start to develop a system for you to navigate changes. Understand that at this point, we are not putting any practical steps in place for changing distracted habits so that you can deepen your focus. Instead, we are preparing for those stages by deepening your awareness so that you can be prepared for any mental or emotional protest you may face as you attempt to give up the distractions in your life.

Using Mindful Awareness To Navigate These Changes

Once you have indulged in developing this level of self-awareness, it will become incredibly challenging for you to lose it, although it is not impossible. For that reason, you want to continue to nurture your self-awareness around your habits so that you do not find yourself losing touch with them again. You also want to maintain this self-awareness as it is going to allow you to recognize any changes you may experience to your habit so that you can take those into account as you begin to navigate the breaking down of your distractions.

Going forward, everything you do surrounding your habit should be done with a certain level of mindfulness. This mindfulness is going to allow you to become aware of, and even predict in some cases, the types of mental and emotional responses that you may have to the process of change. Through this, you can acknowledge these responses, create meaningful ways to approach them, and ultimately recognize that they are temporary and that there is no dire need for you to act on them, even if it feels like you must.

A big part of mindfully navigating the change process is learning how to acknowledge what you are feeling and thinking without creating an urgent need to act on this information. As these inputs are coming in, you want to recognize their arrival and then do what you can to divert your thoughts and feelings to ones that are going to be more centered around your new desired behaviors, rather than your old ones. This way, you are not giving energy or power to your unwanted thoughts and emotions, but instead you are giving it to something that is going to be beneficial for you.

One of the biggest mistakes people make when they are navigating the change of habits is believing that every thought and feeling they have is urgent, true, and must be acted upon. This is not the case and believing this can make changing your behavior significantly more difficult. Instead, you want to realize that thoughts and feelings in relation to habits are also habitual, and that they, too, are a part of what you need to change. In recognizing this, you no longer freak out about these thoughts or feelings, feel intimidated by them, or feel a looming need to act on them in any way, shape, or form. Instead, you can acknowledge them and immediately invest that same energy and attention into your new thoughts and feelings. At first, it may feel strange and it may feel as though these new thoughts and feelings are misplaced, foreign, or you may even feel like they do not actually belong to you. Over time, though, you will find yourself owning these new thoughts and feelings and naturally releasing the old ones.

One specific pattern of thoughts and feelings I want to highlight includes one that often brings about feelings of shame, guilt, embarrassment, frustration or disappointment. If you find yourself feeling particularly negative toward yourself and your behaviors, you are going to end up creating a large amount of negative thoughts and feelings around that behavior. Rather than helping you make a change; this particular experience is going to cause you to become so mentally and emotionally invested in negative thoughts and feelings that you struggle to divert your attention at all. In a sense, you are giving away your power when you do this. Rather than giving away your power, focus all of your energy on neutralizing your thoughts and feelings around your unwanted habits of distraction and focusing all of that energy instead on the change you wish to see. This way, you will be far more likely to disengage from the negative habit and engage with the positive one, instead.

Mindful awareness will go a long way in helping you detach from old thoughts, feelings, and behaviors, so it is important that you always nurture this aspect of yourself as you navigate any change in your life. This way, you will be far more likely to experience a successful change, rather than a failed attempt at a change.

Chapter 4

Neutralize Everything That Distracts You

Distractions are never going to go away. Period. No matter what you do, no matter how minimalistic you choose to live, and no matter how hard you try to change your life to eliminate distractions, you will never be successful. Every single thing that has the capacity to interact with one of your five senses has the capacity to become distracting, and since you cannot submerge yourself in a sensory deprivation tank and live there for the rest of your life, you are not going to be able to eliminate distractions. Furthermore, even if you *could* deprive your senses, there are still built-in distractions such as daydreaming and fiddling with your own fingers or extremities that could distract you from what you are doing. So, at the end of the day, attempting to entirely erase distractions out of your life is pointless.

Beyond the fact of this effort being pointless, I want to draw awareness to the fact that attempting to completely eliminate distractions from your life is also an overwhelmingly negative way to view the process of becoming not distractable. If you are constantly pitting distractions as the problem, and not recognizing that the problem is actually *you* becoming distracted, and not the existence of the distractions themselves, then you are giving all of your power away to the distractions. At this point, you are not taking responsibility for yourself, your mind, or your emotions. Instead, you are mentally existing as a victim to your distractions by believing that only they have the power to help you focus, and they can only do that by ceasing to exist. This mindset is absurd, pointless, and will only go so far as to prevent you from creating any level of accountability within yourself. At the end of the day, this mindset will only set you up to fail.

Rather than giving all of your power away to distractions, you need to reclaim your responsibility and start taking power for yourself by neutralizing every single distraction in your life. You can amplify this work through practical means such as minimizing the presence of distractions in your life, but you should not make that the key focal point of your efforts. Instead, focus more so on your mindset, your feelings, and your own behaviors surrounding the distractions that you are troubled by.

Addressing Your Beliefs About Being Distracted

As your thoughts and beliefs are at the core of everything, learning how to address your mindset surrounding distractions is the necessary step for you to begin neutralizing your distractions. Anything you think in your mind over a lengthy period of time is what will ultimately become your beliefs, and, in a sense, these beliefs are at the root of all habitual thinking or automatic thinking behaviors you experience. You can begin to shift these beliefs by changing what you are thinking over a prolonged period of time. The tricky part, however, comes when you attempt to shift your belief to something that is too radically different from what you already believe. For example, if you believe that you are incapable of leading a life without distraction, it may be too radical for you to immediately transition your belief system into allowing you to believe that you *are* capable of leading a life without distraction. However, it may be reasonable for you to change your belief into believing that it is *possible* that you are capable of leading a life without distraction. This way, you are not attempting to radically shift from one end of the spectrum to another, but instead you are finding a happy medium that creates the potential for change. You would be surprised at how much change can be created through these happy mediums.

In order for you to effectively change your beliefs, you must first recognize what it is that you believe and how that belief is affecting your everyday life. Through this, you are going to start to identify positive beliefs, which reinforce the positive aspects of your life, and negative beliefs that reinforce the negative aspects of your life. Naturally, you want to address and shift the negative beliefs that are keeping you stuck or that are encouraging pieces of your life that you want to move away from, such as your tendency to become distracted rather than remaining focused. Revealing what beliefs need to be addressed is best done by using that incredible conscious awareness-based tool you have already been using to help you identify your thoughts and feelings relating to your habits of being distracted. That is, you can simply ask yourself to become aware of any thoughts you have about the distractions themselves, and any beliefs you carry about these distractions and your capacity to neutralize them or ignore them. Through this, you will rapidly be shown all of your thoughts and beliefs surrounding these distractions so that you can begin to identify what patterns you have that need to be changed.

As soon as these thoughts and beliefs come into your conscious awareness, you need to start addressing them. Begin by identifying what types of new, more positive thoughts and beliefs exist that you could reasonably take on in your life. For example, if you find that you have a belief that you are incapable of ignoring distractions and this is something to be ashamed about, you will want to explore alternative beliefs that are more positive and yet still believable. You may find that you can believe that it is possible for you to try neutralizing distractions, and that it is natural for people to become distracted based on the way our society is structured. Spend some time identifying exactly what new belief or thought could be held that would be more positive and constructive than what you are already thinking, then resolve to choose that new thought over any future negative thought you experience. It will take some time for this to become habitual, but as it does you will find that your beliefs shift and so your entire mindset around and feeling toward distractions themselves shifts, too.

As you begin to effectively shift your beliefs, you will find that you firmly evict your victim mindset surrounding distractions so that you can begin to feel empowered and capable around your distractions, instead. This will go a long way in helping you rebuild your ability to take responsibility and accountability for your behaviors surrounding distractions, which will allow you to have greater control over your emotions and, therefore, your actions.

MARC WALKER and ALEXANDER LARKESS

Understand that if you do not first address your mindset and belief system around distractions, you stand little to no chance of ever effectively neutralizing distractions in your life. Anyone who truly believes they are incapable of eliminating distractions, or who fails to understand their belief around distractions at all in the first place, will fail to have the mental strength required to overcome distractions. This fact is not only true about distractions, either, but about everything in your life. If you are not capable of developing the necessary mindset and beliefs around something, you will always find yourself fighting against your inner belief that it is not possible. Eventually, that negative inner belief system will always catch up with you and drag you back to square one, so it is always best to address it first so that you are not at risk of a significant backslide.

Removing the Power Of a Distraction

At this point, you have regained your power over a distraction by reclaiming your sense of responsibility and accountability for your own actions. Now, you can begin to use this power to completely disempower your distractions, effectively rendering them "neutralized." There are many ways that you can do this, though, as you may suspect these methods all lie within your mindset and your beliefs surrounding the distractions you are experiencing.

The key to neutralizing a distraction lies in realizing that no matter what type of energy you give a distraction, that energy is going to amplify its power. This means that you do not want to think anything negative *or* positive about a distraction, as either form of energy will result in you giving power to that distraction. Instead, you want to practice not thinking about that distraction at all, and if you do find yourself thinking about it you want to practice having indifferent thoughts about that distraction to the best of your ability.

To shine a light on the power that your thoughts give to something, I want you to pause right now and look around the room to identify one thing that you do not like, and one thing that you do like. These objects do not have to be things that you absolutely hate or that you are absolutely in love with. Instead, they simply need to be things that you have a tendency toward liking or disliking. Right now, in this very moment, those two objects had a sense of power over you. One of those objects invoked positive thoughts and feelings within you, while the other invoked negative ones. No matter how subtle those shifts in your thoughts and feelings may have been, they were present, and they affected you. This is exactly what you want to avoid when it comes to creating a neutralizing effect for any distractions in your life.

Most distractions in your life are things that you have a positive experience with, which means that you may be reluctant to neutralize it because you do not want to stop enjoying that particular thing. As we begin neutralizing your distractions, realize that our goal is not to take away the joy that you experience when you engage with that particular item. Instead, our goal is to take away the power that it has to use that enjoyment to drive you to become distracted by this object. In other words, you are desensitizing it's capacity to distract you, not its capacity to bring you joy. This way, you can continue to enjoy using that particular item, you simply won't enjoy it so much that you cannot *not* use the item any time it is around.

In order to create this neutralization effect in your distractions, you must dig into the root of your thoughts with every single distraction and first identify whether that distraction is bringing you a positive or a negative feeling. Even though most distractions are positive this does not mean they all are, so you need to uncover what it is that you are actually feeling in relation to your distractions.

Now that you are aware of your feelings, you need to begin to neutralize the power they have over you. This particular process is going to come from thinking *neutralizing thoughts*. Neutralizing thoughts are any thoughts that you have that will allow you to disempower a distraction. For example, let's say your phone is the distraction you want to disempower. The neutralizing thought you might think could be "oh, it's just a phone" or "hmm." These types of thoughts are not in-depth, they do not afford much energy or attention toward the distraction, and they do not elicit an emotional response from the distraction. Instead, they simply acknowledge it and then provide you with the mental capacity to move on from that distraction and focus on something else.

As you continue to think these simple neutralizing thoughts, you will find that your brain starts to recognize that these distractions are no longer all that exciting anymore. As a result, you stop feeling moved to experience positive or negative thoughts or emotions surrounding those distractions. Instead, they simply are. When this begins to occur, you know that you have effectively neutralized an unwanted distraction.

Going through this process of neutralizing your distractions through your mindset can bring about one mental pattern that I want to shed light on so you can be mindful of it and intentionally avoid it. That is, I want you to be mindful of your potential for falling into the pattern of developing any level of mental excitement when you acknowledge a distraction. I'm not talking about acknowledging the object of distraction, but rather the experience of being distracted itself, or the experience of having the potential to be distracted. It is not uncommon for people to develop an awareness of their distractions and then immediately go "oh I can't think about that, that will distract me" or "oh my gosh a distraction, quick I have to neutralize it." These types of excitable thoughts will drive your energy higher, effectively feeding more attention and either positive or negative awareness into your distraction. In the end, it will provide you with results that are completely the opposite of what you are looking for. Just like with the distraction itself, if you find yourself being stirred to experience any level of excitement over recognizing your distraction, neutralize it. These "no big deal" thoughts surrounding the experience of being distracted *and* the distraction itself will work to completely eliminate any power that these thoughts and objects have over you in your life.

Amplifying Your Results By Minimizing Temptation

While the majority of your work within neutralizing distractions will come from the mindset work you do surrounding the distractions themselves, there are more practical steps you can take to help you neutralize distractions as well. In particular, distractions that have been a major problem for you, or distractions that have built-in features that are intended to tempt you or distract you should be intentionally minimized to avoid temptation.

As you begin to eliminate temptations from your life from this point of view, you are no longer doing so with the belief that the power lies in the distraction and that the only way to deal with it is to eliminate it from your life. Instead, you believe that you have the ultimate power to decide, but you are aware of your natural tendency to become distracted and so you are working within your power and within reason to eliminate distractions. Another reason for wanting to amplify your results through this is that as you work toward neutralizing distractions, it is important to realize that it will take time for this to occur. You cannot erase all of your mental patterns in one go, this is something you are going to have to work toward and put effort into in order to create the results you desire. By minimizing temptations, you are maximizing your ability to create a resiliency toward distractions by neutralizing them altogether. Over time, you may find that you have fewer temptations and, therefore, you do not have to do quite as much to prevent yourself from getting distracted. In the meantime, following this well-rounded approach will ensure that you are getting the results you need, and that you are setting yourself up for success.

Minimizing certain temptations in your life will be easy and straightforward. For example, if you know you tend to be distracted when you work you can create a working environment that is not full of distractions and that instead nurtures your focus. You might remove anything that is particularly stimulating or that may cause you to fidget or get distracted so that instead you can focus on what needs to be done. As soon as the distraction is placed out of sight, it will also likely fall out of mind as there is no easy way for you to reach for it and allow yourself to get distracted.

Other temptations are going to be less simple to remove or minimize and may require you to be creative while also exercising a higher degree of self-discipline in order to create the results you need. For example, you may not be able to leave your phone outside of your office, and you may even need it nearby and "on" so that people can get ahold of you during the workday. In this scenario, you may wish to mute certain notifications, or give important notifications a specific sound that alerts you to realize that these particular notifications are important to your workday. Then, you may wish to put your phone out of reach so that you have to intentionally stand up and go grab it in order to engage with any alerts that your phone gets. This way, you can begin to train yourself *not* to respond to unimportant alerts during the workday, but you can still respond to important alerts during the workday. It may seem more frustrating to have to get up every time your phone rings, but the reality is that even though it may require more work to answer your phone, it will provide you with a greater capacity to pay attention to work outside of work-related phone calls.

Aside from your phone, the internet on your computer, and other similar temptations may be difficult for you to avoid. With every temptation you experience that is difficult to avoid, you will want to come up with a creative solution to help minimize the temptation, then you will want to exercise self-discipline to ensure that you maintain that solution. These more creative solutions that are rooted in self-discipline will likely take more time for you to successfully navigate, so remember to do so mindfully. You can also exercise your neutralizing practices to minimize your level of distraction and keep yourself focused on the task at hand. Over time, you will find that these temptations are no longer such a big deal and that exercising self-discipline is effortless because you have taught yourself to respond this way habitually. By then, you will find yourself experiencing a great deal of consistent focus!

Basic Desensitization Practices To Increase Your Resiliency

In addition to shifting your mindset around distractions and temptations, there are other things you can do to shift yourself into a state of having a higher level of resiliency toward your distractions. These practices are designed to intentionally expose you to distractions so that you can begin practicing neutralizing and ignoring these distractions, effectively supporting you with building up your self-discipline surrounding your level of focus.

It is important that if you choose to engage in these desensitization practices that you only engage in incremental changes, as overexposure could result in you giving in to distraction which would only reinforce your distraction, not your focus. With that being said, follow these basic desensitization practices in order before graduating to the more intense advanced desensitization practices later. This way, you will have far more success in desensitizing yourself toward distraction and temptation.

The first desensitization practice you are going to engage in to help curb temptation and eliminate distractions is simple. You are going to sit in a room, any room, and hold one single object out in front of you. Or, you could sit on the floor and place the object on a table or chair so that it is eye level with you. Then, you are going to set a timer and focus on that object, and nothing else, for one whole minute. If you find yourself getting distracted, you must immediately stop the timer and start again. You will continue practicing this until you are able to focus on the object for one minute straight with no distraction. Then, you are going to start doing this for two minutes. Over time, you will want to increase this until you are focusing on the object in question for twenty minutes.

During this initial practice you want to do your best to avoid having any unneeded stimuli encouraging you to become distracted. Mute your phone and leave it out of reach, turn off the TV, turn off any music that might be playing, and otherwise avoid having any known distractions present. Eventually you will work toward desensitization with those present, but for now you want to build a strong foundation for yourself.

After you have been able to focus on this one object for twenty minutes, you want to make one simple shift in your approach so that you are able to start expanding your desensitization. At this point, you are going to permit just one distraction to be present and available to tempt you during your period of focus. This could be your television, the notifications on your phone, your radio, or anything else that typically distracts you from being able to focus on what you are trying to accomplish. Again, you are going to start at just one minute with this practice and then you can continue to increase by one minute at a time until you can easily get through twenty minutes of focus. You may wish to change the specific distraction you choose during each period of focus so that you are learning to become desensitized to many, rather than to just one.

As soon as you begin to feel confident in your ability to navigate one distraction, try adding a second, and then a third. Slowly begin to increase the amount of distractions that are available during your desensitization practice until you are experiencing the normal amount of distractions that you would during any natural everyday experience. This way, you can start to become used to the level of distraction that will be normal to your everyday experience, and by this point it should start to become easier for you to focus longer on everyday tasks.

Advanced Desensitization Practices To Increase Your Resiliency

Once you have mastered the basic desensitization practices that will support you with improving your resiliency toward distractions and temptations, you need to start working on desensitizing yourself in more advanced situations. These more advanced situations are going to expose you to even more cues and distractions as you are actively trying to avoid them so that you can get used to staying focused during heightened levels of distraction.

The primary approach we are going to use in this particular practice is the same as what you practiced in basic practices, except this time you are not going to sit by and simply observe an item. Instead, you are going to actively engage with it, and you are going to begin engaging with normal everyday tasks, too. What this does is exposes you to real-life experiences where you will typically get distracted so that you can practice staying focused during these real-life experiences. Now, you are starting to move your practice out of the "preparation" phase and into a "practical" phase.

To begin this practice, I want you to pick just one simple everyday task that you need to complete on a day to day basis and practice increasing your level of focus on that task. Try to choose a task that you typically get distracted during, although avoid choosing a task that is *too* distracting as this can lead to you reinforcing your distractions rather than your focus. Remember, you want to increase your exposure gradually over time, not throw yourself off the deep end and hope you figure it out.

Once you have chosen your daily task, I want you to start applying the same mental and emotional strength that you applied toward your previous desensitization practices to this one. When you are ready, begin engaging in the everyday task as usual, and do what you can to stay absolutely focused for the duration of the task. This time, we are not going to expand minute by minute because you already have a fairly solid foundation of focus, and because the task you are doing should already be fairly short and easy. You are going to want to continue practicing this desensitization practice with this particular task until you can see it all the way through.

Once you are able to effectively focus all the way through one task, you will add another one into your day. This time, you might choose another similarly simple task, or you might choose one that might take a little longer, or that might result in you getting distracted more frequently than the previous one. Choose a task that will align with your goal of building up to higher levels of resiliency rather than throwing yourself all in. Then, again, practice seeing that particular task all the way through until you are able to focus on it easily, every single time.

You are going to want to continue to engage in this particular advanced desensitization practice over and over again, applying it to a new task every time. This way, as time goes on, you will be increasing your level of desensitization toward various tasks and you will be finding it easier to continue applying this desensitization toward any new tasks that may cross your path. The more you continue to practice this, the better you will get.

Chapter 5

Detoxify From Hidden Addictions and Compulsions

Your subconscious mind is a master at keeping your habits hidden under lock and key. If you were to look into your subconscious mind, you would likely discover thousands of different habits that exist without you even realizing it. Many of those habits will be effectively contributing to your level of distraction, rather than contributing to your ability to stay focused and see things through. No matter how hard you find yourself working toward uncovering as many habits as you can from your subconscious mind, you are still going to have many more that need to be addressed.

By now, you are well educated on what it takes to engage in the "*take*" part of the give-and-take process of eliminating distractions from your life. You have discovered how to identify habits, eliminate habits, and transform habits so that they are more positive. You have also discovered how to neutralize your distractions so that you can desensitize yourself toward certain things that you may not be able to change as effectively as you wish to. So far, you are doing an impeccable job of eliminating distractions from your life so that you can become not distractable!

Now, we are going to focus on the *"give"* portion of this process. To do this, we are going to address the process of detoxifying from hidden addictions and compulsions so that you can eliminate distractions that may be challenging or even impossible for you to address on an individual case-by-case basis. For this particular part of the journey, we are going to stop focusing so much on what you are moving away from and start focusing on what you are moving toward. By laying the foundation for new habits to exist altogether, we will be creating the perfect landscape for you to officially become not distractable.

Taking Focus Away From Hidden Habits

What you focus on grows, so naturally we want to focus on taking attention away from hidden habits so that you can officially let go of any addictions and compulsions that may keep you engaged in distractions. At this point you may be wondering, "if it's hidden, how on earth am I focusing on it?" That is a great question. How can you focus on something if you have no idea what it is? The answer is actually quite simple. First and foremost, you focus on this hidden addiction or compulsion every time you realize that it has been activated and you realize you are engaging with it, or that you are experiencing the symptoms of it. Immediately upon recognizing that you have engaged with an addiction or compulsion you will find yourself thinking about it and experiencing the mental or emotional patterns you identified earlier, in chapter 3.

Each time you find yourself in this process of recognizing and thinking about the pattern, you are giving attention to it and reinforcing it. As well, when you keep yourself in an environment and associated with behaviors that nurture the addiction or compulsion rather than take away from it, you find yourself reinforcing that addiction or compulsion. So, if you can stop thinking about it *and* shift your environment and lifestyle so that it no longer nurtures this behavior, you can find your way toward eliminating attention and energy from it.

Rather than focusing on how you are going to get away from this habit, then, you should be focusing on what you are going to do instead. By redirecting your focus to something else, you are effectively taking it away from the distraction and giving it to something more meaningful.

To begin doing this, you are going to go through the process of creating a new vision for what it is that you want. In this new vision, you are going to envision that you are no longer submitting to distractions or temptations and that instead you are able to stay focused and see things all the way through. Then, you are going to discover what underlying desires have driven this vision so that you can take advantage of those desires and turn them into an actionable plan that flows in alignment with your human nature. By adjusting your behaviors and your environment to serve your nature, you will find yourself effortlessly taking your attention off of your distractions and putting it into things that serve you instead. All you will need to do then is commit to engaging in this new level of focus for at least thirty days as you engage in a detox, and then you will focus on integrating this new behavior into your lifestyle so that it is sustainable and long-lasting. Through all of this, you will find yourself finally creating an environment for success so that you can embrace being not distractable!

Creating a Vision For the Lifestyle That You Want

In order to put your attention toward something positive, you need to have something positive to focus on! At this stage in your journey, we are going to define what your goals are so that you have a clear understanding of what it is that you are working toward. This is the point where all of your effort is going to start coming together toward what it is that you truly want to achieve, showing you just how far you have really come.

Right now, you are not going to place any focus whatsoever into your distractions or anything that you *don't* want. Instead, you are going to clearly identify and define what you do want so that you can work toward that. You are going to do this by freeing your mind of any worries you have about limitations so that you can freely dream about what it is that you truly want for yourself. I suggest you start by considering the goal you have that encouraged you to read this very book in the first place. What is it that you so desperately want to achieve, yet that you keep getting distracted from? What do you dream about and long for, and wish that you had enough focus and drive to complete? Start there.

When it comes to creating your vision, I encourage you to get as clear as possible and to cover as many different areas of your life as possible. To do this properly, you are going to uncover the eight areas of your life that matter most to you and you are going to define what you want each of these areas of your life to truly look like. These eight areas of your life include: health, wealth, career, relationships, romance, your relationship with yourself, hobbies, and faith. To help you dig really deep, I have included a series of questions below for you to consider. Dig through these questions to help yourself create a vision for what your entire life would look like if you were able to create whatever you wanted, free of distractions.

As far as your health goes, what goals do you have that you wish you could achieve? If you could stay focused and see it all the way through, what would your health routine look like on a day to day basis? What results would you have already achieved?

For your wealth, what do you wish your finances to look like, and what other resources matter to you that you wish to have an abundance of in your life? What would you want to feel like in relation to your wealth? How would you like to manage and use your wealth?

In your career, how would you behave? What types of achievements would you have accomplished, and what level of status would you hold? How would you show up differently, and what type of attention to detail would you bring to the work you do? What skills would you nurture to help yourself maintain a successful career in your desired career path?

As far as your relationships go, what would they be like? How would you interact with other individuals? How would your circle of friends change, and how would you show up differently for those that you care about? What would you do to improve the quality of your relationships with other people? Would you have more friends? How would your relationships with other people look?

In addition to your relationships with friends and family, what about your relationship with your lover? Would you have a higher-quality relationship with your lover? Would you spend more time and attention on them, or doing things that nurtured your relationship with them? Would you invest more energy into finding a partner, and overcoming anything that may be holding you back from finding your dream partner? Would you finally approach the person you fancy?

Your relationship with yourself matters, too. How would you invest quality time and attention into yourself if there were nothing stopping you from doing so? What types of things would you do with yourself, and how would this make you feel? How would spending undistracted time with yourself, taking care of yourself and enjoying your own company, change your life?

Hobbies are very important to our wellbeing, and they can either distract us or become pushed aside as other parts of life distract us. How would your hobbies fit into your life, if you were to fit them in using a healthy manner? What would you focus on, what goals would you have, and what desires would you want to fulfill through your hobbies? Would you change your standards around how you approach your hobbies? Would you spend more time in classes, or being surrounded by people who could help you advance your hobbies?

Lastly, your faith. If you were not so busy being distracted, how would you invest more quality time in your faith? What would you do to nurture your level of belief, and prevent yourself from falling distracted with doubts and uncertainty? Would you learn more, embrace more, or integrate more of your faith into your life? What would your life look like, or how would your life change, with your faith? What goals do you have that are specific to your faith?

By answering all of these questions, you should start to get a clear and direct feel on what it is that you want more of in your life. Through this, you can start to create a vision of what your life would look like, and how it would feel for you, if you were to achieve your goals. After completing this exercise, there is only one more step for you to complete. That is, you want to try to summarize all eight areas of your life into one description of how this would all look. This description should include keywords that pertain to your ultimate goals for your life. For example, you might aim to be more peaceful, more organized, more balanced, more productive, or more relaxed. Creating clarity around what your specific goals are that would reflect how you want your entire life to look will support you with creating greater clarity around what it is that you are working toward. This way, you can work toward something specific, clear, and worthwhile.

Identifying What Your Underlying Desires Are

Now that you have a delightful vision of what it is that you want to create for yourself, we need to dig into the roots of what, specifically, is driving that vision. What are your underlying desires that lead to you having the goals that you have? Knowing the answer to this particular question is going to help you become not distractable in many ways.

First and foremost, if you know exactly what it is that you desire, you can easily adjust your goals as needed while ensuring that they continue to fulfill your desires. This flexibility in your goals is something that many people do not realize is vitally important.
As you grow over time, and as your circumstances change and your personality naturally changes with age, the specific visions you have set out for yourself may not be quite so important to you anymore. When this happens, you may feel lost or confused when, in reality, your desire remained the same but your

method for approaching that desire may need to change. For example, let's say that in your career you said that your goal is to have a high powered, high paying job that allows you to work the hours you want and that gives you paid vacation leave. In defining this, you may have already produced a vision for yourself that declares that you *must* become a high-ranking corporate manager in order to achieve all of this, and so this becomes your goal. While this is a great, clear goal to have, knowing what the underlying desires are ensures that your vision for what all of this looks like can change if it needs to without you feeling as though you have lost touch with your actual goal. Which, in this case, might be to have a job that provides you with an abundance of financial resources, security, and flexibility. If these are your three underlying desires, then you know that even if you cannot or do not want to become a high-ranking corporate manager, you can still look for alternative jobs that will offer you an abundance of financial resources, security, and flexibility.

To get into the core of what your true desires are, go back through every goal you set for each area of your life and ask yourself: "*why* do I want this?" Start looking for deeper, more meaningful answers such as flexibility, security, safety, respect, connection, love, compassion, validation, self-esteem, longevity, the ability to thrive, and anything else really drives these goals within you. Make sure you write down the underlying desires for every single one of your goals, and then ask yourself if there are any further underlying desires you have that have not been adequately expressed in the ones you have already written down. Chances are, you are going to see themes in each of your goals in life that reflect what it is that you truly want, and the actual goals you have set for yourself in each area of your life reflect what you believe needs to happen in order for these desires to be fulfilled.

The last thing you need to do after identifying your underlying desires is ask yourself, "Are the goals I have set for myself the best way to fulfill these desires?" This way, you can ensure that every goal you have genuinely matches what you want for yourself and drives your capacity to create a lifestyle that you will love. If you find any goals on your list that do not resonate with what you desire, or that seem as though they could be adjusted to better reflect what you desire, take the time to shift those goals so that you can work toward something more aligned with you. This way, your desire will activate to deepen your drive to fulfill such goals, effectively allowing you to design the life you truly want. In doing so, you will no longer become distracted because you are doing the things that keep your attention and keep you fulfilled, so you will not feel a longing to look elsewhere in an effort to fulfill your desires.

Creating an Environment That Nurtures This New Lifestyle

With your ideal goals in mind and your desires brought into the limelight, it is time for you to start creating an environment that is going to nurture your new lifestyle so that you can engage in your detox from hidden addictions and compulsions. In this new environment, you are going to create an optimal setting for you to do only what you truly want to do as per your goals, and not what your hidden addictions and compulsions have you doing.

As you go through this detoxification, it is important that you do not attempt to do it on all eight areas of your life at once. Doing so could result in you becoming extremely overwhelmed and feeling incredibly out of place, which can actually magnify your urge to drop into familiar habits and, therefore, strengthen and reinforce old behaviors rather than encourage new ones. Doing this detoxification on just one area of your life at a time will ensure that you are able to see drastic changes while also being able to have enough familiarity in your life that you can mentally and emotionally handle these changes.

I suggest for your first detoxification you choose an area of your life that has a significant impact on your desired changes, but not the one that has the *most* impact on your desired changes. This way, you are affecting change in an important area of your life, but you are not attempting to dig into an area of your life that is going to have such massive changes that the other aspects of familiarity do not feel like enough to keep you comfortable during the detox. Once you can navigate these areas of your life, you will be confidently equipped with the necessary tools to help you navigate the mental and emotional experiences you have with more problematic areas of your life, too.

To create an environment for success in any given area of your life, you need to think about your driving motivation. Each of us is naturally designed to experience two forms of motivation, though one will be stronger than the other and which one is stronger depends on who you are and how your unique psyche works. These two forms of motivation include the motivation to avoid something unpleasant, or the motivation to gain something pleasant. The best way to figure out which you actually are is to look back on your past and identify what has triggered every major change in your life, or every major goal you achieved. Were you triggered to change or reach a goal because you were afraid of what would happen if you didn't? Or were you triggered to change or reach a goal because you were excited about what would happen if you did? There is no right or wrong answer here, nor is either answer better than the other. You simply need to know so that you know how to effectively shape your environment to support you.

In either scenario, you are going to shape your environment to demotivate you from engaging in unwanted behaviors, such as getting distracted, and to motivate you to engage in wanted behaviors, such as focusing and getting the desired task done. However, you will want to lean more toward the direction that naturally motivates you to ensure that your environment is perfectly suited to help you succeed.

The practical steps you will take to shape your environment will depend on what environment you are in, what part of your life you are detoxing, what goals you have, and how much control you have over that environment. The best thing you can do is sit down and plan out what you can actually do to support yourself in generating success in your detox process. If you are trying to detox your health life, for example, what can you do to your environment to help you stay motivated to make a change? You might eliminate junk foods from your environment while buying plenty of tasty healthier foods or take the TV out of your home gym and replace it with a stereo so that you can stay focused. Or, you might change your venue up entirely and go to the gym so that you are motivated to work out while you are there. If you are trying to change your relationship with your partner, you might change your environment by putting your phones away and turning off the TV when you are together and creating ideas of things you can do together. Then, you might add extra things into your immediate environment to support you doing those things together, such as keeping the board games nearby or having some conversation topics handy so you can share meaningful conversation with your partner.

While you may not know every single distraction that will affect you, if you create an environment that minimizes all distractions no matter what they are, you will have the best opportunity to completely detox from hidden addictions and compulsions. This way, you can begin to develop healthier habits for yourself to see all the way through.

Committing To Spending Just 30 Days In That Environment

As soon as you have stimulated the best environment for you to stay focused in and to achieve your goals in, you need to commit to spending thirty days in this new environment. Committing to just thirty days means that you can comfortably be as radical as you need to be in eliminating distractions because you know that these impractical measures will be temporary, not permanent. So, if this means removing your TV from the living room so you can spend more quality time with your family, or taking everything except your laptop, printer, desk, and chair out of your office so you can stop getting distracted while working, you can do this. You simply need to make it through thirty days in these more radical environments, then you can start to integrate your new habits back into your regular life.

The reason behind using a 30-day detox is not exactly a refined science, however evidence does show that it takes a minimum of 8 days to make a change in your habitual routines and a maximum of 284 days to make changes in your habitual routines. The average time it takes to make a change in your habits is 66 days. In this particular detox we will be using 30 days of absolute detox, and around 15-30 days of a reintegration period, which means you will be detoxing for 45-60 days total.

For the 30 days that you detox, it is important to realize that you are going to feel many desires to break your detox and to try to change things back to the way they were. These desires are *not* evidence that you are done detoxing and that your habits are over, no matter how subtle or unemotionally charged they might feel. What they are is your brain attempting to use justification to coerce you into minimizing your days spent in detox so that you can get back into your old patterns and habits, which includes your old hidden addictions and compulsions. Do not believe the part of your brain that suggests you are ready within 3-10 days of being in your new detox. By the end of 30 days, being without the distractions in your environment and with the motivators should feel comfortable and easy, and you should be indifferent to the changes you have made. When you reach a point of neutrality or indifference toward your environment, *that* is when you are ready to move into the next phase of your detox. This could take the full 30 days, or it could take a little longer if you find that your habits are more significant and that your ability to live without these habits feels more challenging. Go with 30 days or the number of days it takes to create a sense of neutrality and indifference, whichever takes longer.

During your period of being in detox, keep a journal handy and take note of any of the urges you feel during this time. Notice where your attention goes to, what distractions you find yourself wanting to reach for, and what behaviors you engage in as you attempt to engage in familiar behaviors that distract you from your goal. Abstinence from all distractions is a great way to start identifying what your truly problematic distractions are, which will allow you to be prepared for these distractions when you begin to reintroduce them into your environment.

Integrating Your New Lifestyle With Who You Truly Are

Once you have reached the point where you are experiencing neutrality and indifference toward your environment, you have reached a point where your distractions, including your hidden addictions and compulsions, are no longer so powerful over you. At this point, you are still vulnerable to them and you could still easily slide back into old habits once you are in a normal environment, but you are now strong enough to begin forming neutrality around your normal environment.

Over a period of 15-30 days, begin to reintroduce all of the distractions that you eliminated from your environment back into your environment. Anything you eliminated in a radical effort to remove all distractions from your environment can now be safely added back into your environment, though you will want to do so a little at a time. Introducing everything back into your environment immediately could result in you having massive urges to engage in old distracting behaviors again, as there are too many cues triggering those unwanted habits back in your environment all at once. Take your time and introduce things based on what is most necessary to least necessary and go from there.

As you begin to reintroduce things back into your environment, you may begin to find that there are certain things that you want to keep eliminated for good. Certain items that were previously in your environment may hold no value to the life you wish to have or the desires you wish to fulfill and may not be beneficial to you in any way. For example, if you want to consume a healthier diet, you may eliminate *all* junk food from your house at first and eat a strictly clean diet for 30 days. Then, you might start reintroducing healthier forms of treats back into your house, but you would not want to reintroduce any unhealthy treats into your house that are not in alignment with your new dietary habits. Doing so would be pointless and would either be a waste of money or a certain trigger to get you eating poorly all over again.

Each day as you introduce more and more into your environment, practice engaging in the desensitization practices from chapter 4. These desensitization practices will support you with being around all of your existing distractions without experiencing such a heightened sense of stimulation around them. As a result, you will be able to comfortably exist around your distractions without feeling any fear around your behavior around them. Instead, you will feel confident in your ability to control yourself, your motivation, and your urges, meaning that you have now effectively detoxified from your hidden addictions and compulsions.

Chapter 6

It's Easy To Tame Your Tools!

Our lives have been abundantly improved through the power of many unique tools and devices that have been introduced to our modern lifestyles. Tools like smartphones, tablets, laptops, AI-based virtual assistants, smart televisions, and other such things are all designed to improve the quality of our lives. These devices give us access to improved methods of organizing our days, communicating with each other, accessing important information, enjoying unique forms of entertainment, being able to achieve work-related tasks more efficiently, enjoying a unique array of hobbies and improving our skillsets, and more. It is safe to say that these devices have given us an ample boost to our society by improving many things and giving us access to many other things that were never even dreamed of as being possible at any given point in the past.

In today's world, the majority of us own at least one of these devices, although most of us own many more than that. It is likely that you have a smartphone, or even two if you have one designated for work. You likely also have a television, a computer, and possibly a tablet, or maybe even more than one if different members of your household have their own tablets. The majority of people are also jumping into the virtual assistant technology, having devices like Amazon Alexa, Google Home, and Apple HomePod.

With access to all of these devices in your life, many great things are achieved. However, they also leave you exposed to experiencing many different forms of stimulation that can make focusing on anything for a significant period of time rather challenging. After all, each of these devices are specifically designed to grab your attention in one way or another to alert you of various notifications, alarms, or other alerts that you have programmed the device to alert you with. If you have even one of these devices prying for your attention it can be challenging to stay focused, but if you have a situation where multiple are attempting to grab your attention for various reasons, your chances of staying focused and getting things done are slim to none.

For many people, their level of distraction around these devices does not start and end with the alerts that the device gives off either. Simply being around the device can leave you experiencing curiosities and feeling compelled to engage in distractions. You may find yourself wondering about random things and searching for answers on the internet or wondering how your friends are doing or if your friend has finally uploaded that picture or video, they said they were going to upload, so you check on that. If you play any games on your devices, you may wonder how the game is going or if anything needs to be done on your game so that you can reach the next level. There are constantly reasons to be distracted by these devices when you have them around, to the point where whether or not they are intentionally alerting you for anything, they are still vying for your attention. Naturally, this is a major problem if you want to become not distractable!

Fortunately, there are many things you can do to tame your tools. As you learn how to tame your tools, you will gain the capacity to use them for the purposes they were intended for without finding yourself succumbing to all of the distractions that come with these tools. This way, they serve as positive tools that can help you achieve desirable results in a modern world. That's right, there is no need to throw away all of your devices or give up on tools that you enjoy and that bring great value to your life. You simply need to learn how to tame them.

Taming Your Smartphones and Tablets

Smartphones are probably the most distracting devices we have in our modern world, with tablets playing a close second if you tend to keep your tablet nearby and use it for things like communication or business. These devices are often loaded with notifications from several different applications, programs, and features, each of which is attempting to prompt you to do something either on the device itself, or offline. For example, notifications about emails and social media will have you wanting to check those applications on your phone, while notifications for your smart watch will encourage you to stand up and walk around or get moving. Regardless of what the notification is, it can be very distracting, and it can often come at times where checking the device or acting on the notification is not ideal.

Rather than letting your smartphone and tablet get the best of you, practice turning it to silent mode, to do not disturb, or to airplane mode depending on the time of day and what works best for your unique needs. Silent mode is a great way to ensure that you hear nothing, regardless of what type of notification it is. Do not disturb is similar to silent mode, though these days most do not disturb features have a built-in feature where people can get through to you in emergency situations by calling you twice. This can be beneficial if you have your phone on you and will need to receive emergency calls but cannot be receiving any other sorts of notifications. Make sure anyone who may need to reach you during an emergency knows to call twice so that they can get through your do not disturb feature. Airplane mode is a great mode to use when you want to experience a complete disconnect from all interactive features on your phone. This way, you cannot receive anything from the internet, nor can you receive any sort of phone-to-phone interactions. So, social media will not disturb you, and people cannot call you either. If you need an alarm to help you wake up in the morning, this can be a great way to keep your device available for such a feature without having to worry about any other unwanted notifications coming through for you.

In addition to adjusting how notifications come through to your phone as a whole, you can also adjust your notifications on an app-to-app basis. In the settings feature on your smartphone or tablet, you can adjust the types of notifications that you receive from each application on your device. This way, you can adjust how each application notifies you. For low priority applications, you can choose low priority notifications or no notifications at all. For medium priority applications you can choose medium priority notifications, and for high priority applications you can choose high priority notifications. This way, rather than being bombarded by notifications all day that suggests that each and every single notification is a high priority, you can teach yourself to respond accordingly, based on the priority level of each notification.

As far as your tendency to grab your phone or tablet to check it or use it as a way to nurture your distractions goes, you are going to need to come up with a system that works for you to minimize your level of distraction on your phone. This could include setting it out of reach or placing it in a drawer where you cannot see it, so it is more difficult for you to interact with your phone. Or, you could train yourself to exercise self-control and self-discipline around your phone or tablet so that you only pick it up for very specific things. In this scenario, you might keep a small notebook and a pen nearby so that anytime you find yourself wanting to check something or look something up on your phone or tablet, instead you can jot a note down about it in the notebook. Then, when you have a reasonable moment to check your device, you can check things or look information up based on what is in your notebook. This can be a great way to deter you from searching up irrelevant information in the middle of important tasks, while also allowing you to gain the gratification you seek at any given point in the future.

Taming Your Laptops and Computers

Unlike your smartphone or tablet which stays with you throughout the day and is highly mobile and easy to use anywhere, laptops and computers tend to be more stationary, or difficult to bring with you when you do take them places. For that reason, many people find themselves already experiencing a fairly limited level of distraction with these devices in that the distraction only occurs when they are on the device itself. While this is excellent news for periods where you can simply turn the device off and walk away, it does not mean that these devices are without distraction. Anytime you are actually using your laptop or computer, it can become incredibly easy for you to get distracted by various things on the device. Notifications for applications you have installed, the realization that you can "quickly" search for anything you want on the internet, advertisements, and the lingering presence of social media and other distracting websites can all make these devices incredibly distracting. In many cases, it takes a great deal of self-discipline to be able to avoid these distractions and focus solely on what needs to get done.

While a large part of navigating distractions on your laptop or computer will come from self-discipline, there are still many things you can do to prevent yourself from getting too distracted when you are using your computer for a specific reason. The idea of using a notebook to jot down things you want to look up or check on is a great way for you to navigate the distractions that come with your computer. This way, rather than opening new browser tabs for your distraction and finding yourself getting carried away with browsing, you can focus only on what it is that you are doing so that you are no longer getting so distracted.

Another great way to tame your computer is to set up your work interface effectively. Many times, when people begin working on their laptops, they open only one platform or application at a time, then when they need to get into other platforms, they find themselves having to navigate to that platform or application. While this may not seem like a big deal, the process of moving from one to the next leaves a great window of opportunity for you to distract yourself with other things along the way. For example, you may intend to open up a web browser to research a subject for a presentation you are giving, only to come across another app that you realize you have been meaning to access to complete a certain task in, and then from there the spiral of distraction grows until you are completely sidetracked from your necessary task. Rather than falling into this distracting experience, you can begin creating an environment that nurtures focus by setting your screen up for success. Consider trying this: the minute you open up your laptop or turn on your computer, open up all of the applications you know you are going to need for this particular experience. Then, arrange each of their windows so that you can see the necessary ones on your screen without having to toggle anything to get there.

For example, your writing program could take up half of your screen so you can see exactly what it is that you are writing, your internet browser for researching could take up one-quarter of your screen, and your notepad full of notes could take up one-quarter of your screen. You can adjust your screen per your own needs based on what applications you require for your work, but the point remains. Keeping your screen set up for all of your applications to be easily accessible means that you will have everything you need right there for you to focus on. Now, you are no longer at risk of being distracted.

Since eliminating distractions on your computer does rely heavily on your sense of self-discipline so that you can avoid logging into social media or engaging in other online distractions, there is more you will need to do within yourself to tame this experience. In particular, setting regular "distraction breaks" for yourself is a great way to keep yourself from engaging in distractions during inappropriate times. This way, rather than justifying that you are only going to check for a quick second, you can encourage yourself to wait until your next distraction break. Often, giving yourself just 5-10 minutes to engage in distraction every hour or so is a great way to keep yourself motivated to avoid distractions in between these breaks. This way, rather than waiting several hours for your lunch break or for your day to end, you are only waiting a handful of minutes at any given time. For many, this shorter wait time makes it significantly easier for you to keep yourself motivated to avoid distractions. Plus, these regular intermissions can help break your intense focus on the work you are doing so that you can come at it from a fresh perspective when your distraction break ends.

If you give distraction breaks a try and you find that you have a hard time getting focused on work again after a distraction break, try setting a timer for eight minutes and being distracted during those eight minutes. Use this time to research the topics you wrote in your notebook, to check in on those distracting apps, and to otherwise do whatever you want to do with your time. Then, when eight minutes are up, set a timer for two minutes. During these two minutes, close your eyes, focus on your breath, and give yourself a couple of minutes of quietness. This will help break up the distraction from your work, while also calming your mind and bringing you back into a centered state. From there, focusing on your work should be much easier.

Taming Your Smart Television and Other Smart Devices

Smart devices tend not to be quite as distracting because they are not generally the types of devices that pressure you to focus on them. However, they can still invoke various bad habits that nurture distractions. For example, you might find that any time you are home you struggle to turn off the television and do anything else because the device itself is so distracting. For these particular devices, there is generally nothing you need to do as far as muting notifications or adjusting your applications to make the devices less distracting. Instead, you need to set up practical measures to prevent yourself from engaging with these devices every time you feel a sense of curiosity or an urge to engage in an old habit of engaging with these devices virtually nonstop.

With televisions in general, a great way to prevent yourself from turning them on anytime you are home is to have a schedule that you use to determine when you are going to watch it, and when you are not. This way, you only watch the television according to the schedule you have set out for yourself, and the more you practice this self-discipline the easier it will get.

Other than that, you can use the process of shaping your environment to discourage distraction as a way to tame this tool. Consider keeping your remote control far away from the couch so you have to intentionally get up and go grab it anytime you want to turn the television on. Then, keep things like books, board games, or other more positive activities near the couch so that when you are sitting there, they are easier for you to reach for. This way, when you are home you will be more likely to reach for a book or something positive over the television remote.

You will need to choose your own unique solutions to minimize the distraction you experience from other devices in your life. The easiest way to do this is to consider how that device distracts you, what your problem areas are with that device, and how you can adjust your environment or behaviors to avoid this problematic device from creating a distraction any further. In most cases, the best solution is to moderate and control your use with the device, *not* to eliminate it from your life entirely. So, focus on finding healthy tools that allow you to moderate and control your usage.

Taming Your Virtual Assistant Speakers

Virtual assistant speakers tend to be very low in their capacity to distract, not unlike other smart devices. However, these devices do have the capacity to create some distraction, particularly if you keep yours programmed to your calendar or if you have it connected to any application that creates notifications through your virtual assistant speakers. The best way to minimize distractions with virtual assistant speakers is to only use very specific notifications and alarms with them. This way, rather than experiencing regular notifications or alarms coming through, you are only receiving high priority notifications and alarms.

Chapter 7

Designate a Room For Silence

With our brains constantly being bombarded with different stimuli, it is reasonable to understand that they no longer truly understand what it is like to be void of stimuli. Many people actually feel uncomfortable or like there is something wrong if they are no longer experiencing drastic amounts of stimuli in their environment, which can actually lead to them creating their own distractions. This cycle can make it challenging for you to break away from distractions because you no longer feel "okay" if you are not being distracted. As you can imagine, this state is extremely unnatural for the human mind and can bring about many troubling experiences that promote your state of distraction, rather than your state of focus.

Learning how to break out of the cycle of needing to be stimulated, or over-stimulated, at all times can help you learn how to bring a deeper and more meaningful sense of peace into your life. This will not only support you in breaking out of the habit of being distracted, but it will also promote positive mental and emotional health in your life. The balance you experience amongst the silence and peace will start to teach you how to be comfortable in the quiet and without stimulation, which means that during your regular day to day life you will find yourself experiencing freedom from the overwhelming need for stimulation, too. In many cases, simply training yourself to experience peace and quiet on a regular basis can go a long way in breaking any cycles you have that keep you attached to habits, addictions, or compulsions that stimulate your distraction.

How Do You Create a Quiet Space?

Your quiet space should be considered your sanctuary, and it should work to help you create enough calm and comfort in your life that you are able to experience freedom from the noise and disruption of the outside world. Ideally, your quiet space should be an entire room, such as your bedroom or a spare room you may have, however if that is not possible you can simply choose a corner or a designated area in your house where you will go when you are in need of some peace and quiet. It is okay if you share your quiet room with others, however everyone who uses your quiet room or space should be prepared to respect the rules of that space by keeping it as a calm and quiet environment.

The number one goal of your quiet space is to remove any disruptive stimuli and instead fill the environment with things that help you feel calm and at peace. Consider looking into sensory experiences that are calming and relaxing and that allows you to feel comfortable in a quiet space. You may include a comfortable chair or surface to sit on, a soft blanket and some cushions to improve your comfort, and a fan or a small heater to ensure that the room stays a comfortable temperature while you are in there. Aside from your sense of touch, consider your other senses, too. In that space you might want to have candles, incense, or essential oils to create a soothing scent for your environment. You may also want to keep to a calm and relaxing color scheme with decorations that are not overly visually stimulating so that your visual senses are not being excessively aroused in that space. To further add to your environment, consider having a speaker that nurtures you with serene, gentle music to set the tone for relaxation and comfort. Or, better yet, do your best to make the room as close to silent as possible. As far as your sense of taste goes, consider bringing a nice cool glass of water with you to help nourish your sense of taste while you are in this room. Avoid having any excessively flavored or snacks in this room, as this will stimulate your senses and you want to stay as close to calm and comfortable as possible.

In addition to what you have in your quiet space, you need to consider what should not come into your quiet space. In your quiet space you should not bring your laptop, your phone, your tablet, or any other devices that have a tendency to draw your attention or create distractions for you. You should also not bring in any forms of decorations or items that will create an overly stimulating environment, so keep colorful abstract art, loud music or music that is anything other than quiet and calming, and overly scented candles or perfumes out of the space. This way, you are not creating an environment that activates any of your senses and leaves you feeling overly stimulated to the people around you.

As well, avoid letting your quiet space become cluttered or messy in every way. Always leave it as clean as it was when you arrived, or cleaner. Take your cups out of there, fold your blankets and put them back when you are done, and arrange your pillows so that they look neat. Keeping this space as clean as possible ensures that it is not only quiet, but it is truly comfortable for you to be in, too. This will all go a long way in helping you eliminate distractions while also providing your brain and body with the much-needed break they require from all of the stimuli of your regular day to day life.

What Should You Do In Your Quiet Space?

While there are no hard and fast rules on how you can or should use your quiet space, there are many things you can do in this space to help yourself break away from distractions and teach your mind to become not distractable. Ideally, you should choose to use your quiet space in a way that feels best for you, while also leaning into practices that will help you get the most out of your quiet space. For example, meditating, reading, or focusing on a specific task that you want to do that you need to be completely undistracted as you do it. Your focus in your quiet space may change each time you enter it, but your goal should always remain the same: to stay quiet, calm, and focused. If you can achieve that in this space every time, you will have created the perfect environment for you and your newfound skill of focus to thrive in.

Intentionally going into your quiet space to meditate is something that you should be doing on a daily basis. During your daily meditations, seek to sit as calmly and quietly as you can, and observe what this feels like. Take inventory of your thoughts and where your natural attention flows to, or what types of urges or feelings you have that invoke a desire to move or engage in something else. Notice how this intentional quiet time affects you as far as your mind and emotions go and see if you can find ways to gently bring your attention away from your desire to be stimulated and toward the quiet moment you are enjoying right now. As you continue to practice this, you will find yourself learning about mental and emotional tools that will support you with gently yet powerfully redirecting your attention on a regular basis. Over time, you will be able to bring these tools into your everyday experiences so that you can stop yourself from becoming distracted and support yourself with staying focused.

Aside from meditating, you may choose to use your quiet space as an area where you can focus on things that matter to you. For example, you might use this space to read, listen to your favorite music, create art, massage your body, or otherwise enjoy some quiet time engaging in hobbies or activities that feel soothing for you. Doing this on a regular basis will give you an intentional quiet space to break away from life and focus on taking care of yourself without distraction. This way, you will be far more likely to genuinely invest in this space of enjoying yourself and, as a result, these meaningful hobbies and activities will have a greater capacity to nurture your mental and emotional wellbeing. For many people, simply setting aside enough time to enjoy themselves without distraction is all they need to be able to fulfill any desires they have so that, later, they can focus with a clearer mind on other things that need to get done.

When it comes to doing specific tasks that require you to be absolutely undistracted while you complete them, there are a series of different hobbies or activities that may require your absolute focus. For example, if you are into building models or working with small pieces to make jewelry, or other meticulous activities that require stillness, focus, and attention. These types of tasks can be done in your quiet space and, in doing that, you give yourself the opportunity to focus solely on this task and nothing else.

It is important that while you are in your quiet space you never bring anything with you that would disrupt the mood of the space, *ever*. You may be tempted to bring a work-related task into this space, or to bring your phone or tablet or laptop into this space, or even wear your smart watch into this space "just once," but understand that it is virtually *never* a good idea for you to do this. Doing it once can disrupt the calmness of your space and can result in you getting into the habit of bringing these distracting devices into your space, which will entirely disrupt the mood. Unlike practices where you are engaging in desensitization so that you can neutralize your reaction toward distractions, your goal here is *not* to teach yourself to ignore distractions. It is to take them all away so that you can enjoy a calm, quiet time with minimal or controlled stimulation. This is necessary for the wellbeing of your mind and emotions, and it is very important that you do not break this rule in your space.

If you need to do work in a quiet space but you want the opportunity to bring something like your smartphone or your laptop there, consider going to your local library and working from there. Doing work at your local library can be a great way to help you enjoy a quiet and generally calming environment, while being able to focus on work-related tasks or other typically stressful projects or activities with minimal distractions, without breaking the rules of your quiet space.

How Often Should You Retreat to Your Quiet Space?

There are varying guidelines around when you should retreat to your quiet space, although exactly how often you choose to and when you choose to retreat to your quiet space is largely up to you. The best way to decide how often you should retreat to your quiet space is to start based on a set of guidelines and then adjust from there so that you are following a system that works best for you. In addition to the guidelines I offer you, also make sure that you consider what is reasonable for you, what makes sense for you, and what is going to give you the best opportunity to get the most out of this space. If you think these guidelines are unreasonable or unachievable, adjust accordingly.

First things first, you should be spending time in your quiet space at least once per day, for at least 30 to 60 minutes. During this time, you can focus on meditating, engaging in a hobby, or simply taking a calm, quiet break to yourself from your everyday activities. It does not matter whether you take this break in the morning or at night, or during any other time of your day. What matters is that every single day you are retreating to your quiet space and enjoying some uninterrupted, undistracted quiet time. This daily retreat is going to offer you a significant boost to your mental and emotional wellbeing which, in turn, will offer a significant boost in mental clarity and your capacity to focus. As you engage in this daily experience of quietness in an undistracted space, you will find that your mind begins to learn how to let go of things and, as a result, it becomes easier for you to navigate the quietness. Now, rather than feeling like you are constantly bombarded by external and internal stimuli, you will start to feel as though you can comfortably and reasonably navigate a state of peace and calmness. If you tend to carry a great deal of stress, overwhelm, worry, or burden on your shoulders, as most of us do, this regular quiet time will drastically help you with processing and releasing that so that you can experience mental and emotional peace. For many, these routine breaks provide them with the opportunity to create acceptance toward what

MARC WALKER and ALEXANDER LARKESS

they cannot control, and a sense of direction and focus toward what they can.

Aside from having regularly scheduled time in your quiet space, you can also use your quiet space as a location for you to retreat to anytime you find yourself experiencing a high level of stress, or a high level of distraction. If you find that you are overwhelmed and it is affecting you, or if you find that you are so distracted that you cannot stay focused on anything at all, retreating to your quiet space for a period of time can help give you a much needed "reset." Here, you can create a space of peace, calm, and comfort, and you can bring calmness to your mind. If you need to, you can give yourself a few minutes to process and unravel in your stressful or overwhelming thoughts so that you can work through them, and then you should focus on following that up with some calm, relaxing time. This way, you are not denying your stress or overwhelm or attempting to repress it, but instead you are genuinely working through it and then bringing peace back to your mind. Using your quiet space in this way is a great way to train yourself to learn how to calm down when you are experiencing heightened levels of stress. Over time, your brain will automatically associate this space with calmness and relaxation and so you will begin to naturally feel calmer and more at peace anytime you step into this space. Having this sort of sanctuary incorporated into your everyday life will give you a great boost to your overall wellbeing and will go a long way in making you not distractable.

Chapter 8

Replace a Limiting Habit With a Fruitful One

Virtually everything we do in our lives is done based on habit. Our brains are so efficient that they have learned to turn everything into a habit so that, rather than having to focus on how to do things, it can focus on other more important things, such as the contents that typically cloud your conscious awareness. While there may be times where you need to create new habits entirely, because the new habits you desire do not remotely look like your old habits and indulge in desires that you are not yet fulfilling with your current habits, there will be other times where shifting your habits is all you need to do. When it comes to shifting your habits, your entire focus will be to move away from engaging in limiting habits that are providing you with limited results so that you can create productive habits that will provide you with fruitful results.

Shifting your habits is not necessarily an easy task, but it is far easier than attempting to create entirely new habits altogether. When you go through the process of shifting habits, rather than creating everything from scratch you will simply make certain adjustments that will allow you to completely transform the process and outcome of a specific habit. From a topical point of view this may seem like the same amount of work, but to your subconscious mind the process of shifting rather than starting anew is much easier and, therefore, much more consistent, fruitful, and sustainable.

A Quick Rundown On the Three-Step Habit Loop

We have already discussed what habit loops are to a degree, but I want to remind you what they are so that you have a deeper understanding of how they work and what needs to happen in order for you to shift a habit without breaking the whole loop. Habit loops are your subconscious mind's way of creating automatic behaviors so that, rather than having to use up energy and attention to do everything consciously, it can all be done automatically. As long as there is a cue to trigger the automatic behavior, then the behavior will happen. You already have many habits, ranging from how you use the bathroom or how you eat during the day to how you engage in certain activities that are relevant to your everyday life. For example, if you make your bed when you wake up, or if you don't, that is a habit. If you wash your hair before your body every time you shower, that is a habit. Or, if you turn on the television every time you get home and immediately turn it to the news, that is a habit.

The habit loop that occurs within your brain contains three steps: a cue, a routine, and a reward. The cue is what triggers your behavior, the routine is the behavior that has been triggered, and the reward is the reason why you engage in that behavior. Essentially, the reward provides you with a primal, intrinsic or extrinsic reward that creates a rush of dopamine, amongst other chemicals, in your brain to facilitate a sense of happiness and fulfillment. Each time you complete the habit loop, this reward is triggered, and it reinforces your habit.

The One Thing You Must Change To Shift Your Habits

Shifting old habits is far easier than creating new habits, because in order to create new habits you must identify a new cue, routine, and reward and integrate this loop into your subconscious mind so that it takes root. Shifting habits, however, only requires you to identify a new routine, and you will keep the cue and the reward as being exactly the same. The end result is that you can develop far more fruitful habits, and it takes a lot for less energy and effort on your behalf to get there.

Identifying a New Routine, Creating New Results

In order to effectively create a new, more fruitful habit, you are going to first need to identify any limiting habits you have that are not bringing you the results you desire in life. Think of areas in your life where you want more, and where you could be creating more, but at the present moment you are not creating the level of results that you desire. Then, think of all of the habits you have in these areas of your life that affect the way you are experiencing this particular area of your life. You should choose to shift the habits that are causing the most limitations in your life so that through only a few subtle shifts you can experience a massive change in the results you see from this area of your life.

Once you have identified your limiting habit, identify exactly what routine is associated with this particular habit, and what cue triggers that routine. You want to be as specific as possible, as the clearer you can interpret the habit the clearer you will be able to change the routine so that you can improve your results.

Now, all you need to do is identify your new routine. Your new routine may include only a few shifts to your present one, or it may include many significant shifts to your present routine. The key is ensuring that it is not so different that it is brand new, but that it is different enough that it maximizes your results. For example, let's say you are currently in the routine of waking up in the morning, having a shake, and going to the gym. While you are at the gym, though, you are slow in the dressing room, and you only manage to get on two machines before you run out of time and have to leave the gym. While you are doing great at actually getting there, you are limiting your results because you are not getting straight into the action as soon as you arrive. You could shift this routine by giving yourself a fixed amount of time to be in the dressing room, or by dressing beforehand so that all you have to do is check your things into a locker before you start working out. Making these subtle shifts to your routine can abundantly change the entire rest of your experience, effectively bringing you fruitful results on a once limiting habit.

Integrating Your Habit Into Your Everyday Life

After you have planned out your changed habit, you need to go ahead and integrate your habit into your everyday life. At this point, you are going to actually follow through on the habit that you have created so that you can start to see your fruitful results. For the first few days, give yourself the opportunity to try on your new routine to ensure that it fits, that it is practical, that it is thorough, and that it does give you the best possible results from your efforts. If you need to make any adjustments, make them within the first week or so of implementing your new routine so that you really are getting the most out of this new practice. Then, from there, you must commit to engaging in this new routine every single time, no matter what. Your level of commitment and consistency is what will eventually integrate your new routine into your existing habit so that it is effective, functional, and repeatable. Over time, you will not even have to think about it, your new routine will come effortlessly to you and your old one will no longer be relevant.

Maintaining Your New Habits

It is important to realize that as you change your habits, your neural pathways for old habits will remain firmly intact in your brain. For this reason, it can be very easy for you to slip back into old patterns and engage in old habits again. It is important that you maintain your new routine so that you can continue to receive your fruitful results over time. The best way to maintain your new routine is to consciously check in from time to time to make sure that everything is still going strong and that you have not experienced any setbacks in your routine. If, during these check-ins, you realize that you have not created the results you desire or that you have fallen back into an old pattern, use this as an opportunity to consciously implement your new pattern all over again. Continue to consciously implement your new pattern as many times as you need to until you achieve the results you desire.

Chapter 9

Build a Stone-Solid and Unassailable Routine

A strong routine is a powerful way to change your life. When you have a strong routine in place, everything about your life becomes a habit of your own intentional creation, which means that you are now the intentional creator of your own results. This way, rather than experiencing your life in a passive manner, you can start to move beyond any limiting habits and behaviors, allowing you to become an not distractable force that smashes through your goals and creates incredible results.

Your life will contain many routines, and it will be up to you to identify routines that are unique to you and create them in a way that provides you with the opportunity to experience the best results possible in that area of your life. Apart from that, however, there are three routines that virtually everyone should have in their lives: a morning routine, an afternoon routine, and an evening routine. If you have all three of these routines fixed in place and organized to serve you with the best results, you will have a much greater ability to reach your goals without any distraction.

Your Morning Routine

Your morning routine is the first thing you will experience on a daily basis, which is why you need a powerful morning routine that nurtures your focus and sets you up for success. People who fail to generate focus and clarity in the morning will bring that lack of focus and lack of clarity with them throughout their daily lives, creating greater challenges for themselves when it comes to accomplishing their goals. If you can start your day off in a clear, concise, and driven manner, you will be far more likely to carry your day out and end it on that note as well.

A morning routine does not have to be complex or overdone, it simply needs to work. For this reason, avoid buying into the belief that if your morning routine is not elaborate and on par with a high-powered CEO's morning routine that you are not going to be successful with it. Instead, think about your unique life, needs, and goals, and create a routine that sets you up for success.

In general, a good morning routine should include you practicing good hygiene, feeding yourself, getting properly prepared for your day ahead, spending a moment nurturing your emotions, spending another moment nurturing your mind, and giving yourself enough time to do all of this without rushing. A great sample of a powerful morning routine would be to wake up, go to the bathroom, make yourself a drink and some breakfast, consume it, shower and brush your teeth, then spend five minutes giving gratitude for the things that make you happy, and another five more focused on your goals. A great way to focus on your goals is to write each of them down on a piece of paper and reaffirm them to yourself so that you can clearly recall what it is that you are working toward, and why.

Your Afternoon Routine

Your afternoon routine should be something simple and quick so that it can be easily fit into your day no matter what you are doing. This way, if you find yourself generally busy in the afternoon, you will still have plenty of time to get your routine done. The entire point of an afternoon routine is to ensure that you have taken adequate care of your body and ensuring that you re-center your focus in case you have become distracted during the earlier portion of your day.

The best afternoon routine should be one where you ask yourself what your needs are and then plan to meet them within the next half hour to an hour, and then where you reaffirm your goals to yourself so that you remember what you are working toward. A simple "how am I doing and what do I need?" will ensure that you can acknowledge any unmet needs you may have that could eventually become distracting. For example, if you find that you feel hungry, thirsty, or in need of a good stretch or mental break, during your afternoon routine would be a great time to acknowledge that need and schedule it into the next hour. This way, you can look forward to it and you can intentionally fulfill that need before it becomes overly distracting. After you have scheduled these needs or fulfilled them if you already have time to do so, you can go ahead and write your goals down again, allowing you to regain focus and stay driven. Then, you can go back about your day as usual.

Your Evening Routine

The purpose of an evening routine is to help you unwind from your day. A strong evening routine will help you eliminate any residual stress or overwhelm you may be carrying with you, bring closure to any unfulfilled desires you have that will need to wait until tomorrow, and encourage your body and mind to prepare for rest. Having a strong evening routine will ensure that you are able to experience full mental, physical, and emotional rest every single night so that you are recharged and prepared for the day ahead. If you skip or underestimate the power of a strong evening routine, you will almost certainly find yourself waking up feeling stressed and overwhelmed from the previous day, which can accumulate over time and cause chaos in your mind. This chaos can, in turn, create distractions and leave you feeling a deep unfulfilled need for true, deep rest.

A great evening routine is one that focuses on calming your mind, body, and emotions. You could spend a period of time in your quiet space as a part of your evening routine, allowing yourself to sort through any unresolved thoughts or experiences from the day and provide yourself closure so that you can release them for the evening. At this point, you may wish to let some things go, or you may resolve to deal with other things at a later date. You can also use this time to sort through any emotions you may be carrying with you from the day, allowing yourself to release them and bring closure to your emotional experience. Then, you can go about taking care of your body and winding yourself down even further. Consider drinking a calming tea, wearing comfortable and relaxing clothing, and engaging in calming activities like reading or listening to quiet music so that you can begin to relax. Once you begin to feel completely wound down, you can brush your teeth, take care of any personal hygiene practices you are involved in, and then go to bed.

Routines That Are Unique To You

Routines are a powerful opportunity to make things simpler for yourself, to stay focused, and to see your goals all the way through. It is likely that in addition to a morning, afternoon, and nighttime routine you may also want to engage in other routines throughout the day that help you prepare for an activity and stay focused on that activity. For example, you may have a routine for what you do when you arrive at or leave work, or what you do when you need to pick up your children from school or engage in any sort of family practice. These routines are important and having them clearly defined ensures that everything gets done and that you are focused the entire time. This way, you can feel confident that you are doing your best, not leaving anything behind, and not leaving anything up to chance. In many ways, these simple routines will bring a great deal of relief to your mind and emotions, making them a powerful tool to help you navigate your day in a way that promotes your wellbeing.

To create routines that are unique to you and your own needs, consider what things in your life happen consistently enough that they would warrant a routine. Then, consider what form of routine would be simple, effective, and productive. Your goal here is to create a routine that will be easy enough to engage in every single day on a regular basis, and impactful enough that it creates the results you desire. If you can find a routine that maximizes the results from your efforts and that is not too elaborate or complex, then you have found the perfect routine.

It is always important that, as you land on a routine, you also consider your mental, emotional, and physical wellbeing. Being realistic about these three aspects of yourself and choosing routines that nurture them, rather than tax them, will ensure that you are choosing routines that are sustainable. While some routines can, should, and must take away from your energy levels, you should always look for ways to minimize this and to offset any depleted energy levels with other routines that nourish your energy levels. This way, you are not driving yourself into burnout.

As soon as you have landed on a routine that works for you and that will be as fulfilling as possible, all you need to do is engage in that routine on a consistent basis. The more consistent you can remain with that routine, the more of a habit it will become and therefore the greater your results will be with that particular routine. You should make as many routines as you feel is necessary for you to experience the best days possible, so that you can maximize your time and energy while also honoring your overall wellbeing.

Chapter 10

Find Focus In a Distracted World and Fly Toward Your Goals

On the enlightening journey toward empowering yourself to become not distractable so that you can reach your goals, I want to draw your attention to something important, and possibly very exciting for you. That is: right now, the entire world is caught in a state of distraction. Few people have taken the time to truly understand how this distraction works, why it is not conducive to their growth, or what they can do about it. Many are fine to live this way, while others are not, but that is not the point. The point is that if you become not distractable in a distracted world, there is *little competition between you and your goals*. The competition, or what would be the competition, is already distracted. They can't get past their habits of checking social media every five minutes, watching television when they are home rather than reading a book, and getting distracted rather than getting focused and making progress. This means that once you learn how to become not distractable, the competition thins greatly, and as long as you are willing to stay committed, your chances for success in any goal you have set for yourself are incredibly high.

If you can become not distractable, then no matter what your goal might be, you are already peeling ahead of the rest of the crowd. At this point, you now have the one greatest power you can apply to any goal in your life: your attention. Through the power of your undivided attention you can accomplish absolutely anything you set your mind to. Once you achieve this skill, there is absolutely nothing standing in your way from you and your ability to successfully fulfill every other goal in your life.

Be Willing To Be Different

Realizing that virtually everyone is living their lives in a state of distraction in this day and age means that if you choose to become not distractable, you need to recognize that you are going to be going against the grain. You will not be doing what everyone else is doing, you will be doing what it takes to succeed, and that is a bold choice to make. For anyone, choosing to be different from the rest of society means that you are putting yourself at risk of having people recognize that you are different, and that you are going to have embraced what it means to be different. While you are not obligated to explain, justify, or defend your differentness to anyone, you are going to need to become confident in your choice to be different so that you do not experience a deep fear around your choice. This way, whenever someone points out that you are different or attempts to get you to be "just like everyone else," you will feel confident in saying *no*. There will be no reason for you to cultivate insecurity, doubt, or uncertainty because you will know for absolute certain that you are doing exactly what you need to be doing in order to achieve the results you want to achieve.

Becoming willing to be different means that you need to be ready to turn down your friends when they are trying to distract you from your work, and that you need to be willing to put down your phone and unplug for lengthy periods of time. You also need to become acquainted with the fact that being different is not temporary, it is going to have to become your new normal if you are going to make these new habits stick. The more you can adapt to the reality that this is how it will be from now on, the more you will be able to create a sense of certainty around your decision as you will be able to deeply and fully commit to it, allowing you to see it all the way through.

Always Look For What Works For You

Since you are going to be taking on the role of being different and choosing to do things in a way that gets you ahead, it is important that you always look for what works for you and that you become your own advocate. At the end of the day, no amount of well-written books, blog posts, or even well-reported speeches are going to address the fact that you are a unique individual with a unique mind, personality, lifestyle, and needs. The best thing you can do is educate yourself and remain open-minded on the information you are receiving, and then apply that in the ways that fit you best.

As you learn, consider writing down what you learn in a notebook and keeping that notebook handy. This way, you can begin to implement things that are relevant to you right away which will allow you to start seeing drastic changes in your level of focus and, therefore, your capacity to achieve your goals. Having these notes written down will also ensure that when you are ready to grow again you can review your own notes and identify new opportunities for growth. As you continue to grow over time, you will find that different pieces of information apply to you, so keep your favorite resources handy and do not be afraid to dig into them again with an open mind at each new stage of your growth. Doing so can help you fully digest all of the information out of these resources so that you can maximize your capacity to achieve your goals and create your desired results.

Stay Flexible In Your Approach

Because of how unique you are, and how you are constantly growing and changing, it is important that you always stay flexible in how you approach things in your life. This remains true for your capacity to remain not distractable so that you can continue to create the results you desire, too. Be willing to accept that what you must do right now to improve your focus may not always ring true for you. You might need to adjust your approach, your practice, or your skills at some point in the future to better serve your growth, your evolving personality, or your changing circumstances.

The more you remain open to the idea of being flexible as needed, the easier it will be for you to embrace change while continuing to remain not distractable. People who struggle to remain flexible often find themselves experiencing a sense of panic and a higher potential for experiencing setbacks anytime something changes in their lives, because they have not remained open-minded and ready for change. You can combat this by remaining open-minded yet committed to your current choices based on your current circumstances.

Create Your Own Results

Lastly, you need to be ready to take responsibility for yourself and create your own results. No one is going to stand over your shoulder and yell at you to focus all day long, and even if they did it would not do anything for you, anyway. Only you can take responsibility for the results you create for yourself in any area of your life, and this includes being not distractable. This means that you need to be willing to hold yourself accountable and push yourself to create your own results, which will allow you to achieve your own goals.

Understand that while you are the one who needs to take responsibility and hold yourself accountable, this does not mean that you cannot have an accountability partner or work together with other people to motivate and inspire each other to achieve your goals. It does, however, mean that you are going to have to realize that no one in your accountability circles can force you to achieve success, and that it is not their responsibility to remember to hold you accountable at all times. While accountability and support groups can be a great benefit, you must never rely too heavily on them as you may end up finding yourself in a position where you do not take responsibility or accountability for yourself, and in that case you are the only one to blame for your lack of results. Have your own back first, that way the support you gain from everyone else is a supplement to your own support.

Chapter 11

Exercises To Become Not Distractable

Finally, I want to provide you with some additional exercises that are going to help you maximize your ability to become not distractable. These activities are ones that you can begin practicing right away, and that as you continue to practice you will find they continue to deepen your capacity to focus and stay attentive to your current task at hand, and your overall goals.

Ideally, you should set aside time for these practices every single day. Get used to practicing them imperfectly at first, as this will allow you to take the pressure off of these new activities and give yourself time to settle in and get used to incorporating them into your daily routine. As you become more accustomed to these daily routines, you will find yourself naturally doing better at them which will only serve to deepen your focus and improve your ability to remain not distractable.

Practice Mindfulness

Mindfulness is a practice that has become somewhat of a buzzword in recent years, though the practice itself is actually quite ancient. To become mindful means that you effectively master the art of living in the present moment and staying focused on what is going on in the here and now. A large part of what distracts us as a society is our tendency to dwell on the past or worry about the future, and this behavior can lead to us worrying about things that are entirely beyond our control. To put it simply, the past has already happened, and you cannot change it, and the future has yet to come and there is no way of knowing what it might bring.

It is valuable to set aside some time to intentionally dig into the past for the purpose of healing and uncovering lessons you can use to help you get through things in your current life better than you may have in the past. It is also valuable to intentionally set aside time to think about the future and consider how your present actions are affecting your future so that you can choose actions that will provide you with the best results. However, these blocks of time should always be intentional, and they should have concrete ends to them so that you do not carry these thoughts with you throughout your daily life. Use them to create guidelines for how you will think, act, and decide in the present moment, and then live in the present moment by following those guidelines and focusing exclusively on what is going on in the here and now. This way, you will experience much greater success in your ability to stay focused without allowing the past or present to distract you.

Exercise Your Body

Your body is full of many things, and amongst those things includes a significant amount of energy. Your body is designed to provide you with energy that will keep you going so that you can accomplish all of your necessary everyday tasks. As you may already realize, our modern lives do not require the same type of energy that our lives used to require. While in the past we needed the energy to engage in hunting and gathering and to complete extensive tasks to take care of ourselves, our modern lives are much simpler as we can easily grocery shop and take advantage of various conveniences which minimize our energy output.

Conveniences are great, and they can make living in our modern world much easier, but they can also lead to us experiencing pent up energy as we fail to disperse our energy as effectively as we once did. Rather than letting this energy build up and turn into distractions, exercise. Move your body every single day, and if you are feeling particularly distracted, take a break and stretch your body out or run on the spot. Using up some of that built up energy will not only help you stay more focused, but it will also provide you with an abundance of health benefits that will serve to increase your focus in the long run, too.

Take Care Of Your Needs

Failing to take care of your needs in an adequate and timely manner is a great way to serve yourself with an abundance of reasons to get, and stay, distracted. When you fail to take care of your needs, your body naturally distracts you from whatever it is that you are doing in an effort to draw your awareness to your unfulfilled needs. Its goal, of course, is to get you to fulfill those needs. Whether you are hungry, thirsty, tired, need to move around, need stimulation, need a change of pace, or need for anything else, your body and mind will do everything they can to make sure you know about it.

The best way to avoid distractions that arise based on your needs going unmet is to identify what your needs are and to keep them fulfilled to the best of your ability. Eat healthfully and stay hydrated. Maintain your hygiene and keep up with your household chores. Make time for entertainment, for building relationships, and for relaxing on your own. Nurture all eight areas of your life by taking care of your health, wealth, career, relationships, romantic life, self, hobbies, and faith. The more you can take care of these parts of your life, the more balanced you will feel and the less your body or mind will feel the need to continually distract you in an effort to get you to fulfill your needs. This way, as you accomplish everything in your life, you do so from the point of focus and intention.

Play Mind Games

Being that your brain is a muscle, it makes sense that you can exercise it on a regular basis to improve your capacity to stay focused, make decisions, memorize things, and otherwise rely on your brain to complete its necessary tasks. Brain games can support you with reinforcing existing neural pathways and support you with producing new ones, which can lead to you creating a stronger capacity to rely on your brain for a variety of things.

Choose brain games like puzzles, memory games, math equations, and science equations. Learning a new hobby or skill is another great way to exercise your brain and improve your focus and memory. You can purchase many of these things at the store, or you can download apps right to your phone that will help you with these activities. If you do download an app to your phone to help you with building your focus, make sure you adjust your notifications so that they are not alerting you at inappropriate times and distracting you from your daily life!

Create a Set Of "Rules" For Yourself

As we grow up, there are rules set out for us and we are expected to adhere to those rules, and in doing so we reach certain results. For example, we get our homework done and graduate school, allowing us to have an adequate education to help us get into the next stages of our lives. Our employers have rules that allow us to reach common goals in our workplace. Even our society has rules that allow us to reach common goals as a society. These greater rules all serve important purposes, and when they are adhered to, they can help us achieve incredible things in our society.

If you are still a "stick it to the system" or "rebel" type, now is the time to step back and realize the value of rules and the power you can gain in your life when you enforce this tool in a meaningful manner. Rather than fighting so hard against the rules, discover ways that you can make rules work for you and then hold yourself responsible and accountable for enforcing these rules in your life.

The best rules to have in your life are ones that are going to gently guide you toward creating the results you desire. For example, rather than simply choosing not to use your phone during working hours (except for work-related purposes,) you could have a personal rule that you will not use your phone during working hours. With this being implemented as a rule and not a choice, this can increase your likelihood of following it as holding something as a personal rule tends to have a little more urgency then holding something as a choice. It is easy to change your mind. It is unwise to break the rules.

Consider making general rules for yourself which will allow you to begin to constructively use your time and energy to achieve greater things in your life. This would be a great time to sit down and intentionally think about your past experiences, behaviors, and patterns so that you can consider what rules would be most effective to keep you on the right path. Then, you can intentionally consider your future and what it is that you want to create so that you can consider what rules would help you get to where you want to go. As with anything, try not to make your life too strict by rushing into the process of enforcing every single new rule at once. Instead, give yourself time to acclimate to each new rule and add more as you see fit, and as it feels comfortable to do so.

Read Long Books Slowly

This specific task has been said to increase your focus exponentially and can provide you magnificent results in becoming not distractable while also creating the opportunity for you to learn new skills and educate yourself in various subjects. Research has shown that in our modern society, we are exposed to a massive amount of short content. Status updates, blog posts, and online articles are often incredibly short and intended to be read in a short period of time. Even eBooks and many novels we buy these days are relatively short because writers know that shorter titles are easier for their readers to get through and, therefore, it is more likely that readers will enjoy the full title.

Unfortunately, this has conditioned us to have a shorter attention span, as well as a heightened need for instant gratification. For many, attempting to read books is challenging because they find themselves getting distracted or bored within minutes of starting and so they put the book down and forget about it. Or, they mistakenly believe that they no longer enjoy reading, when the real issue is that they have conditioned themselves to no longer have the focus or the attention span to get through a whole book.

These same researchers have suggested that if you take a long book and read it slowly, as slowly as you need to in order to get through it, you will drastically improve your focus. Doing this over and over again will also increase your capacity to gain gratification from reading larger books and will condition you to stay focused for longer periods of time. Over time you will find yourself reading faster and getting through these texts quicker, which will only serve to further reinforce your sense of focus and your ability to see these titles all the way through.

Conclusion

If you have read *Not Distractable* to this point, then I want to take a moment to seriously congratulate you on your ability to see this title all the way through. Already, you are taking great strides toward your ability to increase your focus and create incredible results out of that. The very fact that you are at the end of this book means that you have likely already begun taking significant action on the lessons within this book, which means that you are well on your way to becoming truly not distractable.

I hope that in reading this book, you feel a boost to your confidence in your ability to actually achieve all of the goals you have set out for yourself. Hopefully, you now realize that the likely driving factor behind your previous inability to reach your goals was not your laziness or your inability, but the fact that your brain has been wired to remain distracted and keep you from staying focused. Fortunately, there are many great steps you can take to improve your focus and help you stay focused until you get the job done.

Although it may take a significant amount of effort and practice to see these steps all the way through, the more you practice the better you will get at implementing these new skills into your life. Over time, you will discover that your ability to stay focused continues to improve and that you get better and better at achieving every single goal you set out for yourself. As you build these skills, however, it is important that you remain patient with yourself and that you are able to have compassion for your short fallings, while also having enough responsibility and accountability to keep yourself going. The better you can balance your compassion with your drive, the easier it will be for you to motivate yourself to keep going, without completely derailing yourself every time you make a mistake. With self-improvement, progress is always preferred over perfection. Even if you can improve by just 1% per day, that's a 365% improvement every single year.

After you read this book, I strongly encourage you to go back through it and pick one to two areas of focus that you are going to rely on right now. Having a limited area of primary focus ensures that you are not overwhelming yourself or setting yourself up for failure by having too many things that you want to change at once. After you begin to feel confident in these changes and they start to come naturally and easily for you for a period of time, you can begin to implement new practices into your life. This gradual accumulation will be easier and more sustainable in the long run, providing you with better results in the end. It would be a good idea for you to choose "creating a quiet space" as one of your initial focal points, as this is an incredibly valuable practice that can help anyone at any level of skill in this particular area of your life. Having somewhere quiet and comfortable to retreat to will go a long way in helping you build up your ability to release distractions and develop your focus. It is also incredibly soothing for your mental and emotional wellbeing, which can further eliminate distractions from your life.

I also encourage you to keep this book available for yourself so that once you begin to master these initial practices you can implement new ones from this very title. The more times you come back to and reuse a resource you have already invested in, the more value you gain out of that resource in the long run. This way, you truly integrate all of the wisdom that the resource has to offer, and your ability to return to that resource and continue implementing it serves to improve your long-term focus. It is a win-win situation!

THE POWER OF GOOD SLEEP

Improve Your Sleep
For a Better Life

Table Of Contents

Introduction

What is sleep for you? Is it that thing you do between watching an episode of your favorite show and taking a shower so that you can get ready for your workday? Is it your form of self-soothing, or a favorite hobby that you enjoy partaking in as often as possible? Is it a greatly missed memory from days gone by, interrupted now by a busy schedule and growing demands on your life? Or, is it a reward that you get for reaching all of your goals on a day to day basis?

Each of us sees sleep through our own unique lens of what sleep is, how we enjoy it, and how it affects our lives. And while we may all have our own unique relationship to sleep itself, the truth is that at its very core, sleep is the same thing for each of us. It is a necessary, important process that our body needs to engage in on a day to day basis in order to provide us with adequate energy and optimal health to continue living a healthy life. Sleep is when your body engages in many different functions that cannot be performed during your waking hours, each of which is necessary for your wellbeing. This is why when you get a sound, healthy sleep you wake up feeling rested, refreshed, and excited to go about your day. When you do not get a sound, healthy sleep, however, you wake up feeling groggy, tired, and as though the day ahead will be seemingly impossible. Compounding multiple good periods of sleep, or multiple bad periods of sleep, back to back can drastically transform your wellness, and not just in terms of how you feel. It actually changes the way your body functions, the quality of your immunity, your resiliency toward mental stressors and experiences, and many other things.

With sleep being such an incredibly important element of our wellbeing, it is surprising to learn that more people are not already talking about sleep and why we need to be engaging in proper sleep hygiene practices. Proper sleep hygiene practices, by the way, include practices that you engage in throughout the day, before bed, and while you sleep to ensure that you are getting the highest quality of sleep possible. People who have proper sleep hygiene practices notice it, as it changes their lives in ways that can only be understood by someone who has been engaging in these proper practices. People who do not have proper sleep hygiene practices notice it when they feel exhausted, under the weather with no clear reason as to why, forgetful, and generally unwell and miserable on a day to day basis.

Learning how to improve the quality of your sleep hygiene is not just about putting yourself in a better mood so that you do not snap at your family members over breakfast or find yourself too exhausted to hang out with loved ones after work. This is about learning how to take proper care of yourself so that you can improve your health exponentially, providing you with a higher quality of life. The proper way to perceive the importance of sleep is to recognize it as being equally as important as nutrition, exercise, and bodily hygiene practices. As with each of those, sleep also has necessary things that should be done to improve your sleep "diet," effectively giving you the best quality of sleep possible.

In *The Power Of Good Sleep* we are going to dive deep into why sleep is an essential wellness practice, what you gain when you get a good night's sleep, how to get a good night's sleep, and how to continue improving the quality of your sleep in the long run. At first, making these changes may seem challenging, or even a little pointless. As you begin to realize the importance of sleep, however, and as you recognize the tangible impact that a good night's sleep has on your wellbeing, you will begin to realize why this guide and everything within it is so important.

If you are ready to transform your sleep, your mood, and your health, you have come to the right place. Please, grab yourself a nice warm mug of chamomile tea and cozy up to read this excellent, life-changing title, and let's begin!

Chapter 1

Why It Is Important
To Sleep (Well)

If you are diving into this book and your initial thought is something to the effect of: "But I am already sleeping every day, why isn't it enough? Why do I still feel this way?" then you are not that different from others who are still learning about the importance of sleep and proper sleep practices. Many times, people are aware of the fact that there is something wrong with their rest because they feel a general sense of unwellness and tiredness on a day to day basis. They may not realize, however, why they are feeling this way or what they are doing that is contributing to them not being able to get a proper sleep. Even if you attempt to go to sleep earlier or cut your caffeine out sooner, you may have an overwhelming feeling that this is not enough and that you are still not getting the amount of rest that you actually need.

The reality is, there are many different things that can contribute to, or take away from, the quality of your sleep. In order for you to find the optimal sleeping pattern for your needs, you are going to need to develop a more intimate understanding of what happens in your body while you sleep, and how different activities affect these processes. Before we can dig into that, though, I want to address one very important question that you might have: "Why should I take this seriously?"

Upon stumbling into this book, you may have come under the impression that you would simply make a few adjustments to your schedule or your bedtime routine and then be on your merry way with a better sleep and a better sense of wellbeing overall. While you could technically walk away from this having only experienced that takeaway if you want to, I suggest going much deeper into the process of respecting and caring for your sleep cycles. After all, they are incredibly important and they have a much bigger impact on your overall wellbeing than you likely think.

In fact, there are two incredibly compelling reasons that explain exactly why you need to have a high quality of sleep every single night in order for you to feel your healthiest possible. These two reasons include: day to day wellness, and long term wellness. Both your immediate sense of wellbeing and your long term health rely on you being able to get a good night's sleep more often than not. While the odd crummy sleep will not be a big deal in your overall wellbeing, continuous bad sleep can create serious long term side effects that are incredibly difficult to navigate and that can have lasting or even permanent effects on your wellbeing.

The Short-Term Need For Sleep

In the short term, the quality of sleep you have will heavily affect you on a day to day basis. You can already witness this based on how you feel anytime you wake up after a great sleep versus how you feel anytime you wake up after a terrible sleep. For example, think back to the last time that you "slept like a baby," so to speak. Chances are, you had an incredible rest and you woke up feeling nourished, alert, and ready to face the day ahead of you. You may have felt happier, more excited for the day ahead, and more resilient toward whatever happened that day. On the other hand, on a night where you had a terrible rest or nearly no rest at all, you may have woken the next morning feeling grumpy, irritable, and struggling to motivate yourself to get anything done. You may have even felt a headache, nausea, or general achiness in your body that resulted from your low quality sleep.

While these are two incredibly opposite ends of the sleep spectrum, the reality is that even subtle nuances in the quality of your sleep can leave a lasting impact on your daily sense of wellbeing. Having an "okay" sleep, for example, may leave you feeling alright but not particularly great or motivated to face the day ahead. You may have felt like you could do it, but you were not terribly excited for what was yet to come and it was more challenging for you to face hardships that rose unexpectedly that day. Or, if you had a "bad but not terrible" sleep, you may find that you are not in a horrible mood but that you are more irritable and that as the day goes on you have an increasingly more challenging time navigating everyday obstacles.

You may not think that these subtle changes in your attitude or mood would affect you greatly, but the reality is that they can. Being awaken, energetic, and optimistic is not just a mindset that people get into, it is also a state that they create through taking proper care of themselves, which includes taking proper care of their sleep. If you find that it is particularly challenging for you to experience enough energy and optimism to get you through a positive, enjoyable day, chances are you are not taking adequate care of your rest, or other areas of your wellness needs.

The Long-Term Need For Sleep

As with all things relating to your health, even being a little "off" on a day to day basis can lead to significant, lasting side effects on your wellbeing. The easiest way to understand this is to realize that each day, that little bit of feeling off compounds. Furthermore, you are not just feeling off, the actual processes in your body are being thrown out of their natural, and necessary, rhythms which results in you not being able to experience the benefits of them being properly completed. Over time, as these processes continue to go incomplete, the negative side effects of that build up and become increasingly more noticeable.

People who suffer from ongoing sleep troubles often find that they end up experiencing mental, emotional, and physical illness as a result. You may find that your memory begins to deteriorate and that your cognition deteriorates as well. You may also find that you experience an increase in anxiety or depression as your sleep worsens and that they worsen and improve alongside the overall quality of your sleep cycle. Further, you may also find that your digestion, circulation, capacity to get adequate exercise and nutrition, and other bodily functions are reduced or significantly impacted by your limited energy. Some people also find that they experience an increase in general achiness or wellbeing, or even a worsening of symptoms related to other underlying health conditions they may have as a result of a low quality sleep. All in all, many negative side effects can be derived from getting a low quality sleep on a regular basis.

Why a "Decent" Sleep Is Not Good Enough

Because small, frequent disruptions to the overall quality of your sleep can compound and create significant, lasting consequences over time, it is important that you never settle into the belief that a decent sleep is good enough. It isn't.

While there may be periods of your life where getting a high quality of sleep is not possible, it is important that you always do your best to keep the quality of your sleep as high as possible and that you rectify this situation as soon as possible. In situations where you cannot completely improve the quality of your sleep, such as if you have a newborn in the house or if you have recently experienced changes to your lifestyle which have changed your daily routine and sleep routine, you need to do your best to get the highest quality of sleep possible. You also need to be looking to make the necessary adjustments to ensure that these changes do not have a lasting impact on your long term sleep cycle. For example, if you have a newborn then you already know that once that baby begins to get older they will sleep better, so the best thing you can do is sleep the best that you can now and work toward proper sleep training practices to improve the quality of both of your sleep over time.

If you experience a change to your routine, however, it is important that you immediately begin considering ways that you can create a new healthy sleeping routine for yourself that you can integrate per your new schedule. This way, you are not suffering through a low quality of sleep over a long period of time. Instead, you are making it a top priority to get back into a healthy sleep so that you can get back to enjoying the positive benefits of a healthy sleep. Which, by the way, includes your ability to remain resilient toward stress and change, which makes this an even more important topic to consider.

Should you find that you have been experiencing a low quality or limited quality of sleep continually for a significant period of time, it is time for you to acknowledge that what you are presently doing is not working. That way, you can immediately begin to look for ways to rectify your sleep so that you can move from experiencing a "decent" sleep, to an excellent sleep. If that is what you are here for, then you are about to discover some revolutionary new information that will help you transform your sleep for good, no matter what circumstances you are up against!

Chapter 2

How Sleep Works

While you now understand why sleep is so important, you may still be unclear as to what actually happens when you fall asleep. Many people still believe that sleep is simply a necessity to rebuild energy. What they do not realize is all of the processes and stages that go into actually rebuilding that energy in their minds and bodies.

Before you can dig into what is causing this feeling and why your sleep is so unfulfilling, it is first beneficial to understand why a good night's sleep matters. You may be surprised to discover that there are countless things going on in your body and mind when you sleep, each of which is necessary to your wellbeing. When you get a proper night's rest, your body has an adequate ability to fulfill all of these activities and maintain your wellness. When you do not get a proper night's rest, however, your body does not get enough attention on these activities and it can result in you feeling the effects of that incompletion the next day.

While you sleep, your body goes through five separate stages of sleep and it repeats these five separate stages

5-7 times per night, depending on how long you rest. Each stage takes roughly 90-110 minutes to complete, and it must complete all the way through in order for your body to complete every part of the process. If you awaken part way through a cycle, you will find that you feel especially tired because your body was not yet ready to awaken. In other words, you awoke mid-cycle and now your body has to attempt to discard the processes it was engaging in, while they are incomplete, so that it can begin to engage in new processes related to being awake and going about your normal daily routine.

The easiest way to understand the importance of sleep, and the importance in quality of sleep, is to understand what happens in your body during each of these five stages. That way, you can begin to understand what is happening to your body and how your body is being affected during the process.

Stage One: One To Seven Minutes

Stage one of your sleep occurs during the first one to seven minutes of your rest. This stage includes the portion of your sleep cycle where you are just beginning to drift off into sleep. By now, your eyelids are heavy and your head starts to drop. Right now, your brain is still incredibly active which means that it is easy for you to be aroused in case of something going on in your environment. If you had an electroencephalogram (EEG) monitor connected to your brain, you would notice that the monitor starts to slow down as your brain no longer needs to use as much energy.

Each time the sleep cycle repeats itself when you sleep you will come back into this drowsy state, meaning that there will be a few times during the night where you are easily aroused. This is why it is so important to keep your environment quiet, so that you remain asleep through these periods of arousal. If you were in an environment that was noisy, such as one where you slept with the TV or restless music on all night, you would awaken during this stage every single time which would not be conducive to your sleep. If you do choose to fully arouse during this cycle, it can make it harder for you to fall back asleep, especially if you get into the habit of getting up and staying aroused.

Stage Two: Ten To Twenty-Five Minutes

During the second stage of your sleep you are officially in what sleep experts consider to be a light sleep. At this point, your eyes are no longer moving and your brain has begun to slow down even further, meaning that you are now descending into a full cycle of rest. If you were connected to an EEG monitor you would see that the brain waves slow significantly, but there is an increase in their size, as well. There are short one to two second moments of activity that sleep experts call "sleep spindles."

In the second stage of sleep you are somewhat more challenging to arouse than during the first stage, though you are still easy to arouse. This means that if were was noise around you, you would be likely to wake up and investigate what the noise was and where it was coming from. For this reason, people who sleep with the TV on or with significant noise in their sleeping space will find that they actually have around eleven to thirty-two minutes where they are easily aroused. This makes it obvious as to why it is so important to sleep in a quiet, relaxing environment that has no capacity to stimulate you during your rest.

Stage Three: Twenty To Forty Minutes

The third stage of sleep is recognized on an EEG monitor as being the stage where the sleep spindles stop and you are now in a stage of moderate sleep. Now, you are producing delta waves through your brain, with spikes of smaller faster waves occurring between delta waves every now and again. The further you get into your third stage of sleep, the harder you are to awaken.

If you find yourself waking up from sleep during the third stage of sleep or later, you will notice that you awaken feeling groggy, tired, and generally miserable. People who routinely wake up during this stage or later will rarely experience a positive wakening experience as their bodies and brains will not yet be complete with their sleeping cycle. This is where you are really trying to throw the brakes on a train that is attempting to fly full steam ahead, and it is getting harder and harder to do so. In other words, the momentum of your sleep is so powerful that it takes your body a while to adjust to being awake.

Stage Four: Twenty To Forty Minutes

The fourth stage of your sleep is a moderate-deep stage of sleep, and it is characterized as being the deepest stage of your sleep overall. At this point, it is very hard to wake you up because you are in such a deep state of sleep and your body is so deeply invested in its stage four processes. While you can be aroused, people will find it much harder to get you to wake up at this point.

On an EEG monitor, tall, slow delta waves are all that can be seen and your body begins to show proof of this stage of the cycle through slow rhythmic breathing, occasional snoring, and fully relaxed muscles.

Stage Five: Ten To Sixty Minutes

The final stage of sleep is when your brain begins to perk up again, which means that electrical activity starts picking up and it begins to resemble what your brain does when you are awake. During this stage, your muscles are temporarily paralyzed due to something known as "sleep paralysis" which is said to be experienced as a way to prevent you from physically acting on that perky brain activity since you are still technically sleeping. You will also be most likely to experience your dreams during this cycle of your sleep.

The fifth stage of sleep is often called REM sleep, which stands for rapid eye movement, and it is characterized by your eyes literally darting back and forth as you sleep. If you were to watch someone sleeping during this part of their sleep cycle, you would see their eye movement under their eyelids, indicating that they were officially dreaming. Between stage five and stage one a new cycle begins, and effectively puts you back into a state of being easily aroused. This is also the prime time for you to awaken as you have officially completed a full cycle of sleep but you have not started a new one, meaning your brain is ready to be awakened. That is, of course, assuming you have already slept through five to seven full sleep cycles, which is what is needed in order for you to get the highest quality of sleep possible.

What Is Happening In Your Body While You Sleep?

As you sleep, your body is not just going through the process of heightened and reduced brain activity. Your body is also going through many things within your mind and within your body itself that are contributing to your overall wellbeing. Some of these things include cleaning, reinforcing, and rebuilding different parts of your body so that you can awaken in the morning with a clean, stronger body to operate from.

During your waking hours, your breathing rhythm changes in response to what you are doing and what is going on around you. If you are exercising, or if you sense a threat in your general area, for example, your breathing will shallow and quicken so that you can get more oxygen pumping through your body rapidly. This way, that oxygen can oxygenate your cells and help them facilitate whatever processes need to be facilitated based on the situation you are in. If you are sitting or relaxing, however, your breath will be slow and long, and possibly quite a bit deeper in response to this rested state. This is why so many people suggest deep, rhythmic breathing as a way to relax from stress or periods of high anxiety.

When you sleep, your body naturally moves into a slower, more rhythmic breathing pattern that consistently moves oxygen throughout your body at an even pace. In addition to ensuring that oxygen is flowing to your blood at an even pace, it also tells your body and mind to relax deeply, which results in other important processes occurring as you sleep.

Alongside your circulatory system being regulated, sleep allows your body to engage in a process known as autophagy. To put it simply, autophagy is a metabolic process that occurs throughout your entire body in every single one of your cells. This is the process where each of your cells identifies unneeded "junk" within itself and packages it up so that it can be metabolized and broken down into amino fatty acids. Autophagy ensures that your cells are not burdened with unnecessary junk, nor that they are purging this junk into your bloodstream and creating free radicals that can come along with a whole host of different health concerns.

As your circulatory system rests, you also experience a lowered pulse and blood pressure. During this time, your blood vessels and heart are given the perfect opportunity to recover from a hard day of work, while also ensuring that they are ready to face the day ahead, too. With that being said, when you reach REM sleep, your blood pressure and pulse will change and increase until you move back into another cycle of sleep, unless you awaken instead.

Inside of your brain, the deeper states of your rest mean that your brain activity is not firing as spontaneously or actively as it does during your waking hours, or during REM sleep. This is when your neural pathways get a chance to reinforce themselves and clean out any neural pathways that are not being used on a regular basis, which means that your brain essentially optimizes itself for everyday function.

Lastly, your entire brain and body get an excellent chance to repair themselves when you are sleeping. During this time, your immune function is boosted, cells that have been damaged are replaced with new, healthy cells that function properly, and your body in general gets a chance to repair itself. This is why when you are ill or injured rest is recommended, as this is not just a way to reduce your impact on your body but to actually promote your body moving into a cycle where it heals itself.

Chapter 3

The Positive Effects Of Sleep

There are many positive side effects that you gain access to when you have a good sleep. If you have not been sleeping well enough, you may notice that you do not experience many of these positive side effects in your life. Instead, you may actually be feeling more of the negative side effects of a low quality of sleep, which we will talk about in chapter 4. Worry not, though, as you do have the capacity to improve this and experience a higher quality of sleep, so long as you are willing to put effort into learning how and then actually taking the necessary steps to improve your sleep.

While there are many benefits of a healthy sleep, there are ten incredibly positive benefits that you should know about and look forward to. These benefits should also be plenty to motivate you to want to put effort into taking your sleep seriously and genuinely improving the quality of your sleep overall. Some of these benefits are ones we have already discussed, while others will be new and potentially surprising to you. Either way, we are going to discuss each of them in more detail so that you get a better understanding of why, and how, they work.

Significantly Reduced Stress

When your body's natural processes are not completed, many things are left incomplete in your body which can put a huge strain on your natural systems. Through this, you can find yourself compensating for decreased function in certain areas of your body which can result in an increased level of stress and burden being placed on your body. From time to time, this will not be overly bad as you can navigate it and get back on schedule. However, continued strain put on your body's systems means that you are going to have an increasingly more challenging time relying on your body to get you through anything that may further stress you out. This includes anything that may directly stress your immune system, such as illnesses, or anything that may stress your mind, such as pressures at work or in your family.

Ensuring that you get a high quality sleep every single night means that your body will be holding onto fewer stress hormones to help get you through your day to day life. As a result, it will not be quite so significant if you find yourself experiencing day to day stress because you are not already holding onto high-stress levels. Through this, you will find increased resiliency to stress mentally, emotionally, and physically.

Reduced Or Eliminated Inflammation

When you experience high levels of stress in your life, which low quality sleep can create, your body begins to create a significant amount of inflammation. Inflammation is caused by stress hormones and other stress functions in your body essentially damaging your healthy cells and causing them to begin to produce inflammation as a way to protect themselves. While this does not generally happen when you are experiencing healthy, natural stress levels, over time it can begin to develop long term effects.

Experiencing a high quality, healthy sleep on a regular basis ensures that your body is able to minimize stress, and that your body can engage in autophagy. This metabolic process ensures that all free radicals are eliminated from your cells, further reducing your body's need or tendency to create inflammation within your body. Reducing inflammation through a healthy sleep can lead to reduced pain, improved heart health, and many other benefits that help you generally feel better on a daily basis, as well as protect you against long term side effects of ongoing inflammation.

Increased Alertness and Energy Levels

As we have known all along, sleep is a necessary practice for you to engage in on a daily basis in order for you to improve your energy levels. When you sleep, your body recharges and you are able to approach your daily life with a higher level of alertness and a greater ability to get things done. This increased alertness and energy levels can improve your overall motivation, as well as encourage you to be more productive on a daily basis. This can all, in turn, improve your mental wellness, too, as you begin to experience the positive side effects of reaching your goals and experiencing the reward system in your brain to celebrate you reaching your goals. In general, we tend to feel a lot better about ourselves when we take proper care of ourselves and our wellbeing.

In order for you to effectively access these improved energy levels, it is important that you have a complete and undisturbed sleep. This means that you need to experience each of the five stages of the sleep cycle in order and to the highest quality possible, and that you need to experience the cycle at least five to seven times per night, uninterrupted. Your best quality of sleep will ensure that you do not arouse at all during the night and that you sleep all the way through until morning.

Improved Memory Function

While we are starting to uncover the benefits of sleep and what happens during sleep on a deeper level every day, researchers are still largely mystified around why we sleep and dream and what happens in our brains and bodies while we do. One of the things that researchers still do not fully understand is the function of the brain and what is actually going on in the brain when you sleep. However, they have uncovered that one of the positive side effects of the activities going on in your brain during periods of sleep is improved memory.

As you sleep, it is believed that your brain moves through your day in chronological order to identify important memories and links between memories from the day so that it can file them away in your brain. The links that your brain will make during this phase of sleep include links from events, sensory inputs, memories, and feelings, as well as links from this day's events to historical ones that may stand out. By getting a healthy night sleep, which means entering a deep sleep cycle and seeing it all the way through, your brain is effectively able to move through this process and, as a result, retain memories much better.

Supported Cognitive Function

In addition to improving your memories and making correlations between different things in your memory system, your brain also uses this time to actually improve your measurable smartness. The same process that sorts and files away your memories also organizes memories associated with specific knowledge you learned or skills you practiced during the day. This means that the more often you practice something on a daily basis, the more often your brain will reinforce this particular skill or piece of knowledge in your mind, making it easier for you to remember it and engage in that knowledge as needed.

Some research has shown that practicing a new skill or studying before bed can actually improve your ability to retain knowledge from that session. In fact, they have shown that one half an hour session of practice or studying before bed is far more productive than one half an hour session completed at any other point during the day. This is because this information is still fresh in your mind as these sleep processes begin, and because as soon as you enter a deep sleep they are immediately stored within your brain. This is also why it is so important to be intentional about what you do or learn about before going to sleep, so that you are focusing on things that are positive and productive and not on things that may worsen your stress levels.

Improved Heart Health

Did you know that heart attacks and strokes are more likely to occur during the early morning hours, and not during any other time of the day? This is believed to be caused by the way that sleep interacts with your blood vessels, and how that impacts your overall circulatory and heart health. It has been shown that a lack of sleep can cause poor blood pressure, as well as worsened bad cholesterol levels. Both of these are risk factors for heart disease and stroke.

While getting a healthy sleep alone cannot cure your blood pressure or cholesterol levels, they are an important factor in improving these two symptoms so that you can reduce your risk factors. In addition to getting a healthy sleep, you should also be eating a healthy diet and getting regular exercise as both of these factors will contribute to you experiencing improved heart and circulatory health.

Reduced Risk Of Depression

Alongside sleep's ability to reduce stress hormones in your body, sleep can also help bring balance to the rest of your hormonal and chemical system. One of the big chemicals that is impacted by the quality and consistency of your sleep is serotonin, which is the chemical that is known for creating happiness. When you are deficient in serotonin, you can experience depression. Keeping a regular, high-quality sleep cycle ensures that your serotonin levels remain balanced, which can help reduce the likelihood of you experiencing depression.

In addition to getting the proper amount of sleep, exercising is an important part of regulating your hormones and chemicals within your body. Further, you can consume certain foods that are said to be effective at boosting and balancing natural serotonin levels to help alleviate symptoms of depression. Through this three-tiered approach, you may have a powerful impact in reducing the impact depression has on you in your life.

Increased Ability For Your Body To Repair Itself

In addition to being able to eliminate free radicals and unwanted junk out of your cells, sleeping gives your body the opportunity to repair itself from activities throughout the day. As you go through your day to day life, many of your cells experience damage. Some cells experience damage due to aging, while others experience it due to exposure during your day to day life. For example, if you have been exercising, your muscles will have ripped open and, in the process, will have created many damaged cells that need to be removed so that healthier cells can replace the damaged cells. In this way, you find yourself experiencing larger muscles.

When you sleep, your body is able to focus more energy and attention on healing and repairing the cells that have been damaged throughout your daily life. This will happen for cells that have been damaged due to everyday wear and tear, as well as cells that have been damaged due to injury or illness. Ensuring that you get adequate sleep means that these processes are completed effectively and that your body is able to rebuild itself on a daily basis. For a fun fact, this process significantly slows down and sometimes even stops after you reach the age of 65, which is why healing later in life can be so challenging.

Potential Weight Loss Benefits

Some of the many functions that occur in your body when you are sleeping affect your metabolic system, which is responsible for breaking down and distributing nutrients to different parts of your body, and eliminating waste as well. A strong, healthy metabolic system has been shown to make it easier for you to absorb maximum nutrients out of your meals, while also helping you eliminate unnecessary waste from meals, too. When you sleep properly, this system is able to function optimally which means that it may increase your capacity to lose weight more efficiently.

In addition to supporting your metabolic system, it is important to note that sleeping can also reduce stress, as you already know. Unchecked stress levels can disrupt the creation of certain hormones such as ghrelin and leptin, both of which play a vital role in your ability to regulate your appetite. Resting on a regular basis ensures everything is regulated and balanced, which will support you with maintaining a proper, healthy appetite and the capacity to metabolize anything you eat properly.

Potential Anti-Cancerous Benefits

Some studies have shown that not having a proper sleep cycle may put you at a higher risk of developing breast and colon cancer, amongst other types of cancers. This is because when you have an irregular sleep cycle, melatonin becomes imbalanced within your body. Melatonin is a natural chemical that your body produces that stimulates your sleep-wake cycle, and it is essential in keeping balance in your circadian rhythms. It is also linked to having the potential to suppress the growth of tumors in your body.

The best way to improve the anti-cancerous benefits of sleep is to sleep in a dark room, and to naturally reduce your exposure to light over the course of the evening. By lowering the light in your home and reducing your use of electronics and other bright lights and screens at bedtime, you can improve your body's natural ability to produce melatonin which will give you access to the benefit of improved sleep and possible prevention of cancer.

Chapter 4

What Happens When You Get Poor Sleep

When you get a poor quality of sleep, there are many things that happen within your mind and body that can be challenging to navigate. Some of these experiences will be obvious and recognizable on the surface, while others will not be so obvious and, as a result, can compound and create long term side effects that become increasingly more difficult to navigate. It is important that you are aware of the fact that even if you cannot feel or immediately recognize one of these negative side effects taking place, every single one of them occurs when you do not get a high quality of sleep on a nightly basis.

It is also important to note that creating a healthier sleep routine in your life is not going to make underlying health conditions disappear, nor will it completely prevent you from facing future health conditions in your life. Sleep is only one element of your overall wellness, however it does play a significant element in your overall wellness. The best way to avoid developing any long term conditions comes from getting a proper sleep every single night, eating healthy, exercising on a regular basis, and working closely with your doctor to identify and avoid possible risk factors in your life. By including a healthy sleep into your overall wellness routine, however, you will take a huge leap in creating a healthier lifestyle for you in general.

Reduced Immune Function

When your body is thrown through the massive stress that can come its way as a result of limited sleep, it begins to experience reduced immune function. This reduced immune function comes from a few different sources, each of which are ignited and worsened by a low quality of sleep. First and foremost, the creation of stress itself can put a major strain on your body by resulting in your body picking specific areas of "focus" that it will place its attention and energy on. Often, in order to do this, it must take energy and attention away from other faculties which means that you begin to experience reduced functions in certain areas of your body, such as in your immune system.

Another reason why your immune system becomes damaged is because it is during the time that you spend sleeping that your body really gets to focus on breaking down and eliminating anything that may be compromising your immune system. At this point, your body does not need to focus energy on keeping you awake and aware of what is going on around you, as well as interacting with the world around you. Instead, it can focus more closely on what is going on inside of you, such as with your health. If you fail to get enough sleep, and a high enough quality of sleep, every single night, you will find yourself experiencing an increased risk of getting sick as a result of your decreased immune function.

Increased Risk To Your Heart

There are two ways that you can create a risk to your heart health when it comes to a low quality of sleep. That is, if you sleep for less than five hours or longer than nine hours per night on a continuous basis, you are creating a heightened amount of stress on your circulatory system which directly affects your heart health. When you do not get enough sleep, your heart and blood vessels do not get enough of a chance to recover from the work they do every single day to keep your body healthy. Alternatively, if you get too much sleep, they weaken as they are not getting enough exercise to keep you healthy.

Getting between 7 to 9 hours of sleep every single night is optimal to ensure that you are getting all of the rest you need to take good care of your heart without putting it at risk due to not sleeping enough, or sleeping too much. If you do fall on either end of the spectrum on a consistent basis, the damage you are causing can put you at heightened risk of developing coronary artery disease, or having a stroke.

Increased Risk Of Cancer

Not experiencing enough sleep has been shown to share a direct correlation with increased diagnosis of breast cancer, prostate cancer, and colorectal cancer. It is believed that this is caused by your body not experiencing healthy and balanced levels of melatonin, which is a hormone that is responsible for your sleep-wake cycles. This same hormone has also shown to have tumor-suppressing capabilities, as you already know.

The studies that have been done that show these correlations were done with shift workers in an effort to highlight possible health risks that shift workers face by taking on the less desirable shifts in their careers. Through these studies, it was discovered that their imbalanced sleep schedules shouldered by overnight shift workers created abnormal exposure to light and dark, which disrupted their creation of melatonin. This disrupted creation was believed to be responsible for their increased tendency to develop these three forms of cancer.

Difficulty Thinking Clearly

This is a symptom that you likely notice as soon as you experience even one night of reduced quality of sleep. Difficulty thinking clearly is a symptom you get, likely because your brain did not have enough time to recharge and develop enough energy for you to engage in your everyday activities. In addition to difficulty thinking clearly, you might also find that you have a hard time making decisions, thinking rationally, problem solving, and being alert in general. This may also contribute to difficulty regulating your emotions because your thoughts, which are closely tied to your emotions, are disrupted by your low quality sleep as well.

You may notice all of these side effects in your own everyday life as you navigate a day following a night of no rest. In fact, these symptoms are usually what lead people to realize that they had a low quality of rest in the first place, because these symptoms directly impact their day. You should notice these symptoms quickly eliminate as soon as you get a high quality sleep in, or possibly a few if you have fallen woefully behind inadequate rest.

Reduced Memory Function

In addition to experiencing issues with your thinking, you also experience issues with your memory function. Remember, when you sleep at night your brain works to consolidate your memories and organizes them based on what was important and what was not important, and eliminates ones that are irrelevant to you or your wellbeing. When you do not get an adequate night sleep, this process is disrupted and your brain has difficulty navigating your memory as a result of two things. First, it struggles because the previous memories were not consolidated and so past memories may not be stored effectively, meaning that you might not recall things from previous days. Second, it struggles because a lack of energy results in you not having the energy to power your memory. As a result, the part of your brain that is generally "recording" for information is not functioning properly and so it fails to inventory memory-worthy information in a timely manner, or sometimes even at all.

When you experience a low quality sleep at night, reduced memory function may be another clear indicator that you have experienced this low quality sleep. You may find yourself forgetting where you set your keys, forgetting what you were doing, or even forgetting about something someone said to you just moments later. This decreased memory function may also impair your learning abilities, making it harder for you to retain information and learn new concepts, skills, or other pieces of information. Often, this can be alleviated by getting a high quality sleep.

Diminished Libido

As your reduced quality of sleep creates damage in various systems within your body, it can also create drastic imbalances with your sex-related hormones. These imbalances can cause an array of issues, including a diminished libido. Experiencing a diminished libido is not a long term side effect of low quality sleep, either, although many people would not relate this as having anything to do with sleep at all. The reality is that after just one week of low quality sleep can reduce your sex hormone levels by as much as 10 to 15 percent.

In addition to having your libido directly affected, you may also find that you have more irritable emotions which can create further issues in your ability to bond with your partner or a sexual lover. Rather than being able to enjoy and be aroused by your partner, you may find yourself instead fighting with them which can create an even lower sense of libido. The longer this goes on, the more challenging it may be for you to enjoy a healthy sex life with your partner, partly related to a reduced libido due to low quality sleep, and partly related to emotional issues that may arise as a result.

Unwanted Weight Gain

A lack of sleep has directly proven that it has a strong capacity to promote weight gain in people, and not in a healthy way. One study examined the relationship between sleep and weight in more than 21,000 people that were over the age of 20 years old. In that study, they discovered that people who slept less than five hours per night on a regular basis over three years were far more likely to gain weight. Many also crossed over to the point of becoming obese, meaning that they were dealing with significant weight gain that had the capacity to create a variety of other health-related issues. On the other hand, people who slept between seven and eight hours on a regular basis tended to have better weights overall, and therefore were not at risk of weight-related illness.

Getting an adequate night sleep ensures that your body has enough time to engage in important metabolic processes. It also ensures that your body is not being exposed to copious amounts of stress which can affect your appetite and your daily metabolic processes that occur during your waking hours. Through this combination, your likelihood of weight gain is significantly reduced as you have an increased capacity to eat healthier and digest the food in a healthier manner, too.

Increased Risk Of Diabetes

When you sleep, your metabolic process digests any remaining food in your system and delivers it to different parts of your body. You also engage in a sort of fast that occurs overnight, which is broken when you awaken and eat your breakfast. During this fasting cycle, insulin levels will naturally drop as they are no longer needed to help you digest any sugars that may be left in your body. With that being said, there are two ways that you can negatively affect your insulin levels through sleep. The first is by consuming too many sugars before bed, which means that your body does not get the opportunity to properly balance out your digestive chemicals through a fast because it is still digesting. In this case, your insulin levels stay fairly high overnight, and then are retained at higher levels when you consume breakfast the next day. On the other hand, if you do not eat for several hours before bed, then you do not eat through the night and you sleep for a lengthy period of time, you may experience rather low insulin levels, followed by an unhealthy spike when you eat breakfast the next morning. Certain changes in your levels are healthy and natural to your body, but excessive dips and spikes in your insulin levels can drastically increase your risk of developing adult-onset diabetes, or type 2 diabetes.

In a series of ten different studies, researchers found that the optimal sleep length for individuals was between seven to eight hours, as this provides enough time for your body to engage in natural fasting without your levels varying too greatly. In addition to getting a full seven to eight hours of rest, make sure you stop snacking before bed. Refraining from eating for at least two hours before you fall asleep ensures that your body is well into the digestive phase by the time you go to bed, allowing your body to engage in a natural fasting cycle throughout your sleep. The *only* time you should break this and follow a different set of rules is if you already have issues with blood sugar, in which case you should follow the direct guidance of your doctor to avoid facing serious issues within your health. Pre-diabetic or diabetic individuals will need to closely monitor blood sugar levels and eat according to their medical practitioner's guidance, not according to the average standard for sleep.

You Become Accident Prone

A combination of reduced capacity to think, reduced cognitive function, and reduced memory can lead to you experiencing a greater tendency of accidents in your life. In one study, they discovered that you become three times more likely to experience a traffic accident if you sleep for fewer than six hours per night. This means that anyone who works on shifts, or who works lengthy periods of time and does not have much time left for sleep, is far more vulnerable to accidents than the average individual.

With that being said, *anyone* who experiences reduced sleep on a regular basis will experience this same level of being accident-prone. These accidents are not exclusive to traffic accidents, either. You may find yourself more at risk of tripping, dropping things, knocking things over, or making other mistakes as a result of your sleepiness. This is why, in most cases, you are advised against operating heavy machinery or potentially dangerous technology when you are tired.

Potential Skin Conditions

Have you ever noticed that when you get a high-quality night sleep, your skin looks fuller, fresher, and generally better? In many cases, your tone will be more even and youthful, too. This is because getting a good night's sleep really can promote healthier skin overall. Which is why, on the other hand, not getting a good night's sleep can take away from your skin health and leave you prone to breakouts, discoloration, and generally tired-looking skin. You may also get more wrinkles, fine lines, and looseness in your skin in general, as a result of not getting adequate sleep.

Getting at least seven to eight hours of "beauty rest" is an important way to take care of your skin health. You can also incorporate other sleep-related practices into your skincare routine to improve the quality of your skin, including sleeping with a satin pillowcase cover and an eye mask if you wear one, as well as using overnight creams or face masks. These products are proven to help keep your skin healthier and, as a result, looking clearer and better overall.

Chapter 5

The Mystery Of Your Dreams

As we begin to venture deeper into the topic of sleep and what you can do to help improve the quality of your sleep, I want to address the mysterious topic of dreams. Dreams are something that anyone who is getting a proper night's sleep will experience, although not everyone can remember their dreams. As well, not everyone experiences dreams in the same way. Some people experience dreams visually, either in color or in black and white, while others experience dreams audibly or through other senses. As well, some dreams can play out like a mini-movie in your mind, while others seem to just be flashes of pictures or scenes that do not seem to fit together in any sort of coherent manner. Furthermore, some dreams make sense, while others can be confusing or uncomfortable, and some can even lead to nightmares. There are truly so many different elements of dreams that we experience, and we have not even dug into *why* we experience them, or what the point of dreams are, yet. Dreams are, by far, a fascinating topic and they are one that we continue to study on a regular basis as scientists have yet to uncover what dreams really are, or why we have them.

What Are Dreams?

Dreams are something that we are still trying to understand more of on a regular basis. The experience of dreams varies from person to person, and it often varies from night to night, or even from sleep cycle to sleep cycle. Because of how varied the experience of dreams can be, it can leave dreamers confused and uncertain about what the purpose of their dreams are, and whether or not there is anything they need to know about their dreams.

The easiest way to understand what a dream is, is to recognize it as being a story comprised of images that your mind creates while you sleep. These stories can be fun, entertaining, bizarre, romantic, disturbing, and even frightening in nature, and it can vary from night to night. In fact, some people even experience waking up from a nightmare, only to fall asleep and later wake up from a more positive and enjoyable dream.

Dreams are said to last for about fifteen to twenty minutes every night, and every person experiences between three and six dreams per night, regardless of whether or not they remember those dreams. Even if you do tend to be the type of person who remembers your dreams, studies have shown that you will forget as many as 95% of the dreams by the time you get out of bed. Though, you may have flash memories of your dream throughout the day, especially if a certain sensory experience reminds you of a particular dream you have the night before, or even in previous nights before that.

One particularly interesting fact about dreams is that people who are blind, or deaf, tend to experience dreams differently from those who have normally functioning senses. Those who are blind tend to dream more so in sounds or other sensory components, while those who are deaf may see more but tend to hear nothing at all. With that being said, even those who experience normally functioning senses during their waking hours may experience dreams through an array of different sensory experiences.

Dreams are a universal human experience. Even people who do not typically remember their dreams upon waking will know what it is like to dream because they will have experienced at least a few dreams in the past that were memorable. Dreams can create different levels of consciousness in your sensory experiences, as well as in your cognitive and emotional experiences as you sleep. In most cases, you have very little control over the content of your dreams, though in others you may find that you do have a somewhat higher level of control. People who learn how to *lucid dream,* or gain a higher level of conscious control in their dreams, can usually behave intentionally in their dreams, or can even change the content of their dreams if they are not particularly pleased with what is going on. In fact, some people even use lucid dreaming as a means to prevent nightmares so that they can have a more positive dreaming experience.

Because dreams happen when we are sleeping and, therefore, generally unconscious of our surroundings, there is still a lot that we do not know about dreams. Dreaming is the most studied and least understood cognitive state that scientists are still working toward understanding so that they can fully recognize the power and purpose of dreaming as a whole.

As of right now, there are two approaches to dream analysis: neuroscientific, and psychoanalytic. The neuroscientific approach is particularly interested in understanding the structure of the brain and how it is impacted during dream production, organization, and narratability. They ultimately want to understand what structural changes are occurring, whether or not those changes are lasting, and how they affect the overall wellness of your brain. The psychoanalytic approach wants to understand what the meaning of dreams is and wants to use them to create context around the mind of the dreamer. From this approach, they believe that dreams can provide individuals with greater insight into what they may be dealing with in their conscious and subconscious mind, and in some cases they may use that to help the individual facilitate psychological healing, particularly after traumatic events.

Why Do We Have Dreams?

Just as we have a limited understanding of what dreams are, we also have a limited understanding as to why we have dreams and what sort of benefit they offer to us in our wellbeing. This means that we ultimately do not understand why we have dreams, or even what causes dreams to occur in the first place. However, we do have a general understanding as to what *might* cause dreams, meaning that we are starting to narrow in on their benefit and how they impact us overall.

Some people are content with believing that dreams are merely a part of the sleep cycle and that they actually have no significant meaning behind them whatsoever. These individuals believe that the rapid firing of the brain during REM sleep is simply a way for the brain to maintain its overall wellbeing, and dreams are just a side effect of this process.

Others believe that dreams could represent unconscious desires or wishes, that they could interpret random signals from the brain and body during sleep cycles, that they could behave as a form of natural psychotherapy, or that they could be consolidating and processing information from the previous day.

Those who believe that dreams represent unconscious desires or wishes believe that individuals should look to follow their dreams using a dream journal and should use this as an opportunity to spot trends and patterns in their dreams. Then, they can use these as clues to help them pursue things in waking hours that may help them fulfill these desires and wishes.

Those who believe that dreams are merely an interpretation of random signals, or that they are consolidating and processing information from the previous day tend to believe that dreams are a passive experience. In this line of thinking, it is generally agreed upon that the experience of a dream itself is merely an observation by the physical senses in response to what is going on within the brain. Since our bodies are not receiving nearly as much sensory input as we sleep, this gives the brain a chance to consolidate or perform natural functions during sleep that improve health. Some of these functions may trigger sensory experiences, though these experiences are not believed to mean anything.

People who believe that dreams are a form of natural psychotherapy believe that as we sleep, our brains are working on processing and healing from the mental and emotional repercussions of various experiences we have had throughout the day. By using dreams, we are able to work through these experiences so that we can release them, allowing us to move on mentally and emotionally from potentially troubling experiences. In a sense, we achieve similar results as we would in psychotherapy, only naturally on a nightly basis.

Some new research methodologies have also proposed a series of different beliefs around what might cause dreams. These newer beliefs are still being tested and researched, and some hold great merit and could possibly give us a deeper understanding of why we even dream at all. Amongst these possible reasons include theories such as: consolidating and processing memories, preparing for possible future threats, developing cognitive capabilities, simulating real-life experiences, psychoanalyzing unconscious mental function, an all-encompassing state of consciousness that reflects the past, present, and future in one, and a capacity for your brain to bring overwhelming ideologies or notions together in a more conceivable and believable manner.

Each of these theories may provide us with a greater understanding around what dreams may be responsible for as we sleep, however none of them truly give us the exact answer as to why we dream because we simply do not know yet. As researchers continue to look into what dreams are and why we have them, chances are we will begin to discover more and more about this unique state of consciousness and what is happening in our brains during it.

What Do Dreams Usually Mean?

Elaborating on the fact that we do not know what dreams are, or why we have them, we can only assume that we also do not know exactly what dreams mean. However, once again, there are many popular theories that lead to people believing that they know how to interpret dreams and what dreams reflect for the dreamer themselves.

From a psychological researcher perspective, dreams are often interpreted through a few different methods. First and foremost, these researchers acknowledge that dreams could be affected by the thoughts you have immediately upon falling asleep. For example, if you are thinking about your excitement around a new job promotion, you may dream about that promotion and what it will be like. Alternatively, if you are thinking about a scary movie you watched before bed, you might dream about that scary movie.

Another thing that psychologists and researchers have come to recognize is that most dreams have "characters." These characters are made up of other individuals, and they are identified by dreamers in a variety of different manners. In a study that followed 320 adult dreamers, they discovered that forty-eight percent of characters that were witnessed in a dream were individuals that the dreamer knows about and could name during their waking hours. This means they were individuals that the person has known, met, or learned about at some point in their waking hours. Thirty-five percent of those characters were not identifiable by any particular name, though the individual dreaming could identify them by the social role they played, or the relationship they had to the dreamer. For example, the dreamer might recognize a grocer, or they might recognize an individual as being their friend even if they could not identify who the individual actually was. Lastly, sixteen percent of the characters that were identified in an individual's dream was unable to be named or identified based on their social role, meaning they were complete strangers to the dreamer.

Going even deeper into characters that people dream about, the study discovered that thirty-two percent of characters that dreamers could specifically name were identified by appearance overall in the dream. Twenty-one percent of the characters were identified by their behavior, and may not have necessarily been visible or easy to identify based on looks for the dreamer. Another forty-five percent of characters identified in a dreamer's dreams could be identified by facial recognition, and forty-four percent were not identified by how they looked or acted, but instead through a feeling of "just knowing." In fourteen percent of all characters witnessed in these individuals' dreams, they noted that there were elements that were bizarre or unusual for that particular character's typical appearance or behaviors which seemed strange to the dreamers.

Beyond characters in dreams, dreams have also been recognized to contain memories, especially repressed memories that an individual may not be able to reasonably recall during waking hours. These repressed memories can be recalled from the day that was recently experienced, providing the individual with the capacity to consolidate or release that information. They were also gained from a dream-lag effect, which means that the information was forgotten about but recalled about a week later, seemingly out of the blue. It has been estimated that it takes around seven days for dream incorporation to occur so that memories can be effectively processed, and that these processes can improve the function of an individual's socio-emotional adaptation.

Finally, research on dreams has also shown that we experience patterns in our dreams which may help us understand what is going on in our subconscious mind that we need to resolve or be aware of. These patterns can be witnessed through dream content, as well as through themes that may be present in dreams.

Overall, there are fifty-five common themes that people will experience in their dreams, including things like arriving too late to something, a living person being dead or a dead person being alive, the experience of failing something or falling from something, and other experiences. In some individuals, themes remain consistent for years while in others they may evolve over time.

Ultimately, the meaning of a dream largely depends on what the dream is, whether or not it is being repeated or experienced over and over, and how the dreamer feels in relation to having that particular dream. Identifying one specific meaning behind the content of dreams would be challenging, as there are virtually limitless possibilities of what can occur in dreams, what context it can occur with, and what that can mean for the dreamer themselves.

Is There Any Merit To "Dream Interpreters?"

Since the dawn of humankind, there have been various forms of dream interpreters who claim to have the ability to interpret what your dreams mean and, as a result, relay certain pieces of information or messages to you through your dreams. While there is not much information proving or disproving the talent that dream interpreters claim to have, it is important to understand that our limited scientific understanding of dreams means that dream interpreters are taking their best guess at what dreams mean. In other words, they have no guarantee one way or another, they are simply doing their best to help you uncover what dreams mean.

Dream interpreters can come in the form of psychologists or therapists attempting to help you analyze your dreams and use the content for personal growth, to self-proclaimed diviners who interpret symbology in your dreams to give you messages.

Psychologists or therapists who help you interpret dreams will always focus more on how the dream made you feel, what you noticed in particular with that dream, and how that dream may relate to your waking life. In general, they believe that the dreams are revealing information from your subconscious mind and that this can be used to further your healing and your mental and emotional growth and development.

Dream interpreters who use divine interpretation typically have some form of symbology that they believe in and look for in dreams. How symbols are interpreted often depends on where that interpreter comes from, what certain symbols meant to their unique culture or religion, and how the symbol was depicted and experienced in the dream itself. Often, these interpreters will interpret dream symbology as a form of fortune-telling rather than a form of creating a deeper sense of understanding within yourself, about yourself. While some dream interpreters who use this methodology of interpreting dreams have a tendency to be rather accurate in the way they interpret dreams or the messages they relay, there is no scientific basis behind what they are doing. In other words, there is no way to guarantee whether an individual is right or not. As a result, the interpretation of your dreams by dream interpreters should be taken with a grain of salt, or based on your chosen faith and belief system, rather than a concrete experience rooted in any form of scientific explanation.

Chapter 6

Identifying Your Natural Sleep Cycles

Before you can truly begin to make any significant changes to your sleep cycles, you are going to need to identify what your natural sleep cycles are. When you know what your own sleep cycles are, it becomes easier for you to understand where you lack in quality sleep and what can be done to help you improve the quality of your sleep. Understand that tracking sleep cycles is not something that you can necessarily do with perfection, as it is rather challenging to track your own sleep. While there are certain devices you could use that would help you track your sleep, it is important to realize that this entire process is never exact or perfect. For that reason, you need to adjust your expectations and ensure that you are looking for as much information as possible, but that you are also open to discrepancies in the information that you gather.

As you begin to track your sleep, I suggest doing it manually as per the guidelines in this chapter. You can use the added help of a tracking device if you desire, but learning how to track it yourself will help give you a more intimate understanding as to what is going on with your sleep. This way will also allow you to create exact variables for yourself, creating the opportunity for you to decide what specifically you are going to track and how you are going to adjust it to improve your findings.

Know, as well, that what we discuss in this chapter will be a general guideline for the average person who wants to begin tracking their sleep. If you have any unique variables that you want to factor into your own sleep tracking endeavors, you can add that to your own tracking method. We will discuss how to add variables such as mental health, underlying stress levels, chronic health conditions, and other variables into your tracking method in this chapter to ensure that you capture an accurate snapshot of how sleep is going for *you*.

Keeping Track Of Your Own Sleep Cycles

Keeping track of your own sleep cycles is best done with a simple journal and pen. In that journal, you are going to write down a series of variables and you are going to keep track of them every single night for at least two weeks, but up to four weeks, to get a clear image of what your average sleep cycle looks like at the present time. It is very important that you do this for a few weeks, and not just for a few days or one week, as you are going to want to get a clear image of your overall sleep cycles. Since there are so many variables that affect your sleep, attempting to track your cycles for just one week would be ineffective. During that particular week you may have had a heightened or reduced level of stress compared to normal, or you may have even been on your "best behavior" subconsciously, because you want to see positive feedback on your chart. Tracking your sleep cycle for two to four weeks without having made any intentional changes to your sleeping routines will ensure that you get a clear long-term image of what is going on.

For the average person, there are several things you should track when it comes to paying attention to your sleep cycles. Understand that since you may not be able to track your cycle itself in an effective manner, you will want to track things that could affect your cycle, as well as the results you are getting from the sleep you are enjoying. Tracking your behaviors and the side effects of those behaviors will help you understand if you are getting a high enough quality of sleep or not.

The behaviors and side effects that you should be tracking include:

- What you are consuming during the evening and how much

- What activities you are partaking in during the evening and how much
- What your energy level is in the evening
- What your stress levels are in the evening
- What emotions you are experiencing in the evening
- What specific bedtime routine you followed in the hour before bed
- How long it took you (roughly) to fall asleep
- How many times you woke during the night
- How rested you felt when you woke up in the morning
- How long your restful energy lasted during the day
- Whether or not you felt like you needed a nap at any point during the day
- Any noteworthy "symptoms" of sleep you had during the day (i.e. were you clear and energized, or moody and irritable? Did you remember things easily, or were you easily forgetful?)

If you have any unique conditions that may affect your sleep, such as chronic illnesses or mood disorders, you should track those as well. Many people notice that flares in their illness symptoms or mood disorders can lead to disordered sleeping patterns, making it even more challenging for them to get a full night's rest. You can also track medicine, caffeine intake if you tend to drink caffeine on a daily basis, exercise levels throughout the day, general stress levels throughout the day, exposure to stressful events throughout the day, or anything else that may be interrupting your sleep. Having a clear understanding as to how your own conditions are affecting your sleep will go a long way in helping you create a sleeping pattern that works best for you based on your unique needs. It will also allow you to bring this up with your doctor and seek further help if it seems as though your own adjustments are not doing enough to help you get the quality of sleep that you want, and need.

Once you know what variables you are going to be tracking, set up your journal with a chart that is designed to track all of these variables. Then, commit to tracking them every single night and morning for the duration of your test to ensure that you are getting a truly clear snapshot of what is going on. Make sure that you are as reasonably honest as possible in your tracking, too, as you do not want to have your results skewered by inaccurate tracking methods. Remember, this is for your benefit and being honest is the best way to ensure that you make real changes to your sleep cycles.

As you do track each variable, it is a good idea to write down as detailed a description as possible, though you can write the details down in point form. You can also use a scale of 1-10 with 1 being low and 10 being high to help you track the intensity of certain variables, which will help you get a clearer image of what is going on, too. For example, you might track your nightly stress levels on a scale of 1-10 or your morning energy levels on a scale of 1-10 so that you can keep track of them in simple, easy-to-understand terms.

Understanding Your Own Sleep Patterns

At various points throughout your sleep tracking efforts, you may find yourself wanting to look through them to get an idea of what is going on. While you can look through them, I encourage you not to create any conclusive ideas around what is going on until you have completed the entire two to four weeks. Attempting to create any conclusive findings beforehand will, once again, prevent you from getting a clearer image. As well, it may prevent you from getting an accurate image as you may start to manipulate your sleep cycle each night in an effort to begin improving it right away when, in reality, what you are looking for is a clear baseline.

After you have completed the full two to four weeks, though, you can start looking through your sleep charts to see what has been going on in them. At this point, you are going to want to attempt to create a full image for yourself in regard to how each variable is being experienced, and how it is likely contributing to your overall sleep experience. Once you have looked through each variable, you will get a clearer image of what is going on in your sleep cycle overall.

To begin understanding each individual variable, take a look through that isolated variable and see how it has been going. For example, let's say you are checking through the variable that measures your stress levels before bed. You might find that your stress levels tend to be higher more often than not, and you can conclude that this is negatively impacting your sleep. Maybe, as a result of heightened stress levels, you are not falling asleep as easily or staying asleep as well, and you are feeling physically tense and achy as a result of the heightened stress and reduced quality of sleep. At this point, we can see that your stress is clearly having a negative impact on your sleep and that this needs to be remediated.

As you move through each isolated variable, you will find that some of your behaviors are likely to be negatively impacting your sleep more than others. Likewise, you might find that some seem to be completely irrelevant and that they do not seem to affect your overall quality of sleep. Through this, you are going to start noticing your high problem areas and this will make it easier for you to identify what you can do about that and how you can reduce the impact that these high problem areas are having on your sleep.

In addition to noticing where your problem areas are, you may start to recognize patterns between the variables themselves. For example, you might notice that when your stress levels are higher you consume larger amounts of sugar before bed, both of which are negatively impacting your sleep cycles. Recognizing these correlations in patterns is important, too, as it will give you a deeper understanding as to how your problem areas are being affected and what you can do about it.

After you have addressed all of your variables and any patterns you have found in each variable, and between the variables, you need to start organizing which are the most problematic and which are the least problematic. With this priority list, you will know where you need to focus to have the biggest and quickest impact on your sleep quality, and then you will be able to work your way back from there.

It is a good idea that as you begin to make these adjustments, and even after you begin to see results from them, that you continue to track your sleep in your sleep tracking journal. This is going to allow you to get a clear understanding of how your adjustments are working, and may help you make any added adjustments to further improve the quality of your sleep. You may also want to keep the journal handy so that if you notice the quality of your sleep reducing again at any point in the future you can rely on it to help you improve your sleep all over again. At that point, you may also find that your previous findings help you get back on track more quickly, ensuring that you get a better sleep faster.

What Healthy Sleep Cycles Should Look Like

As you begin to track your own sleep cycles, you may be wondering what a healthy sleep cycle should actually look like. Since you are only tracking variables, and actual sleep cycles are not in the variables, it may seem somewhat challenging to identify what a healthy sleep cycle is compared to your own. This can be made even more challenging when you consider the fact that a healthy sleep routine can vary from person to person. Rather than trying to look for a one size fits all guide, look for a sleep routine that: helps you feel relaxed and calm before bed, includes a full uninterrupted rest for 7-9 hours, allows you to wake up feeling energized, and prevents you from feeling excessively tired by late morning or mid-afternoon.

If you study any healthy sleep routine that a person has, which creates a healthy sleep cycle, you will notice that they always include something to help wind down your mind, emotions, and body before you go to sleep. Then, they include necessary measures to ensure that you are able to enjoy a sound, uninterrupted sleep for the duration of your 7-9 hours, or 5-7 full sleep cycles.

Often, they will also include a routine in the morning to help maximize your energy levels to keep you going throughout the rest of the day.

Recognizing Discrepancies Between Your Sleep Cycle and a Healthy One

You will be able to tell right off the bat that your sleep cycle and routine are not standing up to a healthy one based off of what you are doing and how you are feeling afterward. You may even be able to quickly realize that your bedtime routine does not nurture your ability to wind down your mind, body, and energy levels, nor help you prepare for a sound rest throughout the night.

The best way to tell how far off you are from a healthy sleep cycle and routine is to write down what you believe would be the best routine for you. At this point, do not feel the need to write down what someone else says is going to be best, but instead write down what you believe would help you calm your mind, emotions, and body before bed, as well as help you have the highest quality of sleep. Keep in mind things that have been scientifically proven to disrupt sleep quality so as to avoid incorporating these into your ideal sleep cycle. For example, you should not be drinking caffeine later in the day, playing on screens before bed, or drinking too much water before falling asleep as this can cause you to wake up to use the bathroom throughout the night.

Once you have identified an ideal routine, compare your routine to your ideal routine. You may find that you are partially off, or completely off, and that the result of this is the outcomes you are experiencing from your disturbed sleep cycles.

This clear contrasting image between your current sleeping routine and cycles, as well as your current variable patterns, and what a healthy cycle should look like will allow you to recognize what specific actions can be taken to help you start to improve your sleep cycle. For example, if you recognize that your stress tends to be high at night and that your sleep routine completely lacks any behaviors that help reduce stress, you can begin to take necessary action to move toward your ideal healthy behavior. As you continue taking these consistent steps toward change, you will continue to find yourself creating a healthier and healthier sleeping pattern.

Over time, you will find that the healthier sleep pattern becomes routine for you and that it is effortless to maintain. You will also be able to quickly and easily tell if you fall out of sync with it because you will recognize it through the lack of routine behaviors, as well as the side effects or unwanted sleeping patterns that may arise as a result.

Chapter 7

Recognizing Disordered Sleep

As you begin tracking your sleeping patterns, you might be wondering whether your own sleep patterns are normal for disrupted sleep, or if they are bordering on or full-blown into the spectrum of disordered sleeping patterns. It is important that you learn to identify whether your disruptions are caused by a poor sleep routine or an actual underlying cause leading to disturbed sleep patterns, as this will give you an even stronger idea as to what you should do to improve the quality of your sleep. Sleep cycles that are being disrupted as a result of poor sleep hygiene can easily be rectified with an improved sleep routine and a few adjustments to your day which create stronger sleep cycles. Sleep cycles that are being disrupted as a result of an underlying condition, however, are ones that may be more challenging to navigate. While adjusting your sleep routine may help, you may find that you also need to take added steps to rectify the underlying issue that is leading to you experiencing disordered sleep.

Identifying disordered sleep is something that you can begin to do on your own at home, but if you are experiencing disordered sleep as a result of an underlying condition, you will need the support of a doctor to identify exactly what is going on.

The first step to begin to identify what is going on with your sleep is to address the number of disturbances you are experiencing in relation to what your overall sleep patterns look like. If you know that you have an incredibly poor sleep routine and that you are struggling to get adequate rest every night, chances are your sleep routine is to blame. In this case, while you do have disturbed sleep patterns, it is unlikely that you have disordered sleeping patterns. If you find that your routine is fairly supportive of at least a decent night's sleep, however, and you seem to be experiencing incredibly low quality of sleep, this may be an indication that you are bordering on experiencing disordered sleep. Understand, however, that certain variables can produce incredibly poor sleep and so it may not be that your sleep is disordered, but that your variables are simply not favoring a strong sleep. For example, if you turn off your phone and TV well before bed, drink a relaxing tea and enjoy a good wind down before bed but you still feel immensely stressed before falling asleep, the stress may be responsible for your disturbed sleep patterns. While this may still be a sort of disorder, it may also be something that you can rectify at home.

The real way to get a clear measure on what is normal and what is not when it comes to sleeping is to start making changes to your variables so that you are creating a stronger, healthier sleep routine. Then, you want to continue tracking your sleep and see how these adjusted routines begin to support your sleep. If you notice that you do begin to see improvement over time, chances are your issue was with disturbed sleep, not disordered sleep. If, however, you make changes and they do not produce any results, or if you make changes and the results seem to be limited and then they stop improving, you may be experiencing disordered sleeping patterns.

Should you engage in this assessment and discover that, as per your understanding, there seems to be something larger at play, it may be ideal for you to bring this up with your doctor. After all, a continually low quality of sleep can become a serious health issue as you already know. Your doctor may be able to recommend additional practices for you to try, specific herbs or supplements that you could try, a form of therapy that may be beneficial, or possibly medicines that could help you fall asleep. Do note, however, that most doctors will avoid giving out sleep medications as they can affect your sleep hygiene and health in the long run. We will talk more about herbs, supplements, medications, and alternative therapies in Chapter 8.

Chapter 8

Sleep Medicine Or Therapy?

If you do happen to do your homework and discover that you are experiencing borderline or complete disordered sleeping cycles, you might be wondering what you should do about it. While your doctor will be able to provide you with several great recommendations, it can also be helpful and reassuring to do some research on your own so that you can have a deeper understanding into what each of these methods are and how they work. Generally speaking, a doctor will want to try as many natural forms of treatments to alleviate sleep difficulties before moving to sleep medication. This is because sleep medication can be rather strong, and it can have addictive qualities. Further, continually relying on sleep medication can make sleeping without it harder, which can promote your reliance on these medications. While that is not to say that sleep medicines are bad or should absolutely never taken, it does give you a general idea as to why your doctor, and you, should explore other methods, first.

What Forms Of Sleep Aids Are There?

If you find yourself sitting in a doctor's office discussing strategies to help you get a better night's sleep, there are generally four solutions they are going to present you with. The first solution will be to adjust your sleep routine to ensure that you are supporting yourself in getting a positive, fulfilling sleep every single night. Even if you have already been doing this on your own, your doctor may provide you with some additional steps to take to see if these improvements to your routine improve your sleep overall. You will then schedule a follow up appointment so that you can discuss how they have worked, and so that if you need to you can explore one, or a combination of, the other three options that can support you with getting a good quality sleep every single night.

The second option after adjusting your routine is therapy. Therapy is a tool that is used to identify what may be preventing your sleep and approach it from a psychological point of view through using tools and techniques that can aid you with sleeping easier. In many cases, people who end up in therapy with difficulty sleeping will address underlying issues such as high-stress levels, anxiety, depression, or other conditions they may be facing. In doing this, they will generally find themselves naturally beginning to sleep much easier.

The third option when it comes to addressing the quality of your sleep is to consider supplements or herbal remedies. Supplements will often come in the form of a tincture, a pill, or a capsule, and herbal remedies will often be consumed as a tea as this is the easiest way to ingest them. Essentially, they are all the same thing except that the way they are consumed is entirely different. Herbal options are often considered as a less intense form of treating sleep disorders because they can promote natural sleep without the impact of medications. With that being said, you must still exercise caution with supplements or herbal remedies because they can still have drawbacks that may lead to worsened sleep or other issues down the road.

The fourth and final option when it comes to addressing disordered sleep is medication. Typically, your doctor will only offer medication if you have attempted the other methods for addressing your sleep issues and you are not getting the results you desire. If you find yourself at this point, these medications are not a bad thing to be taking, however they do need to be taken with caution and under the prudent guidance of your doctor to avoid running into trouble down the line.

Therapy To Promote a Healthier Sleep

Therapy is often a powerful tool that can provide great benefits to you when you are trying to create a healthier sleep cycle. When people think about therapy, they often think about addressing things like major life events or traumas, and many do not realize that therapy can actually be used for a wide array of things. Relying on therapy to improve the quality of your sleep essentially means that you will be leaning on psychological-based techniques to promote a healthier sleep.

Therapy to address sleep related issues will look entirely different for every single person who tries it. Generally speaking, however, the goal will be to address the underlying thoughts and emotions which may be disturbing the quality of your sleep. The three biggest emotional and psychological threats to sleep include stress, anxiety, and depression. Stress and anxiety have a tendency to keep you awake through worrying thoughts and increased adrenaline levels, while depression can either have the same effect as stress and anxiety or it can lead to you feeling chronically tired yet unable to get a restful sleep. For many with depression, over sleeping can also be an issue which can disturb sleep as you are not giving yourself enough stimulation during the day to create the results for a positive, healthy sleep.

In therapy, you may use talk therapy as well as specific tools to help reduce your stress, anxiety, and depression. Talk therapy in particular includes talking to your therapist so that you can get as much off of your chest as possible. In many cases, simply talking about what is wrong gives you the opportunity to get things out of your mind and can help you generate a great deal of perspective around the troubles you are facing.

If talking itself is not enough for you, there are many tools that your therapist can offer that will support you in navigating your stress, anxiety, depression, or other ailments easier. Some of these tools are going to be ones that you will use during the day, while others will be ones that you use during the evening right before you go to sleep. While these tools may look unique for you, there are a few standard tools that therapists will often offer you.

During waking hours, your therapist may ask you to begin practicing mindfulness and mindful breathing. They may also ask you to start setting aside time to allow yourself to process the stresses of your day well before the evening hits so that you are dealing with your stressful experiences as they arise. The combination of these experiences will go a long way in helping you begin to experience a greater sense of resiliency on an emotional and psychological level, which will help you bring less stress with you into the evening portion of your day.

When it comes to your evening routine, your therapist may ask you to include the aforementioned tools as well as a few additional tools that could help you release some of your energy and relax for the night. You might try journaling, meditation, progressive muscle relaxation, or listening to calming music before bed. These different activities can all help you begin to release some of the emotions you are carrying while creating a state of presence that will allow you to completely shed some of the stress you are carrying with you from your daily experiences. As a result, you will likely find yourself beginning to experience a higher quality of sleep.

If you find yourself dealing with disordered sleep, regardless of what route you choose to take to navigate your disordered sleep, talking to a therapist can be incredibly helpful. This can be especially true when you talk to a therapist who is particularly knowledgeable in sleep-related issues, or in issues related to the specific mental or emotional experiences you are having that are preventing your quality of sleep. Know, too, that therapy can easily be incorporated into any other sleep treatment you choose to use, which is what makes this an excellent option. Even if you do end up using supplements or medications, therapy can help you also build up tools that allow you to rely on yourself for improvements which can further improve the quality of your sleep in the long run.

Supplements and Your Sleep Cycles

If therapy is not enough to help you alleviate the issues relating to your sleep, or if you want something in addition to therapy that is going to help you get a higher quality of sleep, supplements are a great alternative for you to look into. Supplements are easy to access, can have incredible effects on your ability to sleep, and many of them can be used safely on an ongoing basis without any significant repercussions.

It is important to note that while natural supplements are generally healthier than medications, and while many can be used on an ongoing basis without side effects, not all natural remedies are created equally. What I mean by that is, if used incorrectly even a natural sleep remedy can be dangerous. Sometimes, these remedies will interact with different medications or other remedies you may be taking and can cause negative side effects within your body, possibly ones that are emergent and require immediate medical care. Some remedies are also unsafe for people with certain conditions or at certain stages of life to take, which can pose additional threats to your safety and wellbeing. Other times, these remedies are safe in low doses but may be dangerous for you to consume in higher quantities. Knowing what is safe for is important as this will allow you to take them confidently and with positive benefits. Be sure to talk to your doctor about any herbal remedies or supplements you want to try first so that you can feel confident that they will not negatively interact with you or any medications that you may be taking.

Should you choose to explore natural sleep aids that can promote a healthier sleep, there are nine great natural aids that you can look into. These aids can often be taken nightly, or as needed, such as if you are experiencing a particularly high-stress time in your life.

Melatonin

Your body naturally produces melatonin, which is what makes this an excellent supplement when it comes to improving your quality of sleep. When you take melatonin, it works within your natural hormone system to create a response that tells your brain it is time for you to go to sleep. Melatonin has also been shown to improve quality of sleep for those who must sleep during unnatural times, such as people who sleep during the day because they routinely work the night shift. If you choose to take melatonin supplements, it is important to note that some studies have shown that continuous use of melatonin on a regular basis can deplete your body's natural ability to create its own melatonin. For this reason, this supplement should only be taken during short periods of time.

Valerian Root

Valerian root is used to treat a lack of sleep, as well as anxiety and depression which means that this particular herb can be a wonderful all-around sleep aid. If you do choose to take valerian, taking about 300-900 mg of the herb before bed has been shown to drastically improve sleep quality. As with anything, always start with the lowest possible dose and gradually work your way up until you find the exact dose that works for you.

Magnesium

Magnesium is another mineral that is found naturally in your body and it has been shown to play a vital role in your ability to relax yourself so that you can comfortably fall asleep. Those who take magnesium supplements report that restlessness in both the mind and body seem to subside upon taking this supplement, making it easier to relax overall. Generally speaking, taking 200-500 mg of magnesium is ideal for helping you get a good quality sleep. With that being said, talk to your doctor before taking magnesium as taking too much may not be good for your body.

Lavender

Lavender can be used in many different ways to promote your sleep, including as a tea or as an essential oil. As a tea, drinking one cup of potent lavender tea about thirty minutes before bed can help you get a higher quality of sleep that night. As an essential oil, smelling lavender oil for 30 minutes before sleep by diffusing it in an essential oil diffuser can help improve the quality of your sleep. You can also dab a small drop of lavender oil on your pillow (not on your pillowcase but on your pillow itself to avoid accidentally getting it in your eyes) to improve the quality of your sleep.

Passionflower

Passionflower is commonly used as a sleep aid in the form of a tea. When making a passionflower tea, be sure to steep an entire teaspoon of dried flowers for 10 minutes before removing the flowers from the water and drinking your tea. Some studies have shown that taking passionflower as a supplement has not helped sleep quality at all, so it is important that you consume it in tea form. There is no clear understanding as to why this is the case, however it is what has been tracked in research studies to be the case.

Glycine

Glycine is an amino acid that is essential in managing your nervous system. It is believed that this is why it is so supportive when it comes to promoting a higher quality of sleep, too. When it comes to sleep, studies suggest that glycine helps lower your body temperature which naturally indicates to your body that it is time for you to go to sleep. Taking just 3 grams before bed, or consuming a diet high in glycine can help improve the quality of your sleep on a nightly basis. Foods that are high in glycine include meat, poultry, eggs, spinach, kale, beans, and certain fruits like kiwi and banana.

Chamomile

Chamomile is another flower that can be consumed as a tea. Again, steep a full teaspoon for ten full minutes before removing the dried herb from your cup to consume your tea. Research has shown that chamomile plays a relaxing effect on your nervous system which, in turn, makes it easier to alleviate your stress response and experience a calmer mind and body before falling asleep.

Kava

Kava is a plant that is often consumed as a tea or taken as a supplement to reduce anxiety and stress and to aid sleep quality. This root does have positive benefits, however it has also been linked to severe liver damage as most kava is adulterated, or mixed with other substances, before being sold so it is important that you refrain from using this supplement too frequently. As well, if you do use it you should only use it when it has been tested by a third-party organization to ensure that your kava has not been adulterated.

CBD

CBD is a specific terpene drawn from the hemp plant and it has been shown to play an incredible role in helping people have a higher quality of sleep. With CBD, you can look forward to improved sleep, lowered stress levels, and reduced pain in your body if you are someone who struggles with pain. For those who struggle to sleep due to a chronic illness that creates pain in the body, such as fibromyalgia, arthritis, or any other similar conditions, CBD can be incredibly helpful.

Everything You Need To Know About Sleep Medications

Sleep medications are often used as a last resort measure when it comes to aiding sleep. In most cases, they will only be used short term, or they will be prescribed to be used on an as-needed basis. In other words, you will make an effort to sleep on your own but if you are having an incredibly challenging time falling asleep you can use a sleep medication to help you fall asleep.

It is important to note that sleep medications, like any medications, can negatively interact with other medications you take, or with supplements you may use. For this reason, you should always be honest about what medications you take, both prescribed and over the counter, as well as what supplements you take with your doctor. If you consume anything else that could be classified as a drug or natural remedy, that should be mentioned to your doctor first, too. Sleep medications are not something to take lightly, so it is very important that you are fully transparent with your doctor.

When you take a sleep medication, your doctor will often prescribe you the lowest dose of the safest medicine possible. From there, they may adjust your dose or switch you over to different forms of medicine if you find that you are unhappy with side effects or the way that a certain medication is working for you.

Once you find the right dose of the right medication, you should stick with that. Never adjust your dose or try something without explicit consent and guidance from your doctor, as doing so can be very dangerous.

It is also important that you take caution to follow your doctor's exact guidance when it comes to taking your sleeping pills. Taking them the wrong way, at the wrong time, in the wrong dose, or before doing an important activity that requires you to be awake and alert can be extremely dangerous. Always take them exactly as advised. If you do begin to take medication and you notice that upon waking you are tremendously tired and having a difficult time going about your daily activities *do not drive, operate heavy machinery, or do anything ill-advised when you are on sleep medications*. This feeling indicates that you still have a potent amount in your body and you are still at risk of hurting yourself or someone else as a result of the medication you are on. Wait until the feeling completely subsides, then discontinue use and schedule an appointment with your doctor to fix your dose.

As long as you follow all of these necessary precautions, you will likely find that sleep medication is incredibly handy, especially if you have particularly disordered sleep. For many people, sleep medication is a useful tool that transforms the quality of their sleep in a major way. It is certainly not bad to have to take sleep medications if that is what your unique experience is; however, it is important that you exercise caution and that you try other methods first to avoid unnecessary medicating.

Chapter 9

Things That Interrupt Your Sleep

There are many different ways that you can negatively affect your sleep, ranging from behaviors you are engaging in (or not engaging in) to things that you may be ingesting too late in the day. Knowing what interrupts your sleep will help you begin to make immediate changes to your nightly routine which should create the opportunity for you to experience improved sleep right away. If you find that *not* doing any of these behaviors at night seems challenging for you, I would recommend spending time working on breaking these habits before cultivating any specific bedtime routine as this will ensure that you are starting from a clean slate, so to speak.

Eating Too Much Before You Go To Sleep

Going to sleep when you have a full bladder or stomach can massively disrupt the quality of your sleep. This can cause obvious issues, as well as less obvious issues, both of which can disrupt your sleep while also reducing the quality of your sleep. You should avoid either eating too much or drinking too much before you go to sleep. You should also ensure that your final small meal or snack at least two hours before you go to sleep so that you do not have any freshly consumed food resting in your stomach when you lay down to go to bed. You should also stop consuming beverages at least a half an hour before you go to sleep, which includes water, tea, or any other beverage. The only time you may want to adjust this timeframe is if you have a metabolic ailment that requires you to eat or drink at specific times.

The obvious issue with eating or drinking too close to going to bed is that it creates a sense of discomfort. Eating too close to bed can leave you feeling bloated, can increase your likelihood of experiencing heartburn, and can generally make it challenging for you to get comfortable and fall asleep. Drinking too close to bed can have you getting up to go to the bathroom throughout the night when you should be sleeping. As well, having any freshly consumed food in your system means that rather than engaging in natural nightly processes, your body will be working on metabolizing what you recently ate, which is something that should be completed during your waking hours.

Lying In Bed When You Are Not Sleeping

One big mistake people make when they are struggling to sleep is attempting to force themselves to sleep by staying in bed as they wait for themselves to pass out. While giving yourself enough time to fall asleep is important, lying in bed when you are wide awake or clearly not falling asleep anytime soon is a bad habit to get into. As you do this, you train your brain to see your bed as being a place where you can do anything *as well as* sleep, rather than being strictly a place where you fall asleep. In a sense, you train your brain that it is okay to lay there awake, rather than to fall asleep each time you actually get into your bed.

If you find yourself unable to sleep after a certain period of time, it is important that you get up and get out of your bed until you are ready to go to sleep. Try filling your time with a boring activity so that you are not stimulating your brain and wait until you feel tired, then get back into bed. You should also refrain from lying in your bed to watch TV, to read, or to generally hangout. While it may seem fun, it can damage your psychological association with "bed" meaning "sleep" which can worsen any sleeping issues you might be dealing with.

Sleeping In Conditions That Are Not Ideal

Attempting to sleep in conditions that are not ideal for sleep is not a good way to encourage yourself to get a proper night's rest. If the lights are on, noise is blaring out of the TV or stereo, or its too hot or too cold, you are going to find yourself feeling incredibly comfortable and therefore unable to sleep. Likewise, if your phone is sending off notifications every few minutes or your roommates or housemates are up being loud and noisy, you are going to be too distracted to get a good night's sleep.

Instead of trying to force yourself to sleep in conditions that are not ideal for a sound quality of sleep, adjust your environment to give you the ambiance that you are looking for. Turn off the lights and make the room as dark as possible, turn off the TV and if you need a stereo on have it gently playing relaxing music, and do your best to sleep when the ambient noise in your house and neighborhood are quieter. You can also adjust your temperature with a heater, a fan, or the window to help you get a better quality of sleep every single night. If this does not seem to do enough for you, consider creating this calmer and quieter environment about a half an hour to an hour before bedtime so that you can begin to wind down and alert to your mind that it is time for you to rest. Then, completely turn everything off and lower it all down when you are actually ready to fall asleep. This gradual reduction of the stimulation around you can go a long way in helping you create a calm, comfortable environment for you to fall asleep in.

Taking Too Long Or Too Frequent Of Naps

If you are napping too often, or taking too long of naps during the day, you may be completely throwing your entire sleep cycle off. Ideally, humans should be able to comfortably go through a 24 hour period with only 7-9 hours of sleep per night, without needing to add a nap into their daily routine. However, there are many circumstances where napping may be ideal or positive for your wellbeing, so it is reasonable to add a nap into your daily routine if you truly need one. It is important, though, that you nap properly to ensure that you are getting a benefit out of your daily nap without creating issues for your nightly sleep.

Naps should never be too long, taken too frequently, or taken too late in the day. Napping once in the late morning or early afternoon for around 15-20 minutes, depending on how much sleep you need, will give you the best results. The only time you might consider napping longer, for a full 90-minute sleep cycle, is if you tend to sleep on the lesser side of the spectrum on a nightly basis and if you have time to reasonably incorporate one full sleep cycle into your daily routine. If you can do this, then you may benefit from including one full sleep cycle into your daily routine. If, however, you do this and find yourself struggling to sleep at night, your naps are likely reducing the quality of your sleep and leaving you more tired than anything else.

Associating Your Bedroom With Other Activities

As children we often use our bedrooms for many things, ranging from a place to do our homework to a place to play, and of course a place to sleep. As we grow older, though, having this many associations with one space can be confusing and it can cause your brain to stop associating your bedroom with relaxing and going to sleep. For that reason, it is a good idea that you do your best to keep your bedroom as a place exclusively designed for you to sleep in. Refrain from working in your bedroom, watching TV there, engaging in your hobbies there, or otherwise using your time in your bedroom to do anything other than relax and sleep. If you cannot completely refrain from using your bedroom for these activities, then begin to associate only one small area in your bedroom for these activities and do your best to keep the rest of the room strictly associated with you relaxing.

When you associate your bedroom in general with winding down and relaxing, you make it easier for you to immediately begin to feel relaxed and ready for rest anytime you go into your bedroom. Through this association, your brain will begin to trigger certain processes in your brain and body that signal that it is time to sleep, effectively making you tired and making it easier for you to sleep. You can improve this natural association process by doing everything in your power to make your room as relaxing as possible. This way, you maximize your ability to fully rest each night.

Using Alcohol, Caffeine, Or Nicotine Before Bed

Alcohol, caffeine, and nicotine are all substances that can drastically impact your quality of sleep. If you ingest any of these things before bed, you may be causing yourself to experience a poor sleep as a result of your choices. Alcohol can be a stimulant, but it can also create feelings of sleepiness and relaxation which is why many people believe that a nightcap is a great way to end the day and wind yourself down for sleep. The problem is, alcohol can actually fragment the stages of your sleep which results in you experiencing disrupted sleep cycles throughout the night. This worsens as it begins to wear off in your sleep, too, meaning that the quality of your sleep worsens throughout the night. So, while it may seem like it is helping you fall asleep and stay asleep, it is also causing the quality of that sleep to be incredibly poor.

Caffeine consumed through coffee, tea, and even certain snacks is a natural stimulant that can result in you having a hard time properly falling asleep. Some people argue that caffeine does not make them *feel* stimulated so it must not bother them, but the reality is that caffeine in any amount will stimulate your body. Your inability to feel that stimulation simply means that you are desensitized to it, or that you have built up a tolerance for it. Still, your heart will beat faster, your mind will grow busier, and you will be more restless and less relaxed. You should refrain from consuming caffeine for 4-6 hours before bed, regardless of how you believe it is affecting you. Rather than consuming caffeine, opt for a calming herbal tea which will give you the same warm beverage effect without stimulating you. As far as snacks go, refrain from snacking before bed if you can help it, and if you must snack choose items that do not have caffeine and that are low in sugars and carbs so that they do not stimulate you before bed.

Nicotine is another stimulant that can make it more challenging for you to experience a complete night's sleep. As well, as nicotine begins to leave your system while you are sleeping, you can begin to experience cravings and withdrawals in your sleep which can either wake you or reduce the quality of your sleep. Rather than fragmenting your sleep due to nicotine withdrawals, avoid smoking before bed or, better yet, quit smoking altogether.

Disrupting Your Sleep Schedule For Any Reason

It can be easy to make excuses for why you are sleeping less or why you are disrupting your sleep, especially when you are experiencing a particularly busy season in your life. You may feel like a temporary adjustment to your sleep schedule, by reducing the hours of your sleep or changing the quality of your sleep, might not be such a big deal but the reality is that this will have a huge impact on your ability to get a proper rest. Furthermore, the bad habits you develop when you are having a hard time promoting a positive sleep during busier or more stressful periods of your life can be challenging to break which means that even once life settles you may still suffer from low quality of sleep.

Rather than giving yourself excuses to cut into the quality of your sleep or reduce the number of hours that you are sleeping, use busier or more stressful periods of your life as a reason to give yourself an excuse as to why your sleep schedule is absolutely necessary. After all, if you are not getting a proper rest keeping up with a busier or more stressful sleep schedule is going to be incredibly challenging. With that being said, no matter what is going on in your life or what offers come up, always prioritize your sleep schedule over anything else. It may seem harsh or unreasonable at times, but in the end it will always serve your highest good.

Using Your Phone Or Other Screens Before Bed

The blue lights on TVs, computers, tablets, phones, smart watches, and other technology devices can be incredibly stimulating to your brain and can make falling asleep very difficult. While you may not *think* the screens are affecting your quality of sleep, you will notice that as soon as you begin to consistently take them away before bed it becomes easier for you to wind down and relax. While it may be fun to watch videos, scroll social media, or mindlessly play games on your phone before going to bed, trust that there are other mindless things you can be doing to unwind and relax that do not stimulate you or disrupt your sleep.

Consider reading, listening to soft relaxing music, playing cards with your partner or roommates, drawing or engaging in a low stress hobby, or even just meditating and relaxing in silence before going to sleep. These are all great activities that will help your mind naturally wind down, and that will refrain from stimulating you and encouraging you to stay awake.

In addition to pulling these things out of your nightly routine, make sure they are also not capable of waking you up during the night. Mute notifications or put your device in do not disturb mode when you go to sleep and turn it facedown so that there is no chance that your device will awaken you when you are resting. This way, even if you use your device as an alarm clock, it cannot disturb you too much while you are trying to fall asleep.

Not Winding Down Before You Go To Sleep

Staying active until right before you go to sleep is a surefire way to keep your brain stimulated and active for the entire evening. As a result, when you are ready to go to sleep your brain will be so wired that it will be challenging for you to calm down and release any excess energy that you may have created. Contrary to popular belief, your brain and body will not gradually run out of energy as you continue remaining active. Instead, you will abruptly lose energy when you become exhausted because you have completely depleted your energy reserves, which is not healthy and will leave you feeling more tired and restless and less capable of truly resting in the long run.

Rather than expecting your brain to know when to gradually wind down as you continue to remain active right up until you plop yourself into bed, create a nightly routine that allows you to naturally begin to relax and wind down before going to sleep. Since sleeping is a relaxing activity, this will be a great way to help you prepare for it. A good quiet sleep ritual should be maintained for at least 30 to 60 minutes before going to sleep, though anything too stimulating should be avoided for at least 1-2 hours before going to sleep to ensure that you have plenty of time to wind down.

Exercising Too Vigorously Close To Bedtime

Exercising before bed is something that can actually cause your body to generate more energy and remain awake and alert, rather than help you fall asleep. While you do need at least 30 minutes of exercise daily, and while doing it will help you use up enough of your energy reserves that it becomes easier for you to fall asleep, engaging in activity right before bed is a bad idea. Engaging in vigorous activity before sleep will raise your temperature, heart rate, and blood pressure which will indicate to your body that it is time for you to generate energy, not time for you to restore it. Even though you might feel exhausted after a workout, your mind and body will still feel energized and it will be hard for you to get a good, sound sleep each night.

While vigorous exercise is not ideal before bed, you can engage in a simple yoga routine or other slow, quiet exercise routine before bed that allows you to gently stretch out your body and prepare you for sleep. These slow, gentle stretches will help you release any pent up energy for the day without going so far as to stimulate more energy before you go to bed. As a result, you might find that you feel less tense and more relaxed at bedtime, and that your exercise routine does not damage the quality of your sleep on a nightly basis.

Chapter 10

Revisioning Your Nightly Routine

Once you have begun to address any bad habits you may have that have been negatively affecting your sleep on a nightly basis, you can begin revisioning your nightly sleep routine. Revisioning your nightly sleep routine means that you are going to determine an ideal routine that is going to help you create a great deal of relaxation and calmness in your evening so that it is easier for you to fall asleep. The idea behind a strong nightly sleep routine is that you are going to have a routine that provides you with the level of relaxation that you need, while also working with your personality, preferences, and lifestyle. If you can find a routine that you genuinely enjoy, that fits into your lifestyle, and that gives you the results you are looking for, then you have landed on an excellent routine.

It is important to understand that many times you might come across a guide that attempts to assert that there is only *one* way for you to get a good night's sleep and that if you do not follow that exact routine your sleep will suck. This is not entirely true. While there is one specific structure for how nightly routines should look to promote a sound quality of sleep, there are several different activities you can incorporate into that structure to help you get the quality of sleep that you are looking for. It is within the details that you can create a customized sleep routine that gives you the results you are looking for in a way that feels enjoyable and sustainable for you.

Preparing For Your Nightly Routine

The first part of your nightly routine that you are going to do to help you sleep better each night actually starts before the evening even hits. This includes the activities that you are going to take that will improve your sleep throughout the day. During this time, you want to make sure you get any vigorous exercise in, that you engage in healthy daytime activities to reduce your stress and help you stay mindful and relaxed, and that you stop drinking caffeine at least four to six hours before you plan on going to sleep. You can also ensure that you refrain from using your bedroom for anything other than relaxing or sleeping, which means unless you are napping you should be out of your bedroom for the duration of the day.

While this may not seem significant, or it may even seem entirely irrelevant to your sleep overall, you will find that as you continue to maintain these daily routines that your nightly routines become much easier. Now that you are no longer carrying stress, excess energy, or other unwanted experiences into your nightly routine that can easily damage your quality of sleep, you can focus your entire nightly routine on relaxing as much as possible.

One To Two Hours Before You Go To Sleep

In the one to two hours before you go to sleep you want to make sure that all of your loose ends are tied up from the day you just experienced. Now is the time to make sure that if there was something urgent that needed to be completed that it is completed, and that anything else is scheduled into the following day. It is very important that you finish everything within this time period, as this will ensure that you are not carrying the stress of needing to get things done into the final hour of your day. This, in a sense, is your second form of preparing for your nightly routine as you may not be doing anything particularly relaxing, but you will be ensuring that once you reach your relaxing time you are ready to truly relax.

As I mention this being the part of your day where you get everything done that you wanted to get done, I want to assert that this includes finishing up any TV shows, podcasts, or video games you may have wanted to play during the day. You should be tying up loose ends both in terms of errands or obligations, as well as in terms of things you wanted to get done during the day for your own entertainment or pleasure.

Remember, before you go to bed you do not want to be doing anything stressful or anything stimulating. In most cases, errands and obligations can be quite stressful and stimulating activities such as watching TV or playing on your phone can continue to stimulate your brain even if you feel immensely bored or relaxed while doing it. You are going to want to transition away from these types of activities and into ones that are truly relaxing in every way possible so that you feel rested enough to fall asleep that night.

Fifteen To Sixty Minutes Before You Go To Sleep

The fifteen to sixty minute period before you fall asleep is where you are going to start getting really serious about your rest. During this forty-five minute part of your day you are going to begin to engage in the nightly routine that will promote your sound sleep. This is the part of your nightly routine that is often addressed in most "sleep routines," so this is where you are going to see the more traditional recommendations of reading, lowering the lights, listening to quieter music, and so forth.

The entire goal of this forty-five minute period of your day is to ensure that your mind, body, and emotions are relaxed as they can possibly be so that when you hit your pillow you are ready to fall asleep. You should spend these forty-five minutes engaged in no more than three activities that will help you completely wind down so that you are ready to fall asleep. While there are many recommendations for what you can do during this time, the ultimate goal is to keep your routine as simple as possible so that it is virtually mindless for you to follow. That way, you are not stimulating yourself or stressing yourself out by trying to remember what it is that you need to be doing during that period of time.

The easiest way for you to get the most out of these forty-five minutes before bed is to break them down into fifteen-minute segments and dedicate fifteen minutes each to your mind, body, and emotions. Do just one activity per segment for that particular part of your relaxation, and notice how effortless and relaxing this particular routine is.

For the fifteen minutes devoted to relaxing your mind, consider engaging in something such as journaling, meditating, rhythmic breathing, listening to soothing music, or even following a guided meditation. These practices will all help you begin to release the mental attachments you have to any stress or other burdens you may be carrying with you from the day you just experienced.

For the fifteen minutes devoted to relaxing your emotions, consider giving yourself time to simply think about the day you had so that you can process your feelings, listen to music, engage in meditation, or journal about how you are feeling. You might also try engaging in low-intensity forms of art such as drawing or coloring, both of which can help you express your emotions without leaving you with a huge mess to clean up afterward. Through whichever one of these activities you pick, you will find yourself experiencing a soothing sensation on your emotions which will allow you to feel as calm and comfortable as possible.

For the fifteen minutes devoted to relaxing your body, consider using a bedtime yoga routine, meditation, massaging yourself with a calming scented lotion, or doing progressive muscle relaxation. These gentle activities will help you physically relax your body so that you are ready to experience a sound sleep every single night.

It is important that, out of all of the options available, you truly do only pick one activity per fifteen-minute segment. Choose the activity that is going to be easiest for you to follow through on, that is going to be most enjoyable for you, and that is going to bring you the deepest sense of relaxation. If you can do all of this, you will find yourself experiencing a simple and enjoyable routine that gives you everything you need to help you fall asleep.

If you find yourself struggling to pick just one activity per fifteen-minute segment, consider choosing the one that you think will fit best for your nightly routine, then choosing an alternative one to engage in as a part of your morning routine. This way, you are affording yourself the best mental, physical, and emotional self-care that you can during the two most important hours of your entire day.

The Last Fifteen Minutes Of Your Day

After you have engaged in your forty-five minutes of relaxing your mind, body, and emotions you will emerge into the final fifteen minutes of your day. By now, you should already be feeling quite relaxed and ready to go to sleep. So, the only thing that should be left to do is finish preparing yourself for bed. At this point, brush your teeth, slip into whatever you will be sleeping in, turn off the lights, turn on any gentle music you may wish to sleep to, and prepare to go to bed.

It is very important that you do not use these last fifteen minutes to quickly set your alarm, feed your pets, set the coffee pot for the morning, make your lunch for the next day, or do anything else that you feel needs to be finished before you go to bed. Doing any of these things in the last hour of your day, but especially in the last fifteen minutes of your day, can

MARC WALKER and ALEXANDER LARKESS

result in you creating unwanted energy that prevents you from going to sleep. Do not undo all of the work you have done to relax yourself by completing errands that you forgot to do early on. The only thing you should be doing now are the things necessary for you to get into bed and have a quiet, relaxing sleep.

When Your Head Hits the Pillow

As soon as your head hits the pillow, if you are not immediately tired enough to fall asleep, there are a few additional steps you can incorporate into your nightly sleep routine that will help you get the best sleep possible. In fact, there are three great options that you can use to help you fall asleep if you find that you are not immediately lulled into rest. They include: a breathing meditation, a progressive muscle relaxation meditation, or a visualization meditation. If you are going to use any sort of guiding soundtrack to help you through either of these, such as one of the many tracks available on YouTube, you should set this up *before* you get into bed so that you are not stimulating yourself from bed.

Breathing meditations can be used to calm yourself down, especially when they are associated with counting meditations. Generally, these meditations will include several breaths completed with an intentional rhythm that allows you to create a deepened state of relaxation within yourself. As well, you will either count the breaths themselves, or count out the duration of your breaths so that you can experience the full level of peace possible.

Progressive muscle relaxation is a form of meditation that is done where you progressively relax every single muscle group in your body from your feet to the top of your head. This is often used to help people release stress or anxiety, which is what makes it great for calming your body and mind before going to sleep. You can either use a guided progressive muscle relaxation meditation, or you can simply visualize each part of your body relaxing as deeply as possible, starting with your feet then working up through your legs, glutes, abdomen and lower back, chest and upper back, shoulders, arms, hands, neck, and head.

Visualization meditations are often best done when they are guided, though if you are already comfortable with visualization meditations you can always do this on your own without any guidance as you relax in your bed. Generally, guided visualizations are something that allow you to create imagery within your mind that is peaceful and that sets the tone for positive thoughts, and dreams, as you sleep. Guided visualizations are often used as a way to sleep more soundly with people who generally have nightmares when they rest.

Finally, How Do You Want To Feel?

Now that you have a breakdown of the basic structure of how your nightly routine should look, we are going to discuss one last part that is crucial to your ability to revision your nightly routine. That is, we are going to address how you want to feel. If you know how you want to feel, choosing the activities that will help you create those feelings will be much easier for you.

It is obvious that when you are creating a nightly routine you want to feel relaxed and tired, and that you want to be free of stress and anything else that prevents you from sleeping. However, in life anytime we focus on getting away from something we can make it extra challenging to get away from said thing by not deciding what it is that we are moving toward at the same time. In other words, if you know that you are moving away from stress caused by *xyz* but do not know that you are moving toward, you may begin to pick up different bad habits that create stress through *abc* instead. In other words, you may take side steps, or very small forward steps, rather than drastic steps toward something better.

The best way to complete this part of your revisioning is to decide what it is that you do want to feel before bed. Do you want to feel tranquil, relaxed, peaceful, calm, happy, content, accomplished, deserving, valuable? What do you want to feel that is going to counter the stress you have been feeling? Having specific words to help you identify how you want to be feeling will ensure that you are working toward something specific in your nightly routine, which means deciding on what activities to engage in will become easier for you.

Chapter 11

Creating a Healthy Nightly Routine

Now that you know what a healthy nightly routine should look like, and what needs to happen in order for it to create the results you are looking for, you can start working on actually creating your own healthy nightly routine. In this chapter, rather than walking you step by step through creating a routine that you now have a basic understanding of, I am going to provide you with as many examples of activities you could engage in as possible. This way, you can identify the exact activities that are going to help you create the feelings you desire in order to be able to have a sound sleep every single night. So, to create your exact nightly routine, you are going to use the structure from chapter 10 with the activities from this chapter, and through that you are going to have the exact nightly routine you need to have in order to get a good night's rest every single night.

The Structure Of Your Routine, Simplified

In case you prefer to have things simplified even further, I wanted to quickly summarize what your routine should look like so that you know exactly what activities you need to be picking out in order to incorporate into your sleeping routine.

A good nightly routine should look like:

- **One to two hours before bed:** getting everything wrapped up and ready for the next day
- **Fifteen to sixty minutes before bed:** calming down your body, mind, and emotions
- **The last fifteen minutes before bed:** doing everything you need to do to prepare yourself to actually get into the bed

During the one to two hours before bed you will pick any activities that are relevant to your lifestyle and fit them in here. You can also identify additional activities that I may not have mentioned that are unique to your lifestyle and fit them into this part of your day, too.

For the last fifteen to sixty minutes before bed you are going to want to pick no more than three activities that will take you no longer than fifteen minutes to complete. These activities should help relax your mind, body, and emotions.

For the last fifteen minutes before bed, you should pick activities that are preparing for you to actually fall asleep, such as brushing your teeth, turning on calming music, or doing anything else you need to do to prepare yourself for getting into bed.

One To Two Hours Before Bed

Depending on how many activities you need to engage in on a daily basis, you may want to extend this period of time as being one to three hours before bed so that you can allot one hour to the things you want to do, and one hour to the things you need to do. Adjust your routine accordingly to ensure that you are able to accomplish everything you want and need to accomplish on a day to day basis. It is very important that you fully wrap things up and create leisurely time for yourself in the evening, too, as doing so will help you feel a sense of completion on a daily basis.

During the time that you allot to doing the things that you need to do, make sure that you do everything you need to finish that day as well as everything you need to do in order to prepare for the next day. This means that if you had any mandatory errands that needed to be completed, such as homework, a project for work, helping your kid with their homework, cleaning a part of your house, meal prepping, or doing anything else that is mandatory, you want to get it done now. You do not want the pressure of errands looming over you until the very last minute before you go to bed as this will dramatically increase your stress and make falling asleep much more challenging. Not only will you feel overwhelmed by everything that needs to get done, you may also lead yourself to believe that you do not deserve to sleep or have the capacity to sleep until said project is finished. Being in this frame of mind can, naturally, destroy your sleeping patterns and prevent you from getting any significant rest on any night that you do this. The accumulated stress can also cause long term damage to your sleep cycles, making it even harder for you to get a proper night's rest.

If you have any activities that you generally do before bed to prepare you for the morning, you should do that now, too. For example, if you like to set the coffee pot or prepare meals for your pets or otherwise get things ready for how you like them in the morning, make sure you do them before you start your actual nightly routine. This way, rather than filling your leisurely or relaxing time with errands and chores, you can solely focus on filling it with relaxing activities that will help you get a better sleep.

During the time you allot to leisurely activities, engage in things that you enjoy engaging in and that helps you feel a sense of joy. Activities like crafting, reading, watching TV, playing video games, playing board games with your family, going for a walk around the block, calling a loved one, or anything similar will fit perfectly into this part of your day. Giving yourself 30 to 60 minutes to engage in leisurely and enjoyable activities at the end of your day is a great opportunity for you to end the day on a positive note, which means that as you move into your actual nightly routine you will already be feeling good. The better of a mood you can put yourself in on a daily basis, the better you will feel overall and therefore the easier it will be for you to do things such as relax because you will not be harboring so much stress and tension in your mind, body, and emotions. It is generally a good idea to do your leisurely half hour to hour *after* you have done your necessary things so that your enjoyable activities are not being overshadowed by what needs to get done. This way, you can seamlessly move from something enjoyable into something calming and relaxing. With that being said, do not allow yourself to get so caught up with how good it feels that you choose to ignore the fact that you need to engage in your nightly relaxing routine. It may feel tempting to gain the instant gratification of continuing to do what is bringing you joy, but it will ultimately break your routine up and make going to sleep much more challenging.

Fifteen To Sixty Minutes Before Bed

If you view your nightly routine as being a gradual experience of winding down, then this is where you really begin to detach from activities that are outwardly relaxing and focus, instead, on activities that are inwardly relaxing. What I mean is, rather than relaxing to your favorite show or your favorite hobby, you are going to be relaxing to much fewer stimulating experiences that are more calming and private within yourself.

For your mind, you can turn off your electronics, stop checking notifications, engage in a breathing meditation, engage in a visualization meditation, read, journal, write out any worries that you have and "release" them for the night, enjoy a relaxing tea (during the first fifteen minutes of the routine,) pray, or even just relax with your loved ones. Sometimes, light conversation before bed can be a great way to soothe your mind and release any worries you may be carrying with you from the day you recently experienced.

For your emotions, nearly all of the same activities that soothe your mind will soothe your emotions. With that being said, emotions sometimes come with the need to be actually expressed so you may find that things like listening to music, writing, coloring, or speaking with a loved one or praying with the intention of dissolving your emotional charge can be helpful. It is very important that whichever activity you choose, you do so in a way that reduces your emotional charge, not in a way that empowers it. If you find yourself experiencing incredibly charged emotions at night, you will either want to change your nightly routine for relaxing your emotions *or* find better daytime emotional management routines so that you are not bringing such intense emotions into your evening.

For your body, you want to engage in things that are going to physically indicate that it is time for you to wind down. The goal with your body is to create what is known as "biofeedback" which is a process that results in your physical experiences indicating to your body and your mind that it is time for you to relax and get some rest. In a way, this is like reverse engineering your energy levels so that you can naturally lull yourself into a state of rest. You can do this by engaging in a relaxing yoga routine or a gentle stretching routine, by using calming herbs or supplements to help you begin to relax, by bringing your physical body temperature down or even by massaging a calming scented lotion into your skin to physically remove any stress and tension from your body before you go to sleep.

Once again, I cannot stress enough the importance of only choosing one activity per area of focus, as choosing too many is going to be stressful. Your goal here is not to have a productive routine where you get a lot done, it is to have an efficient routine where you get the right things done. You will find that when you spend more time doing fewer things that have a greater impact on your energy levels that you will have an easier time getting yourself ready for bed without accidentally stimulating more stress in your life.

The Last Fifteen Minutes Of Your Day

The last fifteen minutes of your day should be centered around things that are practical for you when it comes to falling asleep. This is when you should brush your teeth, comb your hair, wash your face and apply any moisturizers you use, switch into your sleepwear, and take any medicines you may need to take around bedtime. You can also close your blinds, shut off any music you have on, silence notifications on your phone, and turn off the lights. If you are going to listen to any sleep meditations or anything of the sorts, make sure you put those on before you actually get into bed.

Once you get into bed, make sure you are going through the same motions, too. Get comfortable and then immediately begin engaging in whichever meditation or relaxation experience you are going to routinely use to help you fall asleep. It is very important that you use the same method over and over again, as consistency will ultimately be key when it comes to creating an effortless sleep routine every single night.

Chapter 12

Twelve Additional Steps For Healthy Sleep

By now, you have plenty of great information to help you troubleshoot your nightly sleep routine. You know the importance of your sleep, especially the importance of the quality of your sleep, and you know what may be preventing you from getting that high quality of sleep. You also have a stronger understanding as to how you can improve that quality of sleep, and how you can track those improvements to ensure that you truly are receiving the quality of sleep that you need in order to experience optimal health.

Before you go, I want to make sure that you have as much access to every ounce of knowledge you can get to perfect your sleep, though. For that reason, I am providing you with twelve additional steps that you can take to improve the quality of your sleep. These steps will be both directly connected to your bedtime routine, as well as connected to other parts of your daily routines or health regimens. Each of these steps will help you ensure that you are doing everything you possibly can to experience the best quality of sleep possible.

When it comes to integrating any of these steps, as with all other aspects of switching over to a healthier bedtime routine for a stronger sleep, it is important that you take your time. Gradual and intentional integration will always lead to more sustainable long term results, which is truly what you hope for anytime you find yourself wanting to make changes in your life. With that being said, start with the routines that you think will have the biggest impact on the quality of your sleep, your health, and your life, and gradually build out from there.

Increase Your Exposure To Natural Light During the Day

Like eliminating bright lights and blue lights in the evening can help you sleep better, so can increasing your exposure to natural light during the day. Prior to the domestication of humans, we were motivated in the same way that animals are—through the rising and setting of the sun, as well as through many other primal urges. Relating to sleep specifically, the rising and falling of the sun indicated when it was time to be awake and when it was time to fall asleep. Modern life has led to us spending a great deal of our time indoors, and it has changed the way we access light in our day to day lives. We are no longer woken by the rising of the sun, kept awake by the heightened hours of the sun, and then lulled to sleep by the setting of the sun. This is because we are no longer exposed to the sun in the same way that we once were.

While you may not be able to go back to living in a forest-like we all did at one time in the distant past, you can gain some control over your natural biological rhythms by taking action on the amount of light that you are being exposed to on a daily basis. By increasing the amount of light you experience in the morning and then keeping the lights bright all day before dimming them in the evening, you train your body to naturally rise, produce energy, and then relax at various points during the day.

Focus Carefully On Training Your Circadian Rhythm

Beyond tracking light cycles, there are other things you can do to regulate and train your circadian rhythm, too. Recall that your circadian rhythm is what we call the natural biological "clock" we each have built inside of us that lets us know when it is time to awaken and when it is time to rest. In addition to using light cycles, you can also train your circadian rhythm by going to sleep at the same time every single night and waking up at the same time every single day. This way, your circadian rhythm knows what to expect, is properly regulated, and allows you to naturally wake up when you are supposed to, and naturally fall asleep when you are supposed to as well.

Another way that you can support your circadian cycle is by allowing it to naturally adjust with the changing of the seasons. Our modern lives do not allow us to accurately follow the seasons the way we once did, however doing so can be very important. In the summer months, when your energy is bright and lasting, do not be afraid to schedule more activities in the evening and do more amid the bright hours of your day. In the winter months, however, focus on allowing yourself to engage in slower and more peaceful activities in the evenings when it starts to get dark earlier, as this will also help your natural circadian rhythm continue to work its magic.

Decorate Your Bedroom For a Sleepy Environment

If you are a fan of decorating, then this tip is going to be a big hit for you. When it comes to helping yourself get a better quality of sleep, one great thing you can do for yourself is decorate your bedroom so that it promotes a sense of relaxation and a desire to sleep. While other rooms in your home may be decorated more so on looks and functionality, your bedroom should be designed with the intention of avoiding excessive stimulation and promoting rest. You can do this by intentionally decorating your room in a way that minimizes distractions, allows you to reduce the amount of light coming into your room, and keeps your room comfortable and safe feeling.

If curtains and a lack of clutter does not provide you with enough relaxation in your room, consider adding additional items into your room that can promote relaxation. For example, speakers placed in strategic locations can be played with low music to provide a calmer pace, or earplugs can be worn to drown out sounds that you might be hearing outside of your apartment. You can also include a serene image or two to help you promote the sensation of relaxation, though you should refrain from over decorating your room as this could stimulate your senses. Instead, focus more on bringing soft textures and colors together to create a design that is both attractive and sleep-inducing.

Maintain a Specific Temperature In Your Bedroom

Your body temperature naturally falls as you rest and then rises once again when you wake up. Helping your body engage in this natural cycle will encourage you to experience a higher quality of sleep. It is important to avoid the urge to sleep with excessive blankets or a heater if your room is already generally warm, or to avoid the urge to sleep with an air conditioner or a fan if your room is already generally cool. Adjusting the temperature of the room too drastically could worsen the quality of sleep you receive, making it harder for you to get a sound night's rest.

Studies have shown that your room should be around 20C or 70F when you are sleeping as this will ensure that you have the right temperature to nurture the natural cycle in your body to promote sleep. In addition to maintaining your ambient temperature, make sure that the clothes you are wearing and the bedding you are using in your room are capable of helping you maintain an appropriate temperature, too. This way, you are not accidentally overheating yourself through having too heavy of blankets or too heavy of pajamas as you go to sleep.

Avoid Eating Carbs Or Sugars Later In the Day

What you eat plays a major role in how your body behaves, and this is no different when it comes to going to sleep. One trick that many nutritionists point out as being useful when it comes to many different areas of managing your health, including managing your weight and your energy levels, is timing your carbs, proteins, and fats properly. Carbs, which are sugars, are designed to provide you with quick-acting energy that gives you a boost at any point when you eat them. This is why if you eat something like sugar or white bread you may feel a small sugar rush in your body as a result of what you have eaten. Alternatively, proteins and fats are harder for your body to metabolize which means it takes longer for them to turn into energy for your body. A well-rounded meal should contain all three, technically, as this ensures that you have both short and long term energy.

However, now that we know how these three macronutrients behave and how they affect the body, you can further adjust the way you consume them to ensure that you are supporting the right amount of energy levels when you need them. What I mean is, you should focus on eating protein and fat with every meal, but only eating carbs where you may need a quick boost in your energy. So, for breakfast you may eat a small amount of carbs with protein and fat to ensure that you have energy to get started with your day, as well as energy to last you throughout the rest of your morning. Then, for lunch, you could have a higher carbohydrate intake to support you with creating a boost of energy when you may otherwise have an afternoon "slump" as it is often called. For dinner, however, you should minimize or even eliminate carbohydrates from your meal, depending on how late you are eating it. This way, your body is not getting an immediate boost of energy right before you sit down to relax for the evening, which can result in you experiencing restlessness and, therefore, a lowered quality of sleep. For this same reason, you also need to avoid snacks that are rich in carbohydrates before bed as this can also stimulate your energy levels and leave you struggling to get a high quality of sleep.

Try Taking a Bath Or a Shower

As you know, your temperature can have a large impact on your sleeping levels. While reducing the temperature of your home can help you adjust your temperature accordingly, effectively helping you get a better night's sleep, so too can taking a bath or a shower before bed. Studies have shown that taking a warm bath or shower about 90 minutes before going to bed can help gently raise your temperature, which means that once you get out of the bath or shower your temperature will gradually begin to drop. This natural dropping in your temperature after a bath or shower stimulates a natural level of calmness which can effectively support you with creating a sense of sleepiness, too.

Aside from just taking a plain bath or shower, you can also incorporate relaxing products that support you with feeling more relaxed. Lavender scented products, gentle bubbles, and Epsom salts can all be used to help stimulate a natural sense of calmness. You might also consider using aromatic candles or essential oils as a part of your nightly routine to further calm yourself down, effectively helping you get yourself ready for a sound night of sleep every single night.

Once you get out of your bath or shower, avoid the urge to bundle up in a housecoat or a big soft blanket and instead let yourself rest in comfortable, breathable clothing. This way, your temperature will be able to naturally drop and you will find yourself falling asleep much easier just over an hour later.

Make Sure You Are Sleeping On the Right Bed

While you might be tempted to buy your bed and bedding based on the one that is the most attractive, comfortable, and cost-effective, it is important to note that beds and bedding serve a larger purpose than being merely for decorative purposes. For that reason, it is very important that you educate yourself on what you need and what is going to provide you with the best quality of sleep possible. Generally speaking, people should sleep on the firmest mattress they can comfortably handle, as this will ensure that they are not sinking into their bed, which can put strain on your muscles and joints. With that being said, you do not have to go for the firmest mattress on the market, instead just go for the firmest one that feels the most comfortable for you. As you check for firmness, favor comfort over firmness while keeping firmness in high regard to ensure that you do not accidentally buy a bed that is *too* firm for you.

Pillows are not all made equally, either. You need to have a pillow that is suited for the type of sleep positions you tend to sleep in the most. If you tend to sleep on your stomach which, by the way, is the least healthy sleeping position possible, you should either sleep with a very soft pillow or no pillow at all as this will refrain from you putting unnecessary stress on your neck. If you need a softer surface between your head and the mattress or your head and your arms, use a soft blanket to create a cushiony effect without adding too much height which could cause stress on your neck and spine and, therefore, a bad sleep. If you sleep on your side, opt for a thicker pillow that will have the capacity to hold your head up at a natural height for your shoulder height, without having your head collapse down toward the bed. You might also opt for a small neck cushion to place under your neck to give you more well-rounded support if you tend to sleep on your side. If you sleep on your back, using a medium thickness pillow will ensure that you get enough support under your head without creating a bent spine through your upper neck.

In addition to considering your mattress and pillow, you also need to consider your bedding. Be sure to use materials that are comfortable for the season you are currently in, and change them as needed. Keep them fresh, and use breathable linens and bedding no matter what season it is as this will ensure that air is able to easily circulate which will prevent you from overheating at any point during the night.

Get Some Fresh Air Before Bed

While fresh air in the morning can wake you, fresh air in the evening can help you fall asleep. Again, as modern humans we do not get nearly enough access to the natural elements as we would have before we began living in houses and spending most of our time indoors. Exposing yourself to the outdoors will help naturally drop your temperatures, while also exposing you to the natural darkness that comes from the night sky. This combination of natural darkness and cool fresh air will help let your circadian rhythm know that it is time for rest. Just by spending 2-5 minutes outdoors before bed, you can create a great impact on your overall ability to sleep.

If you have a hard time waking up in the morning, you can repeat this behavior to help you awaken, too. When you first wake up, go outside for a few minutes and expose yourself to the naturally rising temperatures, the fresh air, and the rising sun. This combination will help naturally elevate your energy levels which can help you feel more alert and refreshed after your sleep.

Stop Watching the Clock When You're Trying To Sleep

When you are working toward falling asleep, the last thing you need to be doing is micromanaging the clock and stressing yourself out about how long it is taking. In fact, any behavior you may be engaging in that is increasing your level of stress should be avoided before bed. Rather than checking the clock and stressing yourself out about how long it is taking you to fall asleep, or about how many hours are left until you have to wake up, ditch the clock. Stop worrying about when you sleep and what amount of sleep you are going to get and instead follow all of the valuable tips in this book to begin healing your sleep cycles naturally.

If after several nights or a few weeks of attempting to adjust your own sleep schedules does not result in you getting the quality of sleep that you need, consider talking to your doctor about options to support you with sleep. Otherwise, the best thing you can do is naturally reduce your own stress levels and worrying about the time on the clock is certainly not going to help you any.

Consider Sleeping In Different Rooms

If you have a partner that you live with and share a bed with, you might consider sleeping in separate bedrooms if your sleep disturbances are particularly bad. This may seem like a strange or uncomfortable idea at first, especially if you are attached to the idea of having your partner near you every night, but the reality is that for many people this produces a much higher quality of sleep. A surprisingly large portion of the population notes that sleeping with their partner can lower their quality of sleep for many reasons. Perhaps your partner snores or moves around a lot, or maybe they tend to hog the blankets or shove them all off on you which results in your own temperature being dysregulated throughout the night. You might even find that you and your partner prefer different sleeping conditions, such as a different mattress firmness, noise levels, room temperature or any other number of conditions that affect the quality of your sleep.

If you find that sleeping with your partner in the same bed, or even in the same room is causing you to have a disrupted sleep cycle then the best thing you can do is separate your beds, or even sleep in different rooms. Note that this is not about shaming your partner or creating any sort of conflict between you and your partner, it is simply about helping you have the space to create the conditions you need to create the quality of sleep that you need, too.

Have Your Pets Sleep In a Different Room

Just like sleeping with your partner in your room can be disturbing and can make getting a good quality of sleep challenging, so can sleeping with your pets in your room. Many pet owners love having little Fido or Rover sleep in their room with them, or especially in their bed with them. For many, having their pet nearby is soothing and can actually improve the quality of their sleep, so if this is the case then this particular tip does not apply to you.

However, for light sleepers or those who are already struggling, sleeping with your pet in your room could be challenging. You might find yourself constantly being awakened by the random noises and activities your pet engages in throughout the night as you are trying to sleep, since most pets do not sleep as long as you. Each time your pet shifts, gets on or off the bed, or goes to engage in any natural activity that they engage in during the night this could disturb you and, as a result, disturb the quality of your sleep. Creating new boundaries with your pets or sleeping with the doors closed may seem unkind at first, but once you get used to it you might find that it is just the change you need to help you get a much better quality of sleep each night.

Eat Dinners Or Evening Snacks That Encourage Sleep

While there are plenty of things you want to avoid because they can make falling asleep harder, there are actually various things you can eat that can encourage your natural sleepiness. You might find that eating dinners or evening snacks that encourage sleepiness help you naturally adjust your circadian rhythm so that you are tired in the evening and so that you can get an adequate sleep every single night.

There may be more, but in general there are 15 foods that you can easily access that will help you naturally promote your desire to sleep. Incorporating even one of these into your evening meal or snack is a great way to help yourself increase your feelings of sleepiness. These fifteen food items include: honey, tea, nuts, beans, dairy, bananas, whole grains, cherry juice, yogurt, chickpeas, poultry, eggs, grapes, leafy greens and oats.

Conclusion

Congratulations on completing *The Power Of Good Sleep!* This book was designed to help give you a more intimate understanding of what sleep is, why it is so important, and how sleep can have a massive impact on your overall health.

I hope that through reading this book you have found a greater level of understanding around why your sleep matters and how you can take practical and necessary measures to improve the quality of your sleep. You may have come here with the intention of simply feeling better in the morning by being more well-rested, and having enough energy to get you through the day, but now you know that sleep is about so much more than that. Your feelings of being well-rested and having enough energy to get you through the day are merely a symptom of the better underlying health you enjoy when you have a high quality of sleep on a nightly basis. For that reason, well-rested is definitely what you should aim for, though you should know that you will be experiencing so many more benefits from a positive sleep, too.

It is important that you understand that it can take time for any changes to really be visible when it comes to naturally improving your sleep cycles. You might notice right away that you begin to feel more rested, though it may take a while for you to notice a massive change in your energy levels. The quick boost may be great initially, but take heart if it is not followed by continuous improvements in your energy levels at first. As you continue to make these improvements and continue to maintain them, you will find yourself experiencing better energy levels over time, too.

If you do continue to make adjustments to your sleep and feel as though you are not seeing significant improvements, or if you feel as though you are experiencing even worse sleep over time, you may be dealing with a sleep disorder. In this case, it would be beneficial to communicate with your doctor to see if there are any natural or therapeutic measures you could take to further improve your sleep quality.

Take heart in knowing that while it can take some time to troubleshoot your sleep ailments, virtually every sleep condition can be resolved and you will find relief. Continue doing what you can and looking for answers and, before you know it, you will be experiencing healthier and higher quality sleeps overall.

One thing I do want to stress before you go is that if you are putting all of this work into improving the quality of your sleep, it is essential that you continue to put the work in over time. You *must* turn this into a new routine and be willing to maintain it forevermore, as the minute you stop engaging in your new sleep routine and instead start engaging in old patterns, you will be feeding the cycle of poor sleep again. It may seem challenging at first to maintain such a new schedule, but the sooner you do the better your sleep and health will be in the long run. If you notice yourself falling off track with your new routine, make sure you address this immediately and get back on track so that you do not begin to experience major setbacks from reduced sleep quality.

It is very important that you take your sleep seriously, as it truly can contribute to a much higher quality of life. The sooner you can begin to contribute to experiencing a better quality of sleep, the better.

Finally, before you go, if you have liked our book, we kindly ask that you please take a moment to review MISTAKE FREE LIFE on Amazon. Your honest feedback would be greatly appreciated, as it helps us to create more great titles for you, while also helping others gain access to all of this incredible information.

Thank you, and best of luck!